# Split Second

### Real Life Experiences
### From Behind The Thin Blue Line

## Jeff Garland

GOWOR
INTERNATIONAL PUBLISHING

*Split Second Real Life Experiences From Behind The Thin Blue Line* © Jeff Garland 2014

www.splitsecondstory.com

The moral rights of Jeff Garland to be identified as the author of this work have been asserted in accordance with the Copyright Act 1968

First published in Australia 2014 by Gowor International Publishing

www.goworinternationalpublishing.com

ISBN 978-0-9924977-8-1

Any opinions expressed in this work are exclusively those of the author and are not necessarily the views held or endorsed by Gowor International Publishing.

All rights reserved. No part of this publication may be reproduced or transmitted by any means, electronic, photocopying or otherwise, without prior written permission of the author.

**Disclaimer**

All the information, techniques, skills and concepts contained within this publication are of the nature of general comment only, and are not in any way recommended as individual advice. The intent is to offer a variety of information to provide a wider range of choices now and in the future, recognising that we all have widely diverse circumstances and viewpoints. Should any reader choose to make use of the information herein, this is their decision, and the author and publisher/s do not assume any responsibilities whatsoever under any conditions or circumstances. The author does not take responsibility for the business, financial, personal or other success, results or fulfilment upon the readers' decision to use this information. It is recommended that the reader obtain their own independent advice.

This book is dedicated to all of the brave men and women of the NSW Police Force, past, present and future, who selflessly risk their lives, each and every day, just so that we can feel a little safer.

To my gorgeous girls, Rachael, Teagan, Keely & Beckah — you have added meaning to my life and are the only reality that truly matters.

Without you, this book, as well as my own survival, would not have been possible. I love you all so very much.

To Clara, Kerry, Simone, Katie and especially Esther and Teagan: thank you for taking the time to read my manuscript and provide positive feedback and encouragement.

# A Personal Note from the Publisher

To the reader,

As the Founder of Gowor International Publishing, I make it part of my practice to offer a personal review for each Author about their book. The reason why I do this is so that you, as the reader, can glean a further understanding into why this book is so valuable to you in your life.

Let me start my personal review of *Split Second* by saying that I cried many times while reading it. When I say I cried, I mean that I had tears running down my face, not just a tear in the eye! As I turned the pages, I felt myself deeply drawn in to Jeff's incredible story. I was moved to the core as he revealed incident after incident during his time working in the NSW Police Force. And, in many moments while reading, I felt as though I was watching an action movie unfold.

This book is a testament not only to the outstanding work that Jeff performed while on duty and working to uphold the law but to what I believe can only be described as his true courage. Jeff's inner strength to overcome his own personal battles, and his willingness to care for people and make a difference through raising awareness about PTSD is nothing short of inspiring. It is and has been an honour to work with Jeff personally in bringing this powerful book to publish.

*Split Second* will change the way that you see the police – and life – forever. It will leave you with an increased appreciation for those who look out for us, and for what it means to be alive. You will reconnect with the people you care about through Jeff's story… and find deeper meaning in your own.

This book is one that you won't be able to put down.

Enjoy the read!

With inspiration,

**Emily Gowor**
Founder of Gowor International Publishing

# Contents

Foreword ..................................................................................... 11
Introduction ................................................................................ 13
Preface ........................................................................................ 19
Chapter One: College of Knowledge .................................... 23
   My First Posting ................................................................. 29
Chapter Two: Redfern Days ................................................... 35
   The Meeting ......................................................................... 39
   Dog Attack ........................................................................... 41
Chapter Three: Black Market Murders ................................ 45
Chapter Four: Redfern Riots ................................................... 59
   In The Line Of Duty ........................................................... 63
   Shots Fired ............................................................................ 65
   Not My Gun ......................................................................... 67
   Birthday Pursuit .................................................................. 70
Chapter Five: The Voir Dire .................................................... 75
Chapter Six: Signal One .......................................................... 81
Chapter Seven: The Trial ......................................................... 89
Chapter Eight: Field Intelligence ........................................... 95
   (aka) Brocky ......................................................................... 97
   City East Rampage ........................................................... 102
Chapter Nine: Loose Cannon ............................................... 107
   Hire Car .............................................................................. 111
   Burning Saab ..................................................................... 114
Chapter Ten: Waterloo Riots ................................................ 119
   Work Smart ........................................................................ 123
   Crazy Man .......................................................................... 125
Chapter Eleven: The Ute ....................................................... 127
   The Aftermath ................................................................... 142

Chapter Twelve: Return To Work .................................................. 145
   The Fatal ......................................................................................... 149
   Stress Shoot ................................................................................... 152
Chapter Thirteen: Full Circle ........................................................... 157
   Retraining ....................................................................................... 158
   World Champion I ........................................................................ 160
Chapter Fourteen: Next Step ........................................................... 169
   Prosecutors .................................................................................... 170
   Shafted ............................................................................................ 175
Chapter Fifteen: Returning to the Front Line .............................. 181
   Acting Sergeant ............................................................................. 185
Chapter Sixteen: Crackneck ............................................................. 189
Chapter Seventeen: The Entrance Channel .................................. 197
Chapter Eighteen: Welcome Back ................................................... 213
   Going Off ........................................................................................ 215
   The Sentencing .............................................................................. 217
   World Champions II and III ........................................................ 218
Chapter Nineteen: It's Not Fair ....................................................... 223
   Attempted Suicide ........................................................................ 229
   I've Had Enough ........................................................................... 231
Chapter Twenty: The Promotion ..................................................... 235
   The Hardest Day ........................................................................... 238
   Special Fixture .............................................................................. 243
   The Beginning Of The End ......................................................... 247
   Karma .............................................................................................. 253
Chapter Twenty-One: The Decision ............................................... 257
Chapter Twenty-Two: In My Opinion ............................................ 273
   PTSD and Me ................................................................................. 275
Chapter Twenty-Three: Reflection .................................................. 281
   Lessons I Have Learned .............................................................. 289
Epilogue ................................................................................................ 291
Honour Roll ......................................................................................... 307
Service History ................................................................................... 311
   Promotion History ....................................................................... 311
   Awards/Notations ........................................................................ 311
About The Author .............................................................................. 315

# FOREWORD

Being thrown into the cauldron of the mean streets of Redfern was difficult enough even for those of us deemed 'experienced hands' and knockabouts, in those post-*Cop It Sweet* days. For eager, inexperienced 'young guns', the cauldron became exactly that — a veritable melting pot of suffering caused by all the deprivations commonly found in such an extremely low socio-economic community, aggressively fanned by the greed of drug suppliers hell-bent on decimating the predominantly Aboriginal population within the Block and surrounds, where the perception was that all police were racist.

The experiences of one such officer are laid out for all to see here in Jeff Garland's story. Places like Redfern are but one part of the trials and tribulations most young police undergo in their initiation years. Yet, endearingly, Jeff has let us into his innermost thoughts from his experiences at Redfern and his continued career, which provides a passionate resonance to his journey. I congratulate him for having the courage to record these thoughts and for allowing us into his world.

I similarly congratulate the many Team Leaders, Supervisors and Commanders within the New South Wales Police Force, both past and present, who through their strong leadership have allowed junior officers, such as Jeff Garland, to safely navigate those early years and provide them the opportunity to get on with what policing is and should be all about — locking up the crooks.

I commend this book to the reader. It provides the layperson with an extremely passionate, warts-and-all human insight into the most dangerous occupation in the public sector.

**Peter Parsons APM**
**Assistant Commissioner**

# INTRODUCTION

It was just after 10 a.m. on Thursday, October 13th, 2011 when I received the phone call that no serving officer who still loves their job wants to receive: that my policing career would end before the month was over.

It wasn't like I hadn't been expecting it, but for the phone to ring where it did and when it did was like a convergence of time, where memories of the past collided with my present day realities. It was also poignant because at that precise time and moment I was standing on the edge of the cliff…gazing down at the jagged rocks below… feeling the cool ocean breeze against my face…listening to the waves thunder against the coastline…contemplating life, not death.

For me, it was a time for reflection. A time to confront my demons and to change what they meant to me. It was a time for me to let go and move on. You see, it was just before Christmas 2007 when I responded to a report of a male actually contemplating suicide at this exact location, Crackneck Lookout on the NSW Central Coast. After almost an hour of 'physical' negotiation and despite his best efforts to kill both of us, he involuntarily changed his mind and, ultimately, the course of my career.

The reality that I couldn't be a policeman anymore was devastating. A flood of memories washed over me, filling my senses with sounds, tastes, visions and feelings of my career serving within the 'thin blue line.' It was a long way from the mean streets of Redfern where I had earned my stripes, or from the middle of the Pacific Ocean where my career would ultimately end, but for me it was my reality—my ground zero.

But just as the news of my pending departure sank in, so too did my changing neuro-association of Crackneck Lookout. Compared to that warm and sunny December morning, the cliff and landscape was almost unrecognisable. The scars of the day were blanketed with a layer of green, like it had moved on, encouraging me to do the same. The steep slope and loose rocks underfoot were no longer visible beneath Mother Nature's caress. The bitter memory that I had almost died there that day was gone. As the sun broke through the gloomy clouds, I felt a warmth, a strength inside me that proffered reassurance that everything was going to be okay.

And just as I turned to leave, feeling optimistic, I saw out of the corner of my eye a guy run to the edge of the cliff…and jump…right beside me! Luckily, he was strapped to a hang glider. It lacerated me from my reflections, to the extent that I started taking photos of him on my phone, soaring effortlessly above, oblivious to the impact he had just had upon me. Not only had he helped change my confronting memories of Christmas four years earlier, but he had also given them new meaning. The transformation was complete, and deep down I honestly believed I saved a second life on the cliff that day — mine!

I guess to the majority of men and women who make the decision to become a police officer it's a lifelong career and not merely just a job. For me, it was exactly that — my past, present and foreseeable future. But sometimes the cruelty of mankind and the horrors associated with 'the job' can be too much for even the bravest and toughest soul.

I loved pulling on that uniform each shift, with every day offering an exciting new challenge. But most of all, as I'm sure other emergency service officers can attest, I felt like part of a family. I know it's not the most glamorous of jobs and that the police are always the first to 'cop' slack when things don't go right, but deep down I knew I was making a difference in my job, to my community, to myself and to my colleagues. I would always push myself beyond the limits of my own expectations, striving to succeed. But sometimes my passion for the job got the better of me, and consequently I got a bit too involved on more than a handful of occasions.

Throughout my career, I was almost stabbed, shot, run down and drowned; I arrested drug dealers, armed robbers, murderers and escapees; I was involved in riots and high-speed car pursuits; wrestled with armed offenders and suicidal males; I was spat on, kicked, punched, bitten and verbally abused; my own life and that of my family was threatened by violent, drug-affected, mentally ill and intoxicated 'customers.' But that's my job, and I loved and was very good at what I did. But there comes a time when you need to be honest with yourself and accept that you aren't coping and need to ask for help.

Hmph! You know as well as I do that as a 'bloke,' we are not supposed to admit that we aren't coping—it's not what we do. It's even harder to do when you are a male police officer. I didn't talk about what I was 'feeling' because I didn't think anyone would understand and I thought that I would be adversely judged and labelled by the rest of the 'family.' I felt embarrassed and ashamed because I wasn't coping. I had chosen to ignore my feelings for far too long to fit into the policing mould. "You've had a bad experience; deal with it and get over it." And that's what I had done throughout my career, and I'm sure a lot of other police have too. But enough was enough.

I was first diagnosed with Post Traumatic Stress Disorder (PTSD) in 2001. I didn't know much about the condition at the time other than that it wasn't a label I was happy to have. Although there is some conjecture as to whether PTSD is a mental illness, a brain injury or an anxiety disorder, it is not a sign of weakness. The truth is that PTSD is a normal reaction to a highly abnormal event; it is an invisible wound as real as any physical injury; it is a serious and debilitating condition that affects thousands of people every year, particularly those in the emergency services and the military. It doesn't discriminate who it targets, whether male or female, young or old, single or married. But if diagnosed early enough, and with the appropriate support mechanisms in place, it is something you can learn to live with.

Sometimes referred to as 'the sadness,' PTSD changes who you are and can prevent you from leading a normal personal and professional life. It can overwhelm you with emotion and fear. You don't want to socialise, answer the phone, spend time with your friends and family, leave the house or look after yourself. You suffer from constant flashbacks and nightmares, sweating and severe mood swings. It can lead to addictive behaviours such as alcohol or drug abuse and gambling; it can result in marital or relationship breakdown, domestic violence, loss of employment, financial hardship and even suicidal tendencies. Although I don't have any tertiary qualifications as a psychologist in this area or claim to know all the answers, from a personal point of view, from someone who has been both a victim and a survivor of the condition, I can convey to you my experiences, both negative and positive, in the hope that you may change your mind about this disorder, but more importantly in the hope that you may change your mind about your friends, family or workmates who have succumbed to its torment.

I think that one of the hardest things about being a cop is the culture that doesn't allow you to show that you aren't coping or to express how you feel. Policing is one of the most confronting, dangerous and stressful jobs around, and it takes a truly special person to make that sacrifice and become part of the thin blue line. I have been amazed, especially over the last twelve months, to see the quantity and quality of experienced police that are succumbing to PTSD—tough cops I fought alongside who had been reduced to nothing more than a blubbering shell of their former selves.

By its very nature, the NSW Police Force, and I suppose law enforcement in general, has developed from a male-dominated history where weakness was a sign of failure. Such arrogance is now reflected in the high levels of stress-related attrition and suicides within the policing family. I felt that I had conformed to the 'police image', dealing with tough times and then throwing myself back into the job headfirst. But I never relied upon my past experiences as an anchor to draw from, instead taking the next risk a little bit further, and each time was always another step too far, too risky. Well, why not? I survived, didn't I?

Some of the things I have done throughout my career may make you grimace as you read my story, but I still stand by the decisions I have made with conviction because I believed in what I was doing at the time, believed that it was the right thing and that it was worth the risk. It's strange how things always seem so much clearer after they've happened and you've had time to step back, consider your options and analyse your efforts absent of the threat. That's the benefit of hindsight. A lot of the time, you are confronted with a situation in which you have to make a *split second* decision that can make all the difference in preventing a crime, making an arrest or saving someone's life—sometimes even your own! In making that *split second* decision, you must rely on your own experience to survive—and then learn from it. It's what we do with this newly acquired knowledge that makes the difference. We don't always get it right and things don't always go according to plan.

At times you tend to forget about your own mortality in this job and believe you are invincible. Not to the extent that you feel that you are above the law, not by any means, but you've got this inner confidence, almost bordering on naivety, that good will always triumph over evil. And I guess I am guilty of that. I never thought I was above the law, but I started taking more risks because I didn't have the support to understand that what I was doing wasn't safe and wasn't smart. Risk-taking became part of my inner self, and after being knocked down and getting back up so many times I felt encouraged to take another risk and push myself just that little bit harder, that little bit further. Nothing seemed to deter me.

As I said, things look so much different when you get a chance to reflect. Throughout my career there have been a lot of incidents to look back on, having been involved in about twenty-five major incidents that have threatened my life and my beliefs and affected me both personally and professionally. I guess this is the underlying reason why I needed to write this book, to allow me to express and accept, even confront, all the feelings that have arisen from these ordeals.

It's also an opportunity to share with everyone my experiences and to provide an insight into frontline policing so that others can appreciate the risks that police take when they pull on their uniform — what I call their 'blue armour'. I am not aiming to glorify my career or the way I perform my duties, just to give expression to my story. I certainly wasn't perfect and made my fair share of mistakes, which I am happy to share with each and every one of you. Everyone is different, and the way each officer polices is dependent upon his or her own experience, work location, resources and abilities. We all do the job in our own unique way and I am very proud of what I have achieved and of the way I executed my duties. And I believe that you only get out of this job what you put into it. But for me there was no in between — it was either all or nothing. I'm sure my wife would agree that I have changed as a person and as an officer. But there comes a time when you have to stand back, take a moment and reflect upon what you've been through and how it has affected you.

This is the moment, and now is the time…

# Preface

It was early Monday morning, July 30th, 2001, when I made my ritual two-hour commute south from my home on the Central Coast to the streets of downtown Redfern. It was a journey that I had made every shift for the past four and a half years. I loved my job — chasing crooks and fighting crime — so having to travel wasn't an issue, plus I was only a few months away from being promoted to Senior Constable. But for some reason, that morning I couldn't shake the feeling that it wasn't going to be a good day.

I arrived early, as always, to prepare for my shift. I changed into my uniform, wrapped my appointments belt around my waist and went to the gun safe to load my six-shot .38 calibre Smith & Wesson firearm, as I had done routinely before. Next, I went into the station area to sign out a portable radio and greeted the Supervisor, who looked tired from a busy night and who was obviously looking forward to going home. When checking the roster I noticed I would be working with a Probationary Constable and that our assigned area was around Redfern Railway Station, in the spot commonly known as 'the Block,' using call-sign Redfern 45 (RF45). Although I hadn't worked with him before I knew that he was keen and was looking forward to getting out on the road.

About 8.30 a.m., at the start of peak-hour traffic in arguably the busiest city in the country, what I had earlier dreaded had become my reality.

> RF45: Redfern 45 urgent, I'm in the back of a stolen vehicle, Charlie Alpha Mike 0-6-2, on Cleveland Street.
>
> Police Radio: Yeah Redfern 45 did you say that you were in this vehicle?
>
> RF45: I'm in the tray at the back radio, can I get some assistance quickly? North on Cleveland Street.

BEEP (audible tone)

Police Radio: Standing by further Redfern cars, any car in the vicinity, to make their way to Cleveland Street, northbound, Redfern 45 is in the rear of a confirmed outstanding vehicle, Charlie Alpha Mike 0-6-2, urgent assistance required, further Redfern cars thanks.

Police Radio: Redfern 45, your current location and a suburb thanks.

(silence)

Police Radio: Redfern 45, your current location thanks…

We had made regular patrols of the Block and Redfern Railway Station for about an hour when I noticed a white 4WD Ute parked in the vicinity of Eveleigh Street. Such a sight wouldn't have aroused my suspicion in other areas of the Command, but since it was in a location renowned for its high levels of crime and drug activity I suspected that it was stolen. Because I hadn't seen the Ute parked there earlier in the shift or previously in the Block, I decided to confirm my suspicion that it was stolen, and of course it was.

After cruising around the Block for a short time, hoping to catch someone inside the vehicle, I noticed the same utility driving north towards us, with two males on-board. I yelled at my partner to stop the truck and block the vehicle against the kerb. As the utility turned towards us, I jumped out, hoping for an easy arrest. I came around to the front of the Ute as it squeezed past us and drove off down the street. The driver and his male passenger glared at me. I shouted "Stop, stay where you are," standing only a few feet away from the driver's open window. The driver ignored me and accelerated away.

The next thing I knew I was in the tray of the Ute looking back at my partner, who was looking bewildered, as we rumbled down the street. In a reflex action I must have grabbed hold of the back of the Ute and flung my bulky frame into the tray. I was in, and there was no turning back.

I was glad that I had remembered my portable radio. I scanned my surroundings to assess what options I had, but there clearly weren't many. The tray was about two metres wide and three metres long and had three large metal toolboxes on each side and one against the window. There was a small corridor for me to crouch in, so I leant forward and called on my portable, "Redfern 45, urgent. I am in the back of a stolen vehicle, Charlie Alpha Mike 0-6-2, on Cleveland Street."

The radio operator's tone and intensity reflected the situation. She immediately called for urgent assistance after realising that I was in fact "in the back tray of the stolen vehicle!"

> Police Radio: Standing by further Redfern cars, any car in the vicinity, to make their way to Cleveland Street, northbound, Redfern 45 is in the rear of a confirmed outstanding vehicle, Charlie Alpha Mike 0-6-2, urgent assistance required, further Redfern cars thanks.

The driver of the vehicle looked at me over his shoulder through the back window and seemed surprised to see he had picked up a hitchhiker. He slammed his foot on the brake. The Ute jolted forwards, throwing me onto my chest. I managed to scramble to my knees as the driver accelerated quickly for a short distance and again slammed on the brakes, forcing me against one of the toolboxes. He looked again through the back window to see if I was still there with both fear and anger in his eyes. Adrenaline was pumping through my veins, but I was terrified. I was a hostage trapped in the tray of that Ute, and the last thing I wanted him to know was how frightened I felt. His intentions seemed clear — to throw me from the tray so that he could escape. It was the beginning of a long battle…

## Chapter One:
## College of Knowledge

For as long as I could remember I had always wanted to be a policeman, and here I was, living the dream. I had come such a long way, metaphorically speaking, from where I had grown up in the mini-metropolis of Belmont on the NSW east coast, just south of Newcastle. My mum and dad divorced when I was really young, which was hard on us kids, but nothing unusual in those days. It left mum with the unenviable task of raising my elder sister, twin brother and I on her own.

Growing up in the 1980s was like living in another realm. It was before mobile phones, the internet and social media had been invented; it was safe to play outside until the street lights came on and drinking from the garden hose was part of the experience of childhood. Unfortunately, so were the ravages of puberty, which scarred me not only physically, but emotionally too, having to contend with the bullying and name-calling that my acned appearance caused.

My entire scholastic existence subsisted within the boundaries of the local infants, public and high schools, where I was more studious than popular. My efforts helped me achieve notable results on the Higher School Certificate in 1991, especially in legal studies, economics and history. My first job was as a 'checkout chick' at the local Coles supermarket when I was about sixteen. It wasn't anything cool but was still a great initiation into the workforce. I also found employment as a cleaner, pizza delivery boy and expert 'trolleyologist' (trolley collector), which, needless to say, didn't satiate my dreams of making a difference in the world.

I loved playing sport, particularly soccer (even though I was built like a matchstick and weighed about 49 kilos) but I liked to try my hand at everything, including AFL, hockey, tenpin bowling, cricket and tennis. I had a close-knit bunch of friends that I hung out with and my share of love interests, but nothing serious.

During my last year of school and my first year after graduation (1991-1992) I pursued my other passion, which was raising money for the less fortunate. My first endeavour targeted the national issue of youth homelessness but on a local level. So whilst studying in Year 12, I organised and participated in the 'Ride for Nobody's Children Project,' which was a 1,200 km charity bike ride from my hometown of Belmont to the sun-baked shores of the Gold Coast, Queensland. I don't think I had ever gone that far on a holiday, let alone on a pushbike!

It was a lot of hard work, both physically and mentally, especially when I fell from my bike riding down the Toowoomba Ranges — doing about 80km/hr — when my brakes jammed as I was passing a truck. Luckily it was a near miss and I escaped with relatively minor injuries. I was conveyed to hospital for treatment as a precaution and ironically ended up next to a male who had been beaten up by the same 'underprivileged' group of people I was raising money for. Awkward! But overall, considering my age and limited experience, it was a marvellous expedition and the start of a new philanthropic chapter.

The following year I produced my first concert at the age of eighteen when the 'Get On Your Feet Charity Spectacular,' with over five hundred performers, rocked Newcastle University. I guess you could say it was like the first ever 'Eisteddfod/Dance Spectacular.' As a result of these endeavours I was nominated for the Young Achievers Award in 1992, which was unexpected but a great honour.

From mid-1993 to early 1995, I was involved in my first 'serious adult relationship,' which momentarily diverted my attention from my desire to join the thin blue line but proudly resulted in the birth of my first daughter, Teagan Rae. I can still remember how proud and raw I felt holding her for the first time in the hospital. It was an amazing experience being a dad for the first time, even at age twenty. There was so much I had to learn, but I was so excited about the opportunity. She was the first baby I had ever held and undoubtedly the love of my life.

Sadly, on the same day I was accepted to start my policing journey I learned that her birth mother had taken my eighteen-month-old daughter away and that their whereabouts were unknown. It took all my strength not to fall apart, but I promised myself that I would never give up searching for her. About eighteen months later, with the help of my solicitor and the Courts, I discovered she was living on the Sunshine Coast of Queensland. Although it was an unexpected and difficult separation that dragged on for more than four years through the Family Law Court, I am honoured to say that my beautiful daughter has been in my full-time care now since 1999 and has blossomed into a gorgeous and level-headed young lady.

Losing my child was a difficult time for me. Not knowing where she was or whether she was safe tore me apart inside. I knew I had to find her, but to afford that I needed a steady income, so I refocused on my ambition of becoming a policeman. In 1995 I took part in a number of police-funded training courses that were designed to prepare applicants for entry into the Police Service. I found them valuable because they allowed a 'behind the scenes' look into policing that most recruits or members of the public don't get to see. I also got involved in a new government initiative known as 'Volunteers in Policing' in the Lake Macquarie area. This allowed me to work within a police station and provided me with a first-hand view of life as a police officer. This opportunity offered me something that most officers never have the chance to experience before joining the police service.

I worked hard to get into the police, especially physically. I knew that it was important to have a commanding physical presence, so I needed some serious work on my scrawny physique. It also helped to channel my energy into something positive until I found my daughter. Within months, I was able to transform my 50-kilo frame into 76 kgs of muscle thanks to healthy eating, exercise and time at the gym.

In December 1995, at age twenty, after successfully completing all of the physical and psychological requirements, I was accepted into the February 1996 intake at the NSW Police Academy, Goulburn, as a student of Class 265. My journey was about to begin.

Although the long drive down to the Academy was filled with nerves and anticipation, I will always remember my time down there, especially my first day. It was like being at school again, with lots of large brick buildings encompassing the aspirations of men and women from all over the state, looking for their chance to fulfil an ambition. I felt a sense of pride, and at the same time uncertainty, as I entered the campus. The first afternoon I spent nervously unpacking and getting to know some of the other cadets I would be training with. It was a new experience for us all, but one we could survive if we worked together.

The next morning was bitterly cold as we paraded into the main hall, where we were split into subclasses. About 250 men and women had converged in this school, affectionately referred to as the 'college of knowledge.' It was a different way of life from the moment I drove through the front gates, and a realisation of something I had wanted for most of my life.

The course was physically and theoretically challenging; we had to learn so much about the law, procedures and police powers. It went on for eighteen months and was broken up into four different stages—much different to how it is now. Phase 1 was eight weeks at the Academy, where we studied the principles and ethics of being a police officer and began to bond with our fellow classmates. The course ran from Monday to Friday, sometimes late into the night, with each day commencing with morning parade and inspection. The days seemed long with so much information to digest, so I savoured driving home on the weekends just to get away and enjoy an old-fashioned home-cooked meal.

I was lucky enough to be part of Class 265 Bravo with a great bunch of people. We all got along well, which helped us survive the freezing cold and endless lectures. Every day we practised marching, which was tedious but at the same time enjoyable. One of the drill instructors made the lessons quite entertaining with his humorous quick wit. I was even conferred the 'Virgil' award for looking most like one of the 'Thunderbirds.' I honestly thought I was good at marching, but perhaps I looked a bit awkward.

There was a lot of emphasis placed on physical training during Phase 1, which is understandable. There wasn't much sense in knowing your powers if you weren't strong or fit enough to do your job. With pushups, running, sprints, gym sessions, a timed obstacle course, strength training and, yes, more running, the type and amount of exercise was enough to challenge anyone, but the frosty cold mornings and demanding, pain-seeking trainers added another level of intensity. They knew the importance of physical fitness, and throughout my career, I did too.

Phase 2 was four weeks working at a station close to your home. It was a good break to get away from the monotony of Academy life. I returned to the Lake Macquarie area, where I had spent time in the Volunteers in Policing before joining the service. Knowing the other police in the station made it a lot easier to fit in and gave me the confidence to ask sometimes obvious and practical questions. As Student Police Officers, we weren't issued with police appointments such as firearms or handcuffs (for obvious reasons); I was just there to watch and learn. It was an observation phase during which I made mental notes to hopefully apply to my studies and future career.

During this rotation, I had my first encounter with a number of dead bodies when we visited the local morgue not too far away from the Newcastle Police Station—unforgettable, and not so much in a good way, although the officer who took us seemed to enjoy our pale expressions. Although it wasn't the first dead body I had seen, it was the first I had seen in this context.

It was a large room with an overwhelming smell that assaulted my senses and was hard to ignore. Each of the bodies lay supine on a cold stainless steel slab, waiting to be medically examined. The high-pitched sound of a saw cutting through the skull to expose the brain and watching a person's face being pulled from their chin to their forehead are two extremely powerful images I will never forget. But the sight of a young baby's body was the most difficult of all and a reminder of just how precious life really is. It was a sobering experience to see a part of life that not many people ever do, and it was confronting to realise that as part of our chosen career, these sights, and even worse ones, may be our frightening reality. Although I enjoyed the rotation, four weeks just wasn't long enough.

Phase 3 was sixteen weeks back at the Academy that included weapons training, self-defence and lots of study and role-playing. The incidents and scenarios seemed easy enough in the classroom context, working with my mates in the absence of any obvious threat. Although I knew that it wouldn't be so clear-cut out in the real world, it helped give us an idea to work from if we were ever placed in a similar situation. For me personally, I believe hands-on policing is one of the most important things that you need to learn as a rookie. Real-life skills, the ability to think and react quickly on your feet and being able to cope well under pressure are important attributes to have when contemplating a career in the police. You don't have to be an Einstein or a university graduate, just street-wise, physically fit, ethical and determined.

In this study phase, the concepts of corruption and stereotyping were waved about like a flag used by a one-eyed supporter at a football match. It was the era of the Royal Commission into police corruption, and we were branded as the 'new breed' of honest coppers. There was a lot of pressure put on us and we were force-fed the importance of values, ethics and integrity. To say these issues were well covered would be an understatement; when you are young and keen all you want to learn about is firearms, physical combat and how to arrest crooks.

And the food, don't ask about the food! The Academy buys it in bulk, cooks it in bulk and serves it in bulk. Some nights were okay, but other nights I was glad I was getting paid to study so that I could whip into town for some fast food or a counter meal and a drink. The Academy bar and the local nightclub, Tully's, were popular hangouts for police and the locals. It was the place to be on a Thursday night.

The night before our confirmation as Probationary Constables was the time to tie up loose ends and bid farewell to the good friends we had made. It was exciting but at the same time overwhelming. After six months of intense training we were ready to be released into the community, with guns.

The morning of the pass-out parade was hectic, after a nervous night's sleep. We were issued with our appointments and given words of encouragement from our mentors and principal. We donned our police uniforms for the first time, with pride, standing in front of the mirror conductors of our own success. What we had trained so hard for was upon us. The weather was beaming as I met my mum and brother at the carpark. It was a proud time, and I felt so lucky to be able to share the moment with my family.

Once the dignitaries and families had assembled around the parade grounds, we knew there was no turning back. With valour and honour we marched into the arena to applause from the crowd. With our caps in our hands and our hearts on our sleeves, we recited the Oath of Office. With precision and timing we marched past the podium before the final farewell. As the junior class lined the road towards the hall, we marched six abreast and tall in stature. And to the sounds of Auld Lang Syne, Class 265 came to a halt with a stomp. At the sound of the cheers and the official farewell, a wave of police caps thrown into the air with elation, pride and some relief.

There was only twelve months of on-the-job training remaining before we returned to the Academy for completion of our course and were rewarded with our first stripe as Constables of Police. No longer were we lower in importance than a flea on a police dog. We had become part of the future of policing and taken one step into our own destinies.

We had achieved what we had set out to accomplish and had completed the first transition. We had successfully survived the 'college of knowledge' and joined the rank and file of the NSW Police Service. 'Probationary Constable Garland' — I liked the sound of that!

## My First Posting

I remember when it was for me that my concept of policing changed from the 'warm and fuzzy' rhetoric of the Goulburn Police Academy to the harsh reality of frontline law enforcement.

After I had graduated as a Probationary Constable, I received my initial posting at Gosford Police Station on the New South Wales Central Coast at age twenty-one. I was assigned a senior and more experienced officer, referred to as a 'buddy,' whose role it was to continue my on-the-job training and assessments. He was huge, built more like a brick wall then a mentor. He was very likeable and funny, but not someone you would want to meet down a dark alley, especially if you were a crook.

On one of our first shifts together, we were called to a domestic dispute, where I naively attempted to impress my buddy with my 'college of knowledge' education and training. There I was, holding a radio in one hand and a torch in the other, trying to reason with the alleged crook. Within seconds, the naked felon, who was standing only a few feet in front of me, spat blood in my face and threw a volley of punches that luckily missed more often than they connected. It caught me off-guard. But, with the assistance of my buddy, the perpetrator was not so politely restrained and was brought before the Courts. From that moment on my love for 'the job' and my desire to be involved intensified. I also realised that life on the front line wasn't like anything I had read in a textbook or been taught within the sanctity of the Academy. I had survived my first real taste of frontline action and learnt from the experience. Luckily for me, I was able to load my first six months as a Constable of Police with many such opportunities to 're-educate' myself.

Perhaps for me the most memorable and intense incident I was involved in whilst at Gosford occurred early one night shift. We had received information about an alleged escapee hiding within the area. After a short briefing we formed a posse and headed for a suburb near

Wyoming, which was a highly populated housing commission area. The escapee, who was in custody for armed robbery offences, had fled from the juvenile correctional facility at Kariong. He was described as being sixteen years of age, Aboriginal, with dark hair and a thin build. Although I hadn't had much contact with Aboriginal people prior to this incident, the description seemed to depict most teenage Aboriginal youths.

We arrived at the location under cover of darkness and set up a perimeter. The house was on the northeastern corner of a T-intersection. It was a single-storey brick residence with lights illuminating from the inside. With two other police I went to the front door. There was some confusion about how we were going to execute the arrest, so some quick thinking was required. My partner knocked on the door.

A young voice answered, "Who is it?" My partner quickly said, "It's Jimmy." The voice from inside replied, "Hang on," and opened the door.

It was too easy! At this time we identified ourselves as police and a number of youths came running from the house. I heard someone yelling that the escapee was jumping fences into adjoining properties. The description came over that he was wearing a black jumper and black tracksuit pants with white stripes. This was not a positive thing considering it was in the middle of the night and most of the streetlights had been destroyed by rock-throwing kids.

I ran into the yard directly to the south of the location, where I scouted around. Without success, I went back to the street when a resident from the yard I had just come from yelled out that the youth had jumped their back fence. All the other police were busy, so I decided to go it alone. I jumped the six-foot timber fence at the back of the property, which led to a vacant lot in a parallel street. I then remembered that I had forgotten my portable radio, so all I had was my torch and my youthful exuberance. Not very good officer survival (OS) skills on my part!

As I walked along the street, I saw a willow tree in the corner of the vacant lot. The branches of the tree were leafy green and hung almost to the ground. I looked at the tree once, then again, and developed my first 'gut feeling.' I walked closer to the tree and shone my torch on the branches. Somehow through the leaves I could see a shimmering of white, which was the escapee's tracksuit pants glowing in the light of my torch.

I yelled out, "Police, stay where you are." From behind the tree ran a shadowy figure. I yelled, "Stop. Police," but he kept running, so I made a *split second* decision to chase him. With no radio to rely on it was him and me, one on one.

It was difficult to see where I was running because it was dark and the grass was long. The crook jumped over the fence with me in hot pursuit. I scaled the fence and saw him leap into the neighbour's yard. I had no idea where I was or if he was armed. As I approached the fence the light came on in the backyard, followed by a loud splash. I looked over the fence and saw the runaway pulling himself out of a swimming pool like a drowned rat. I climbed the fence and almost fell into the pool myself as I dropped to the other side.

He scampered across the yard and hurdled onto a trampoline. Before he could scramble over to safety I bounded behind him and grabbed his arm, balancing like a seesaw on top of the eight-foot fence, wrestling with him dangling above the ground below me.

He looked right at me and I could see fear and frustration in his eyes. I said, "Stay where you are. You're under arrest." He began to lash out but I held on. He was soaked from the pool and started to wriggle out of his jumper, so I threw myself over the fence and pinned him to the ground, only inches away from yet another pool. He continued to wave his arms and legs about, but with me sitting on his back there wasn't much chance of him getting away. I said jokingly, "You are under arrest and have the right to remain wet."

Just then, a rather savage looking Rottweiler came up to the gate where we were and began barking loudly and wildly. I just sat on the crook and waited, hoping the gate was closed properly and locked. I was too afraid and tired to move. Just then, the lights in the house came on and a middle-aged man brandishing a broom came to the top balcony.

He yelled out, "Who's there?"

"I am a Police Officer and I need some help. There are police around the corner, can you get them please?" I yelled.

The man went inside and a short time later came into the backyard with a Probationary Constable, who helped me handcuff the crook and lead him out the front where my offsider was standing with a big grin on his face. I could tell he was pleased. The escapee was taken back to the police station, where he was charged with numerous offences, including resisting arrest.

Back at the station, the crook said to me, "Ya know, cuz, you are the only white fella that's ever caught me. You mighty quick."

Not a bad compliment from someone you just sent back to prison. It was a memorable moment in my early career, probably because it was my first foot pursuit, but mainly because it was the first time I had to rely on my own abilities to make an arrest under difficult circumstances.

As they say: all good things must come to an end, but before my stint at Gosford finished and I was thrust into policing on the mean streets of Sydney, I had the opportunity for one more slice of action. My most vivid memory of my time at Gosford came when I worked with a very experienced Senior Constable from Highway Patrol. He had been seconded back to general duties to 'retrain' him in the latest police methods on the off chance he wanted to return to frontline policing.

He was very friendly and, like me, keen to get involved. One night shift in January 1997 we were rostered to use a sedan, which is like waving a red flag at a bull. This meant that we could go 'hunting' for stolen cars because sedans were the best cars for a pursuit. The night was pretty quiet, so we took the opportunity to conduct some random breath testing (RBT). It wasn't the most exhilarating job, but it helped fill the hours and ensured safety on our roads.

As we were patrolling around the Erina area east of Gosford, we heard that a pursuit was heading south from The Entrance. It was only fifteen minutes away, and the main road led right to where we were. So, like bunnies in a paddock, our ears pricked up and we began monitoring the locations as they were broadcast.

One of the last transmissions said that the offending driver had been involved in a shooting incident a short time earlier and that he was believed to still be armed. The pursuit was terminated on a number of occasions due to the speed of the offending vehicle and the category of the pursuing vehicle. All police vehicles were categorised for their suitability to engage in pursuits: category one (fully marked sedans); category two (unmarked sedans); category three (police caged trucks) and category four (police escort vans/buses, etc.). Naturally, category one vehicles were the most suitable, with caged trucks only allowed to engage in a pursuit if there were no other more suitable vehicles available.

The pursuing vehicle in this incident was an unmarked Detective's sedan (category two). The Duty Operations Inspector (DOI) at the Police Radio, who is responsible for monitoring radio transmissions and police pursuits, terminated the pursuit due to the danger to other road users.

The vehicle was last seen along the Entrance Road towards Erina. It was an old-style sedan, mustard in colour, which would make it easy to locate. We took a position near Erina and waited. And what do you know, not that long after, a mustard-coloured sedan went careening past us. I pointed it out to my eager offsider, who accelerated after it as I activated the warning lights and sirens. I informed the Police Radio that we were in pursuit and heading west towards Gosford. This was my first ever car pursuit, so I was a little nervous, but I was intent on doing things the right way and doing a good job.

We chased the vehicle through Gosford and over the Brian McGowan Bridge at speeds of up to 100km/hr. The driver was swerving all over the road and I regularly informed Police Radio of our location, speed and traffic conditions. As we climbed Kariong Hill towards the freeway it appeared that the vehicle was going to stop. As we rounded the bend at the top of the hill the road was blocked with a line of police cars. The vehicle slowed down but mounted the median strip, heading back down the hill to Gosford. At this time a fully marked Highway Patrol (HWP) car took over the pursuit with us right on his guard.

As the pursuit headed back towards the Brian McGowan Bridge, the sedan tried to squeeze between a couple of cars but lost control. It swerved and rammed the driver's side of the lead police vehicle. The HWP car spun around in front of the offending vehicle, causing it to drive onto the garden strip in the middle of the road in an explosion of dirt and dust. I jumped out of the car and ran towards the vehicle. I saw my partner and the other HWP officer had their service revolvers drawn and pointed at the driver. They couldn't get the driver's door open because of the accident damage, so I ran to the front passenger side and pulled at the door, which was also jammed. But, somehow, I managed to rip the door open and grab the driver by the shirt, dragging him from the car just as he leant forward and reached under the seat. I restrained him on the ground with my handcuffs whilst the other police searched the car.

I'll never forget the moment when a HWP officer came over to us and said, "You guys are lucky. This is what he was reaching for under the seat."

The officer held up an old-looking shotgun with a shortened barrel.

"And he's got one loaded in the barrel," he continued to say.

At that stage, my heart sank. A lot of 'what if' thoughts started running through my head. What if he had been able to reach the gun? Or what if he had started shooting at me? I took a few seconds to gather my thoughts as I looked at the carnage around me. It looked like a warzone with twisted and damaged cars, dirt all over the road and red and blue lights filling the night sky. To have such an exciting and successful result to my first ever car pursuit, which included the arrest of an armed and dangerous criminal, made the experience all the more meaningful, and a fitting end to my time at Gosford.

Unfortunately, the memory became bittersweet when I learned that the two HWP officers who took over the pursuit momentarily before he was arrested were awarded Commissioner's Commendations for Bravery for the incident, while my partner and I weren't even mentioned in the report. What made matters worse was that the presentation of the award was made at my graduation ceremony at the Police Academy when I became a Constable of Police!

It was hard to believe that my first six months of frontline policing had ended. The things that I had witnessed and been involved in you just had to see to believe. It was a frightening reality that the majority of the public would never experience divorced from the security of their own lives. It was a huge step for me to take too, stepping out of my own comfort zone and comparatively raw and passive existence.

This one-time study nerd, weighing less than fifty kilos wringing wet, was now out on the frontline literally tackling crime head-on, armed with my newly acquired knowledge, strength and commitment. There is no way I could have achieved or even contemplated doing the things I have before I joined the police.

## Chapter Two:
## Redfern Days

As my training stint at Gosford was coming to an end, we were told of our next postings in the Sydney metropolitan area. I was given the City Central station, which is in the heart of Sydney, opposite Darling Harbour. It may have been a good station to work in, but after my adventures in Gosford I wanted to be in the thick of things and where the action was. So after a few phone calls and swapping between some of my colleagues from the Academy, I got the posting I wanted — Redfern.

Redfern was a unique place to work. The types of crimes and the extreme levels of social deprivation that riddled parts of the community meant that as an officer you needed to be prepared for the uncertainty.

But, surprisingly, there is a lot of history in Redfern, besides the clashes between police and the local criminal element. It was originally a 100-acre plot of land owned by a local surgeon, William Redfern, in 1817. It was a town characterised by the migrant population, with the Aboriginal people migrating to the area in the 1920s to seek work on the railyards. This led to the development of 'the Block' opposite the former Eveleigh Railway, renamed Redfern Railway Station in 1972 when the Whitlam Government transferred ownership to the Aboriginal Housing Company. This became a unique project in Aboriginal-run housing and the focal point for the reconciliation movement. However, over time, the ravages of heroin took its toll on the area and its people, making it a 'hotspot for violence, crime and fear.'

I transferred to Redfern in February 1997 after I finished my tenure 'on the streets' at Gosford. The two places were like chalk and cheese.

The Central Coast was about two hours north of Sydney and more like a holiday vista than an urban jungle. Although it did have its problems with crime, Gosford wasn't as intense compared to the challenge I had just accepted, despite having a large area and population.

The Redfern Patrol bordered the south of the heart of Sydney (which I may refer to as the City), home of the iconic Harbour Bridge and Opera House. It was, at the time, one of the most volatile areas in the state, renowned for its violent clashes between the local Aboriginals and police. For months the newspapers and televisions were riddled with images of police battling with the Aboriginals in the Block as a result of our new English-born leader, Commissioner Ryan's 'positive policing' approach. It was just another area of policing where crime was high and resistance was regular. It's where I wanted to be. This was my chance to get involved and an opportunity to confront serious crime head-on and make a difference.

A learned Sergeant from Gosford told me before I transferred that "If you do well at Redfern, you can do well anywhere."

This was something I would always remember when times got tough. And more often than not, they did.

My first day at Redfern was a beautiful sunny day and I arrived early. I walked into the police station, which was in a small one-way access, number 30 Turner Street. The building was old and decrepit and as I entered I remembered some of the footage I'd seen from the infamous recordings of *Cop it Sweet* (where police were filmed for a documentary and widely criticised for making racist comments towards and about the Aboriginal community in Redfern). I realised then that before I even started my first shift at Redfern I would be branded the same, but I couldn't let that stop me. There were a few police sitting behind the counter. They just seemed to grunt and go back to what they were doing. It was like walking into a different culture, unlike the one I had experienced on the Coast. It felt like I would be seen as an outsider until I had proven that I was worthy enough, and that wasn't going to be easy.

The first day was an orientation where other first-day Probationary Constables and I were introduced to the staff around the station and taken on a tour of the area. One of our first stops was, of course, the Block. It was nothing like I had ever seen before. Rows and rows of houses were tattered and in ruin, and yet they were homes. It was like another world, a forgotten time when the police were seen as more of a hindrance than a help. It was one of the 'hot spots' of the state, and from the television footage I had seen, it was where all the riots were taking place and where the police were getting injured.

We were shown the full-time mini bus that was positioned at the top of Eveleigh Street and close to the Redfern Railway Station, where the majority of the crime was being committed. It was an initiative aimed at proactively reducing crime by virtue of a constant and high-profile police presence. It was the responsibility of the two police stationed there to monitor the area and act as a deterrent to crime. But, of course, while they were working from the bus, watching the railway station, crimes were being committed down the other end, closer to the City. It wasn't the easiest of jobs, and not many police liked working there, but I was looking forward to the challenge.

The Redfern Patrol, or Local Area Command as they call it these days, is quite a big area that covers both residential and industrial zones. The majority of the crime committed in the area was opportunistic, with the most prevalent offences being bag snatches, break-ins and stealing from motor vehicles. These are crimes that don't take much planning but that require anonymity and awareness. The drug problem is also a big concern in the area, with the Block being one of the biggest distributors in the state of illegal narcotics such as heroin, cannabis and cocaine, comparable to Kings Cross and Cabramatta.

The close proximity of Eveleigh Street to the railway station made it easy for offenders and drug users to come into the area, purchase their 'gear' and slip through pretty much undetected. Policing the area was tough, so enthusiastic proactive coppers were needed to get involved. Initially we had a problem with the security guards at the train station because they used to warn the local crooks when we were around or looking for them, but with time they became a very valuable asset.

There were about 140 police at Redfern, most of whom were very junior and generally inexperienced. But, importantly, they were dedicated, professional and reliable. The levels of enthusiasm and initiative shown by the majority of the police at the station were commendable and inspiring to say the least. As at Gosford, I was given a 'buddy' with whom I was supposed to work. But we didn't hit it off from the beginning. I found it difficult to fit into the scene of the station because there was a lot of bravado floating around and a lot of competitiveness. There was one group in particular, which included my buddy, that was referred to as the 'cliquey group.' You were either in it or way out of it. These officers believed they were better than everyone else. It caused a lot of tension at work, and if you were doing well, you had to look out. I had a few run-ins with them because I was eager and loved my job. I copped the brunt of their cynicism on more than one occasion. It was devastating to be branded and lynched by a group of your fellow workmates, especially when you were new and had done nothing wrong.

One particular morning, I found a gay magazine in my pigeonhole with comments suggesting I was a homosexual scribbled over it. I can't remember what it said now, but I was shattered. I couldn't believe that I was being bullied at work. This type of irresponsible and childish behaviour was something that you would expect (unfortunately) to see in a school playground and certainly not within the structure of the NSW Police. I definitely wasn't gay and was deeply offended to be labelled and find such trash at my place of work. I reported the incident to the Commander and had a very good idea who was responsible. But being so junior at a new station, I felt that if I had gone ahead with an official complaint, it could have negatively affected my career. I was told that the matter would be fully investigated if that was what I wanted, but I was too afraid of being alienated. I loved my job, and so despite its going against my moral grain, I chose to ignore the incident and accepted a 'warning' being given to the entire station.

It probably didn't help that I was young and fit with streaked blonde hair and had inherited the nickname 'Judy' whilst I was working at Gosford. It wasn't because I wore ruby slippers or hung around with munchkins, just that my last name was Garland (funnily enough my mother's name is Judy Garland by marriage and my daughter Teagan was actually born on the real Judy Garland's birthday). The nickname has never bothered me and has provided some interesting looks and funny moments throughout my life. It's just another example of unique police humour. My friends and family still call me Judy even today, some more often than they call me Jeff. It's just the discriminatory labels and treatment I got that really hurt. Things eventually improved, especially after the officers whom I believed were involved were transferred from the station. But it left me feeling disheartened very early in my career.

## THE MEETING

The first few months at Redfern were pretty slow for me, both personally and professionally. One thing I was warned about before I joined the force was never to get involved with another 'coppa,' especially one you worked with. This was easy at Gosford because there weren't too many young female officers, but Redfern was a little harder. There were some quite attractive female police at Redfern, but none that really caught my eye. That was until…

It was the morning of May 19th, 1997, and I was sitting in the station area waiting for a charge to be verified by the Supervisor. It was a busy night shift, with four arrests, and I was buggered. But it was the morning the new Probationers were to start their orientation at Redfern, so I had something to look forward to, which kept me awake. It wasn't that I was interested, just a bit curious. Before long, two young, red-headed females walked through the front door. I didn't pay much attention at first, but then they came around the corner into the station area. For perhaps the first time in my life I was lost for words, which is quite an achievement. She was the most beautiful woman I had ever seen, with the biggest brown puppy eyes and the warmest smile that could light up the darkest room. And she looked great in uniform. It was too good to be true. I thought I was just tired. I remembered what was said to me about getting involved with workmates, so I finished my charge, went home and had a good, long sleep.

Over the next few weeks, I managed to find out that her name was Rachael and that she had come to Redfern straight from the Academy. It took me a while to work up enough courage to talk to her, and when I did, I was glad I had. I was working down Redfern Railway Station doing beats with my partner when I saw Rachael and some other officers walk onto the concourse. I asked her partner if he needed a lift home to the Coast and was pleased to find out that Rachael was from there as well, so being the gentleman I was, and for no other underlying reason, I offered to drive her home, and she accepted with a smile.

On the way home that afternoon, the three of us talked about work and our lives before we joined the police. It made the two-hour trip home feel shorter and more enjoyable. By the time we reached Gosford train station we knew each other pretty well, but I was regretting having to say goodbye to my new lady friend. I dropped our 'third wheel' off at the train station and offered to take Rachael to her front door. I only lived about five minutes away but thought that if I drove her home we could talk some more. She was so friendly and approachable, but I was crushed to find out that she was already engaged. As she leant between the front seats to say goodbye I felt this uncontrollable urge to kiss her. But my conscience got the better of me, and thankfully so.

We said our goodbyes. Rachael got out, but then opened the front passenger door and leant in. She looked so beautiful, so sweet and innocent. I wanted to tell her what I was feeling but said nothing in light of her current relationship status. She grabbed her books and got on the train. I went home and had a very cold shower.

Over the next few weeks, Rachael and I grew very close. I was going through a tough time trying to locate and spend time with my daughter, and Rachael was always there for me to offer support. I felt like I had shared my soul with her, and yet at the same time I wanted to push her away. I knew deep down that Rachael was someone with whom I could spend the rest of my life, but this was early days, and as far as I knew, she wasn't available.

I remember the first time we went out to the movies to watch the not-so-romantic Jean Claude Van Damme thriller, *Double Team*; she was wearing a chocolate brown shirt with white jeans. Very sexy! She told me later that night that she had split up with her fiancée, so naturally I did everything I could to console her. I wondered if she had left him to be with me, but if she had she wouldn't admit it. After the movies we went back to my place, where I spoilt her with a home-cooked dinner. We also shared the sweetest and most sensual kiss. We both realised from that point on that there was no turning back.

We spent more time together and began getting intimate with each other, but didn't consummate the relationship, although unofficially we were dating. After about six weeks we shared our first night together, and it was like losing my virginity all over again. Rachael was one of the most passionate, sensual and intense lovers I had ever experienced. Let me just say that she was late for work the next morning. I took a risk in July and asked Rachael to come away with me to Queensland to see my daughter, which she agreed to. It was a big step for me, but I wanted Rachael to become part of my life. I picked her up from her home and met her mum, dad and younger brother, who all seemed quite nice.

The trip to Queensland was great. We talked and joked around a lot, which helped us get even closer. It was very special for me to have Rachael sharing my time with my daughter because I felt that she would play a big part in both our futures. We had such a good time, and both the girls got on like a house on fire. She was a natural mother.

Over the following few weeks I began to create some space between Rachael and me because I was worried that I was getting too close to her too quickly. We had never actually decided to have a relationship but simply to be good friends. I started seeing other girls at the time on a casual basis, which Rachael knew about. I don't think she was too impressed, but we still spent lots of time together talking and mucking around. I guess this distancing was my way of trying to stop myself from falling head over heels in love with her.

After about five months at Redfern I headed back down to the Police Academy in July 1997 to be confirmed as a Constable of Police and given my first stripe, referred to as a 'hook.' We had been on the streets for almost a year and it was time to catch up with our fellow classmates who had survived the first twelve months. It was still cold in Goulburn and not much had changed. But it was good to hear all the war stories from police around the state. Even though there was still some training to do, it was like a big reunion. I had been looking forward to it for some time.

My family came down on the morning of the confirmation ceremony and met Rachael for the first time. (I found out years later that Mum knew straight away that we were right for one another and believed that one day we would be married).

I will always remember my graduation day. I had an overwhelming feeling of achievement and of belonging to a culture of sacrifice and service. After years of hard work, I had accomplished my goal and was beginning a new life, with a new family of colleagues and the prospect of never-ending opportunities. It felt like Rachael would be part of my future too.

## Dog Attack

Not too long after my graduation on a beautiful sunny Saturday I was in the station area completing some of the endless paperwork when an urgent message came over the police radio. It was unusual because it wasn't an 'armed robbery' or 'break and enter' in progress, but rather a report of a dog attack. Over the confusion of the station noise I could make out that a large dog was mauling a puppy in Waterloo. I ran from the station with my partner and headed for the area of concern under lights and sirens. As we pulled up at the front of the house there was a crowd of agitated and panicked onlookers yelling and screaming.

Waterloo was a big problem area within the Redfern LAC. It is a neighbouring suburb within the Command that over time had grown into a festering cesspool of crime, thanks to the high levels of unemployment and delinquency amongst the youth. It hadn't reached the limits of chaos it later achieved, but this was only the beginning — well, for me, anyway.

I got out of the police truck and by this time a number of other units had arrived. In the front yard of one of the townhouses a large ferocious dog was attacking a small puppy, about three months old. The large dog had the pup around the back of the neck and was shaking it savagely. A burly Senior Constable drew his service baton and walloped the large dog over the snout. It seemed to do the trick. The dog dropped the pup and momentarily appeared dazed, but then it just shook its head and snatched the pup into its mouth. The Senior Constable hit the dog again, but there was the same insignificant result.

By this stage, the crowd was becoming upset and accusing us of not acting quickly enough. It appeared that the only option was to shoot the attacking dog, but there were too many bystanders to take that risk in case the bullet ricocheted off the walls or ground. The Senior Constable took another swipe at the dog and again the pup fell from its jaws. The pup was still alive but suffering from shock. As the large dog walked stunned around the front courtyard I made a *split second* decision. I jumped the side fence and into the courtyard as the dog headed towards the pup yet again.

I lunged at the dog and grabbed him around the neck from behind. He began thrashing his body around and snapping his jaws in an attempt to bite me. I knelt down and tried to keep his head pinned to the ground, which took all my strength. I looked to see that the other police and onlookers were just standing there in disbelief. They couldn't believe what I was doing, and frankly I couldn't believe it either.

Rachael was standing on the outside of the fence screaming at me to get out, but I couldn't. My hands were frozen on the back of the dog's neck, trying to keep parts of my anatomy intact. She leant over the fence and grabbed the pup to safety. By this time the dog was really getting cranky and began stalking around the courtyard. I tried to keep him still but it wasn't easy. My hands were tiring. Luckily someone had grabbed a dog lead, which helped me see an end to the nightmare. Rachael grabbed the lead and called me over towards the fence. I wanted to move but I was too afraid that if I did I would lose my grip and the dog would finish off with me what he had started with the pup.

I dragged the mutt over to the fence as Rachael tied the leash to its collar. Once I knew it was safely restrained I ran from the courtyard and threw myself over the nearest fence. My hands were stiff and cramped and I couldn't straighten my fingers because I had been holding on so tight. I was exhausted.

An officer walked up to me and said, "Judy, that was one of the bravest things I have ever seen. You're a fucking idiot!"

The owner of the dog came over to the front yard where we were all standing. The crowd had grown, which seemed to inflame the situation. The owner was agitated and abusive towards the police. I tried to calm him down, which may not have been the best thing to do, as he started pushing people and yelling at us to let his dog go, but thankfully some of the crowd restrained him before things got out of hand.

And that was my first encounter with one of the members of the Waterloo Boyz — but more about them later. The Council took the dog away and I think it was destroyed. Rachael and I took the pup to a vet and it made a full recovery.

Not long after this incident, I was injured at work following a bungled arrest in Eveleigh Lane and had six weeks leave. I spent most of the time at Rachael's place, gratefully receiving her tender loving care. Over that period I grew closer to Rachael and her family and was pleased to be able to reciprocate her support when she later faced a tough time when her parents divorced. My parents had divorced when I was young, so I could empathise with what she was feeling.

Later that month, Rachael and I went to the 1997 Rugby League Grand Final in Sydney to watch the mighty Newcastle Knights snatch a last-second victory over the hapless Manly Sea Eagles. We had a fantastic time together, and from that moment I knew that I couldn't live without her. So I asked her parent's consent and planned the perfect evening to propose. I took Rachael to dinner in Sydney, to the opening of Les Miserables and the Sydney Casino, and then, on bended knee, on the 24th floor of the ANA Hotel overlooking Sydney Harbour, I asked her to be my wife.

I wrote on a card to her, "You are my world, you are my life, I love you so very much, will you be my wife?" And after a moment of silence, she tearfully accepted.

## Chapter Three:
# Black Market Murders

One of the things I loved most about policing was the unpredictability of the job. You never know what may happen next. Sometimes you find yourself in situations you could never have foreseen, as was the case in November 1997. It was an early Sunday afternoon. The venue was a local nightclub, a popular spot renowned for its skimpily clad patrons, sexual fantasies and high levels of drug use.

It was also 'Open Day' at the Redfern Police Station. We were told by the Supervisors to make ourselves scarce because we wouldn't want to give the public the opinion that we were lazing around on a beautiful sunny day when we should be out fighting crime. My partner and I were supposed to be performing beats around the Redfern area, but I managed to swindle the use of a marked sedan for the shift. We made the usual never-ending patrols around the Block and Chippendale areas hunting for criminals, but with little success.

The local nightclub, the Black Market Café in Chippendale, was very popular on Sunday mornings after all the other spots in the City had closed. It was an alternative venue for those who liked to be a bit different. We drove around the area for a while and noticed that things were unusually quiet, which was not a good omen.

By now, it was 12.45 p.m. and getting close to lunchtime, and we decided to do one last lap before a break. As I drove along Regent Street, I felt that something was about to happen. I hadn't had this reaction since the foot pursuit with the escapee at Gosford. I looked to the service station opposite the nightclub and noticed a crowd that had gathered and was looking down at the entrance to the club. It seemed something wasn't right, but I didn't know what. As I drove around the block towards the service station, my 'gut feeling' got stronger.

We approached the intersection of Regent and Meagher Street, where I saw two men running away from the front of the club. This was not necessarily unusual for this area, but these men didn't fit the regular type of partygoer for the club. The place was a hangout for young adults, and both men were in their late thirties or early forties. Moreover, it was the middle of a hot sunny day in November and one of the men was wearing a dark-coloured trench coat. The fact that both the men stopped running when they saw us also piqued my curiosity. My initial reaction was to stop the police vehicle and get out. I wanted to speak to them and find out what was going on, but something made me stay in the car, where I waited and watched. It was a decision that I believe spared my life and that of my partner.

The man closest to the club was aged in his late thirties, about six feet tall, medium build, with long brown hair. He was wearing a dark trench coat and had his hand concealed inside his jacket, as if he was hiding something. The other man was in his early forties, of solid build and a little shorter. At this stage I was parked in the middle of the street and could clearly see both men.

They slowed to a walking pace after noticing the police car. The taller man approached the passenger door of a silver Porsche, which was parked about two car lengths in front of us. He opened the door and got into the car without removing his hand from his coat. I had a strong feeling that the two men were armed and had just committed, or were about to commit, a serious crime. The other man got into the driver's seat and within seconds the Porsche had pulled out onto the street.

We performed a check on the car's registration number, but it had not been reported stolen. Nevertheless, we decided to follow it. As we approached an intersection, the traffic lights turned red and, without warning, the Porsche took off. We activated our warning lights and sirens and initiated a pursuit. I didn't expect it because the car wasn't stolen, so considering my earlier observations, they were obviously running from something.

We chased the Porsche along Cleveland Street towards the Eastern Suburbs, where it increased speed to about 100km/hr, running a number of red lights, driving onto the wrong side of the road towards oncoming cars and narrowly missing a police caged truck. As my partner updated the speed of the Porsche, traffic conditions and locations to Police Radio, the Porsche drove onto the incorrect side of the road again, turned left through a red light and accelerated back towards the City, with us in hot pursuit.

The felons were swerving over the road and speeding past the few cars that were around. Suddenly the Porsche swerved, made a harsh right turn through a stop sign and accelerated to about 100km/hr in a 60km/hr zone, before running another red light, swerving into oncoming traffic and heading towards King's Cross. It was clear that these males were determined to escape capture for whatever crime they had just committed, but I wasn't letting them get away…until the Duty Operations Inspector at Police Radio terminated the pursuit. Begrudgingly, we deactivated the warning lights and sirens and watched as the Porsche continued on its course for freedom.

My instinct that the men were running from something serious intensified as the Porsche began to swerve between traffic, forcing other cars from the road, even though we were no longer in pursuit. I watched as it mounted the median strip and turned off into a side street. I knew I couldn't give up, so even though I had been told not to continue the pursuit, my initiative got the better of me and I followed the fleeing car over the median strip and into the narrow side street. But the Porsche was nowhere to be seen, just a row of traffic ahead. I thought that we had lost them. But my police thinking kicked in; if they weren't in front of us, then they must be beside us, somewhere.

There was only a little laneway and a street, so, working on instinct, I turned down the street, and suddenly the man wearing the trench coat walked around the corner. I couldn't believe my luck.

I got out of the car, said, "Mate, don't move," and held him against the wall.

I still didn't know what the men had done, but because of what we had seen outside the nightclub, the possible concealment of an unknown object/weapon inside the overcoat and the subsequent pursuit, we had reasonable grounds to 'stop, search and detain' him.

I held the offender face first against the wall and spread his legs apart. I asked my partner to keep him against the wall while I peeked around the corner for the driver. I informed Police Radio that we had one man in custody as I walked the couple of metres to the laneway, where I could see the Porsche, but no driver. As I turned back towards my partner, the apprehended man pushed off the wall and ran down the street with my partner still attached to his coat, before breaking free. I wished I had handcuffed him!

We chased him down the street towards the main road, where an elderly gentleman was walking his bike along the street. Without hesitation, he threw his bike into the path of the male, causing him to stumble. We forced the man to the ground and following a violent struggle managed to restrain and handcuff him.

At that time, I noticed that he had dried blood on his left wrist; I asked him how it got there, but he didn't reply. My partner notified the Police Radio that the offender was in custody. Shortly after, when a police truck arrived, he was arrested for resisting police, cautioned and conveyed from the scene.

We had just been involved in a high-speed pursuit with a car that wasn't stolen, followed by a foot pursuit with the passenger of the vehicle, who was bleeding from a wound to his wrist. We honestly had no idea what was going on, but because the offender had resisted our attempts to lawfully stop and search him, we had sufficient reason to investigate further.

I gave a brief description of the driver of the Porsche through the police radio for broadcast and requested the assistance of a dog squad officer to search for the other male. I went back to the Porsche and found a pair of gloves on the front seat.

About fifteen minutes after the initial pursuit, my partner and I were still at the scene waiting for the dog squad to arrive when over the police radio we heard that a firearm had been thrown out of the Porsche during the course of the pursuit and had been handed in at the Mounted Police Station.

One of the other police at the scene said to me, "What have you got yourself into, Judy?"

I didn't know, but it began to sink in that these males were involved in something far more serious than just traffic matters.

Then I did something stupid. After listening to the advice of other police from Redfern, I called off the dog squad vehicle because it would be near impossible to track someone in such a high-pedestrian area. I knew at some level that this wasn't the best course of action, but my inexperience and respect for authority blinded my judgement. It may not have resulted in locating the other male, but considering what was about to transpire I should have at least tried.

Ten minutes later, I heard a 'double beeper' over the police radio. (A 'beep' is a high-pitched tone designed to co-ordinate police responses to jobs. One beep is designed to focus your attention or broadcast a memo; two beeps signifies an urgent, life-threatening job and three beeps means 'Signal One' and that an officer needs urgent assistance.)

> *Beep Beep: "Redfern car, any car in the vicinity, reports of a shooting at the Black Market nightclub in Chippendale."*

I knew right then that the men we had pursued were involved, but I didn't acknowledge it. I don't know if it was through inexperience, being overwhelmed by the reality of the situation sinking in or believing that Police Radio somehow already knew. The radio operator even asked me about the description of the offenders, and not once did I inform him that that was where I had first seen the men and where the pursuit had started, or that the offender in custody from the Porsche from which the firearm had been thrown was bleeding. At that moment I simply forgot that the other police hadn't witnessed what I had seen. I just wanted my tow truck for the Porsche.

A short time later, it was confirmed that there had been a shooting inside the nightclub, with two people confirmed dead and another in a serious condition. Although, only half an hour before, we had been involved in the detection, pursuit and arrest of a murder suspect who could have, at any time, turned a firearm on me or my partner to aid his escape, I wasn't afraid until I had a chance to reflect on what might have happened.

Once the Porsche had been towed away, my partner and I went to the Sydney Police Centre, where our offender was sitting in the dock. I will refer to him as Adamson (not his real name). He complained of soreness in his left wrist, and I arranged for ambulance officers to attend to him. My partner and I began to make notes about what had happened to piece it all together. I was fielding questions from other police in the charge room about the pursuit and arrest, but I still didn't have the full picture.

I was in shock and rang Rachael. She was at home having lunch with some girlfriends and when I told her what had happened she just laughed.

"Why doesn't that surprise me?" she said.

It was good to talk it all through with her. She was calm and level-headed and gave me the opportunity to reflect on my actions. With hindsight, I could clearly see the dangers we had unwittingly faced, and it honestly scared me.

The ambulance officers arrived and treated Adamson. He required surgery on his wound and needed to go to hospital. My partner and I stood guard at the hospital until the lead Detective, who was handling the investigation, arrived. I told him about my observations outside the nightclub and how I believed that Adamson was one of the shooters. Adamson had declined to be interviewed about the matter, but after seeking legal advice he consented to a blood sample and swab and the retention of his clothing for examination and evidence. Here I was involved in the arrest of the main suspect of a multiple shooting homicide, and Detectives and professionals were turning to *me* for information.

Adamson was found to be a former member of an Outlaw MotorCycle Gang (OMCG) I will call 'the Fetts' (not their real name). The fact that he was wearing a Fetts belt was evidence of the fact he was entitled to life membership. The four victims of the shooting were the National President, Sergeant at Arms and two probationary members of an opposing OMCG I will call 'the Vaders' (not their real name). I know they are Star Wars analogies, but they are representative of the evil dark side of our society. My partner and I stood guard for hours and then escorted Adamson to surgery to have fragments of bone and hair removed from his wound, which he conceded was from a gunshot. After the surgery, my partner and I were relieved by other police and were stunned to see armed State Protection Group police manning the doors of the hospital. Apparently there had been a few members of Adamson's gang banging on the windows of the hospital, attempting to free him.

When we got back to Redfern Police Station, we completed our statements and started the paperwork to ensure Adamson would be charged with resisting police when he was released from hospital. The following days passed in a blur. I did a lot of overtime and spent most nights sleeping under a desk at the police station.

---

Up until this incident, I had never had much to do with OMCGs. There is no doubt they were well organised, not restricted to budgetary constraints and certainly not afraid of the police, which over time has proven true. I had heard rumours that during a police raid on an

OMCG clubhouse they found photographs and intelligence of police officers working within the area, including home addresses and the names of their children and where they attended school. I guess one of the 'attractions' of being a member of an OMCG was that, unlike the police, you considered yourself 'outside the law' (hence the term 'outlaw') and part of the one percent (one-percenters) of the community who operated outside of society's legal conventions. It is rumoured that the first OMCG originated in the USA in the 1940s. Almost seventy years later it is believed that there are about forty OMCG gangs active in Australia, 'allegedly' involved in organised crime such as drug manufacture, money laundering, vehicle rebirthing, extortion, illegal firearm use/trafficking, prostitution, fraud and murder, to name a few.

The oldest OMCG is the Hell's Angels (1948). They are believed to be the first 'Master Chefs' of methamphetamine (speed) during the 1980s made by bikies in Australia. The largest OMCG in Australia are the Rebels (1969); with about 2,000 members, they have chapters dotted over the Australian landscape. The most infamous of the OMCGs are the Comancheros (1973) and Bandidos (1983), following the Milperra Father's Day Massacre in 1984 in which seven people were killed and twenty-eight people were injured. The newest and perhaps most active OMCG in Australia are Notorious (2007) from Sydney, who are predominantly youth of Middle Eastern background who wear expensive runners and fashionable t-shirts and are clean-shaven, which is in distinct contrast from the traditional OMCG image of denim jackets, leather boots and beards.

The nature of OMCGs has become more sophisticated and has evolved over time in response to a changing criminal environment and more advanced law enforcement. They are like businessmen, aware of the concept of supply and demand and running international franchises. According to the Australian Crime Commission, the OMCGs are no longer isolated amongst the members. They provide their criminal 'expertise' to traditional organised crime groups and also 'recruit' external expertise, such as chemists, accountants and lawyers, to assist in the manufacture, concealment and defence of their activities. OMCGs have also recruited members who don't even ride motorbikes, making the infamous Harley Davidson 'optional extras' just to keep the police on their toes.

This certainly was a prodigious introduction for me, not only to the existence of OMCGs in everyday society, but also to the considerable and real threat that they posed to anyone who stood in their way.

A few days after the shooting, a third victim died in hospital. The shooting sent shockwaves through the police, as reprisals were likely. Adamson and his 'mate' had murdered two of the highest-ranking members of an opposition OMCG in cold blood. It was likely that retaliation would be swift and harsh. Although we didn't know the motive, we believed it must have had something to do with drugs or weapons…or did it?

About two weeks later, I was given a copy of the pursuit tape for the brief of evidence. At the time of the incident I had been too busy driving to listen to what was happening, focused on finding the Porsche while my partner calmly and professionally called our locations. I pushed the tape into the car player as I was driving home with Rachael one evening and was totally unprepared for what I heard.

I think that for the first time, the reality of that day hit me. All my suppressed fears came to the surface. I broke down in tears and had to stop the car so that Rachael could drive. I kept thinking, What if I had gotten out of the car and stopped them? What if they had started shooting at us? Why didn't I say anything to my offsider? Why didn't I search and handcuff the male before I looked for the Porsche? It was like reliving the incident all over again. For the next few weeks, I was a nervous wreck. I couldn't sleep and suffered nightmares from which I would wake up in a cold sweat, screaming and crying uncontrollably.

Rachael was a wonderful support. We talked and talked and she held me when I needed comforting. The Police Service had offered me counselling in the days following the murders, but I didn't take it up because at the time I didn't feel like I needed it. But this was weeks later. I felt like I couldn't approach anyone for help, as policing is not the type of job where showing emotions is accepted. It's frowned upon by the culture as a sign of weakness or 'unpolice-like behaviour.'

By the end of December, the other murderer had been identified but was still missing. Apparently Adamson had dobbed him in. In February 1998, my partner and I were summoned to the Supervisor's office and asked to convey a prisoner from the Sydney Police Centre charge room to Central Local Court. When I looked in the dock I couldn't believe my eyes. The person we had been sent to convey was the man who had been driving the silver Porsche in November. I was 100 percent positive it was him, despite the fact that he had shaved his hair off. It was strongly prejudicial against him, as an accused person, to be identified by me whilst being charged with a triple murder. I spoke to the Crime Agencies Detectives and confirmed that he was the other man at the club. The shorter murderer I will refer to as Doyle (not his real name). He was a very large, frightening man whom I wouldn't want to meet in a dark alley or the basement of a nightclub!

I finally felt as if we had come complete circle. We had arrested the first offender and had been disappointed and annoyed about losing the second. But here he was. He had been stopped by Customs in Botany Bay onboard a freight ship attempting to leave the country with a fake passport and a lot of cash. When he was taken back to the local cop shop it was discovered he was wanted for the homicides. He was caught by freak chance, as was the timing of our patrol around Chippendale. If we hadn't driven past the nightclub at the moment the gunmen were running out, who knows what may have happened? But that's the importance of being proactive and being on the frontline.

Although the offenders had been arrested and charged and were in custody, it was still going to be some time, littered with numerous Court appearances and legal arguments, before the matter would proceed to trial, if it even got that far.

As I was only involved in the arrest of the murderers and not the actual investigation, I have done my research and read all of the Supreme Court decisions from 1999, 2000 and 2003, as well as the Criminal Court of Appeal decisions from 2001 and 2005, which has given me great insight into what happened and why.

The iconic Black Market Café, or Hellfire club, as some knew it, would best be described as a 'day club.' Once the nightlife of Kings Cross and the City had been interrupted with the break of dawn, that was where the party would continue until mid-afternoon. It was an imposing two-storey brick building on the corner of an arterial road, only minutes away from the hustle and bustle of the Sydney CBD.

From the outside it looked like a 'haunted house' from an amusement park, splattered with charcoal and black on the towering outer walls with rows of metal bars lining the side and the arched entryway. Inside was nothing short of shambolic, more like a house gutted by fire then a trendy Sydney nightspot.

Its ash-coloured interior, stained timber floors, paint-chipped walls and décor were almost medieval for its time and place. The lack of lighting just added to the sense of foreboding. I mean, it was dark. It certainly wasn't the typical chic 'café' you would expect to find on the outskirts of the most beautiful city in Australia. Although I had patrolled the area numerous times throughout my short career, I had only ventured inside once to make a foot patrol and was seriously affronted by its appearance, smell and choice of entertainment. From memory, after you walked through the entry and into the club there was a cloakroom to the right hiding a concealed set of concrete stairs that led to the basement where this ambush occurred.

As I have stated, I never visited the crime scene, so I am basing my opinion on the decisions of the NSW Supreme Court and NSW Criminal Court of Appeal, my observations relating from my own involvement in the incident and as a result of an episode of *Gangs of Oz* called 'The Bikies: Taking Care of Business' shown on Channel 7 in 2010, during which there was a re-enactment of what police alleged occurred in the basement based on an extensive forensic reconstruction of the crime scene and on the available physical evidence.

Doyle, thirty-three, was a member of the Fetts OMCG at the time of the murders. He was born in Greece and emigrated with his family to Australia in 1969. He had convictions for drug supply and minor traffic matters on his criminal record; Adamson, thirty-nine, was a former member of the Fetts OMCG (1985-1996) at the time of the murders. He had served for three years in the armed forces, had no prior criminal record and was working as a tattooist.

Interestingly, the defences raised by Adamson and Doyle during the proceedings changed, and at times they even 'dobbed' each other in. At the initial Supreme Court trial in 1999, Doyle's alibi was that he wasn't at the club at the time of the shooting, and he appeared to turn on Adamson. He admitted going to the Black Market Café with his girlfriend and Adamson on the morning of November 9th, 1997, but left prior to the shooting, leaving the keys with Adamson, who remained at the club. He said that he returned home with his girlfriend, had a sleep and only heard about the shooting after hearing about the murders on TV and seeing his Porsche being towed away.

Adamson, however, contradicted Doyle's version by 'almost' adopting the account he made to police in the ERISP the day following his arrest. Adamson recalled that Doyle had driven him to the Black Market Café in his silver Porsche that morning. He stated that he was drunk at the time and that after leaving the toilet and entering the cloak room his hand was hit 'violently' as he tried to remove his jacket. He then left the club, noticed his hand was injured and bleeding and was grabbed by Doyle, who led him to the Porsche parked nearby to go to the hospital. Although he admits Doyle was driving fast, he denies throwing anything from the vehicle and doesn't recall breaking free of the police.

However, Adamson further added in evidence, somewhat contradictorily, that Doyle's girlfriend was with them at the club. He admits to being affected by speed and cocaine, as well as alcohol. He agrees that they returned to Doyle's house about midday but returned to the Black Market Café a short time later so that Doyle could meet a female. He also stated that he didn't remember the 'car trip' or seeing the police because of the pain and his level of intoxication but remembered being left in the stationary Porsche by Doyle and then attempting to escape from Police because he was "scared and confused."

None of this the Jury or Court believed due to other available witness accounts and physical evidence. Not surprisingly, there was another twist in the tale. Both Doyle and Adamson had a new account of what really happened on the 9th of November 1997 at the Black Market Café. But this time, both of them knew who was responsible, and it wasn't them, or each other. It was another member of the Fetts OMCG, whom I shall name Gibson (not his real name).

Both Doyle and Adamson gave evidence that Gibson wanted 'back-up' at the Black Market Café because the National President, Sergeant at Arms and two probationary nominee members of the Vaders OMCG had arrived. Fearing that there might be trouble, Gibson went to Doyle's house, where he drove them back to the nightclub in the Porsche, picking Adamson up on the way. Gibson then directed Doyle to wait outside to keep watch and told Adamson to stand guard at the basement door. Gibson and another Fetts OMCG member (whom they were too afraid to identify because he was "still around") went into the basement. A short time later, gunshots were heard, the door was suddenly opened and Adamson was shot in the wrist. They then assert that Gibson, "panicking," gave the pistol to Adamson and told him to get rid of it. Adamson admitted to throwing the pistol from the car during the subsequent police chase, but Doyle denied knowledge of a second pistol or of taking any guns to the club.

Doyle admitted in the witness box that the alibi defence he raised in the first trial was false because he feared reprisals against his family if he gave evidence against Gibson. Adamson also admitted that the version he told police in his ERISP and evidence he gave during the first trial was also false. The reason for this revelation was that the person they were now accusing of the murders, Gibson, was dead, and so they felt they were able to tell the truth (and because he wasn't alive to defend himself against the allegations). Unfortunately, both of them had known that Gibson was dead for some time before they told their solicitors at the commencement of this final trial.

Although the learned Judge identified that both versions were now consistent with each other, Adamson denied fashioning his evidence to "dovetail" with Doyle's. The Defence counsel, however, accepted the possibility that the accused persons may have "put their heads together to tell a mutually false account." It was held by the trial Judge, and a subsequent Criminal Court of Appeal decision, that these lies were sufficient evidence of consciousness of guilt. Ultimately, the Court concluded on the available evidence that:

Adamson and Doyle were, or had been, members of the Fetts OMCG. They travelled to the Black Market Café in Doyle's Porsche on the morning of November 9th, 1997. An off-duty doorman (also a member of the Fetts OMCG) obtained keys to the basement. Members of the Vaders OMCG were told that the doorman and Doyle wanted a meeting with them in the basement. The three deceased went to the basement whilst the other Vaders member waited inside the club. According to ballistics, seven 9mm shots (three from a Berretta and four from a Smith & Wesson) and one .25 calibre shot was fired.

It is believed, based on the forensic reconstruction of the positioning of the deceased persons, shell casings, blood and other available physical evidence, that Doyle (armed with the Smith & Wesson) and Adamson (armed with the Berretta) were already present in the room at the time the Vaders OMCG members entered, Doyle was behind the door and Adamson at the far end of the room to draw their attention. Once inside, Doyle fatally shot the 'Sergeant at Arms' once from behind in the left side of the head above the ear. A physical struggle then ensued, during which time Doyle shot the probationary nominee, who was present, in the side of the neck below the right ear, and Adamson shot the National President in the right arm/wrist. Adamson then shot the probationary nominee in the forehead 'execution style,' killing him instantly.

It is believed that upon hearing the shots the other probationary nominee entered the basement and shot Adamson in the left wrist with a .25 calibre firearm. The nominee was then shot in the arm and neck by Doyle before running up the stairs and being taken to hospital by taxi. Adamson then shot the National President once in the head at close range before he and Doyle exited the basement, leaving the bikie icon mortally wounded and clinging to life.

A short time later, Doyle was seen running from the basement with Adamson, who was waving a gun. Doyle and Adamson were then seen by witnesses and police (that's me and my partner) running from the front of the Black Market Café towards the Porsche, with Adamson attempting to conceal something inside his jacket. Police pursued the Porsche, during which time two firearms, a 9mm Beretta and a 9mm Smith & Wesson, were thrown from the vehicle and later recovered by police. The pursuit was terminated due to high speed. The Porsche was found abandoned. Adamson was arrested, but Doyle escaped. Sometime later a male (subsequently charged with being an accessory after the fact) obtained a ticket for Doyle to travel by sea to Japan. Doyle was arrested in February 1998 on the vessel, carrying a stolen passport, a driver's licence in a false name and a large amount of cash. He was taken to a police station where he was fingerprinted, correctly identified and charged with multiple homicide.

Although Doyle had managed to avoid arrest for a few months, investigators already had an idea he may have been involved thanks to the courage of a lone female witness who was able to identify and willing to testify against the two cold-blooded murderers. Only a few days after the shootings, police had executed a search warrant on Doyle's premises, where they located decisive evidence, including a photo of him holding two firearms that were similar to the ones used in the shooting and thrown from the Porsche.

As a result, police were able to identify the rural property in Queanbeyan where the photographs were taken, which revealed crucial pieces of evidence. They discovered that Doyle had travelled to the property a few weeks prior to the murders and used both a Beretta and a Smith & Wesson firearm for 'target practice.' Ballistics were able to prove, from casings located at the property, that they were the same firearms used in the Black Market murders.

Although the majority of such incidents involving OMCGs are related to power and control over drugs, money and territory, it has been rumoured that the Black Market Murders had a more banal motive—a female. There was suspicion that one of the murdered Vaders OMCG members was having an affair with a woman who was connected with the Fetts OMCG. It was also rumoured that because the Fetts controlled the security at the club, they controlled the drug trade as well, and the violence erupted when the Vaders wanted a piece of the action. Although the Court adverted to both possibilities, they were not able to come to any identifiable conclusion.

However, the Court did go on to say that "All three of those killings were deliberate executions" and "Although highly likely to have been a previously planned execution to which the deceased were lured, [this] was not a killing or killings which arose at the scene as a result of some attempt to reach some agreement, or to discuss some proposition which went awry."

## Chapter Four:
# Redfern Riots

The Christmas break from December to February was usually our busiest time. It provided an opportunity for school-age offenders to fill in their holiday boredom with a wave of mini-crime. Each year it was a predictable event and was met with an ever-increasing police presence. Things usually came to a head on the 26th of January. Most people celebrate that date as 'Australia Day,' but to the residents of Eveleigh Street and the police within Redfern Local Area Command, it is referred to as 'Invasion Day.'

Before I began working at Redfern, I had seen the violent clashes between the police and the local Aboriginals on the television and in the newspapers. It was a frighteningly harsh reality that such savage behaviour could exist just a stone's throw away from the largest capital city in Australia: Sydney.

Australia Day in 1998 was no different. It was hot, the beer was flowing, and the locals were restless. We made regular patrols of the Block area during the course of the day, not in an attempt to aggravate the locals, but to act as a deterrent and maintain a visible presence on the streets to satisfy the locals that we were doing our job. However, our actions seemed to have the opposite effect. It felt like a time bomb was waiting to explode.

As the shift progressed, the number of clashes between the police and young Aboriginals in the area intensified. I was in the station completing paperwork when I heard a call over the police radio.

"Redfern 80 urgent, foot pursuit, Eveleigh Street."

It was two of our officers in foot pursuit down at the Block. Like a reflex action, everyone available in the station dropped what they were doing and ran to the nearest car.

There was a convoy of red and blue lights channelling along the main street of Redfern. (Speaking from experience, there is nothing sweeter than hearing the wailing of a police siren when your safety is under threat). I got out of the car at the top of the Block, near the railway station, and ran into Eveleigh Street, where I was confronted with a sea of rage and fury. Hundreds of Aboriginals were converging in the area as a symbol of revolt. I couldn't see the officers needing assistance, and the Police Radio was having trouble contacting them.

The Sergeant and I walked into a laneway that ran parallel to Eveleigh Street known as Eveleigh Lane. It was like a cauldron for police. From out of nowhere you could be showered by bricks and bottles and set upon like lambs to the slaughter. Police from other areas treated it as a no-go zone because they didn't understand its intensity and weren't familiar with its history.

We couldn't find the missing officers, so we searched through some abandoned houses that were used as 'shooting galleries.' We called them 'empties,' and if you saw them you would know why. As we walked onto Eveleigh Street I heard a lot of shouting coming from the southern end. We ran down the street and saw a number of uniformed police and marked police vehicles under a tirade of heavy abuse. As we got closer, one of the police caged trucks sped off into the distance. This just seemed to infuriate the locals more, and out of nowhere people emerged and began to crowd around the police. They were yelling obscenities, which, for the area, was not uncommon. But this was different. It wasn't like the usual name-calling or idle threats. This was anarchy.

One of the Aboriginal youths I had dealt with in the past came up to me chest to chest and attempted to intimidate me.

He shouted, "What's your name and number?"

I replied, "Jeff from Redfern."

He was one of the leaders of the revolt and believed to be involved in drug dealing in the area.

After a while the crowd began to disperse and we decided to make a strategic retreat from the area to prevent further confrontation. We managed to get back into our car and patrolled the surrounding streets just in case problems flared again. A crew from a neighbouring patrol stopped us in an adjoining street and warned us that things were escalating once more. As we drove north into Eveleigh Street, I could see about sixty Aboriginals gathering around the police and their cars. I saw my 'friend' again, this time jostling with another officer in the heart of the melee.

As we approached, a number of Aboriginal youths began hurling abuse and calling us "fucking white copper cunts."

This time the hatred was more intense, and it was out of control.

My partner and I walked to the crowd only to be confronted by my young friend again saying, "Come here mate. You think you're tough."

I ignored his taunts as I saw the two officers who had originally called for assistance being surrounded by a violent mob. We saw one of the officers chasing a woman into a nearby park. The trail of saliva down the back of his shirt explained what had happened. As he spoke to the woman, a large man grabbed his arm and began standing over him. As I had dealt with this person before I was able to convince him to move away without too much difficulty. The officer led the woman to the back of a caged truck to the jeers of the masses. He was whipped on the back by a handbag from one of the locals for his actions, which he ignored.

As we made our way back to our cars, the tide began to turn.

The large man began running to the laneway yelled, "Pick up the bricks. Pick up the bottles. Let 'em have it."

It didn't take much to realise what was about to happen. As I looked around at the sea of faces, things seemed to move in slow motion. I had my back to the laneway at the time and spun around to see a young boy about five metres away pick up a sizeable rock and peer at me. I walked towards him, pointed and said, "Put the rock down, mate," which he did.

But as I turned towards the safety of the police cars nearby, I looked over my shoulder and saw the youth next to him pick up a rock and throw it at me. I felt it whiz passed my right ear as it bounced off the rear passenger window. I looked back and saw the first boy throw a rock at me, which also missed and hit the police car. That was just the start of it, the lull before the storm. As I ran for cover behind the row of marked sedans, I saw a barrage of bricks and bottles land at my feet. The riot had begun.

All around the police vehicles was a deluge of rubble. I ran to the car and crouched down low, yelling out to the other police, "Get down. Get down."

It all turned so quickly. These were the images I had seen on the news, but this time I was in the centre of it. I didn't have time to be afraid because my adrenaline was pumping. You could hear the impact of the bricks and bottles as they hit the police cars and shards of glass sprayed everywhere. As I looked up, I saw that directly behind us was another group of Aboriginals who could have seriously changed the outcome of the confrontation if they had chosen to get involved. But thankfully they didn't.

I worked up the courage to peek through the driver's side window of the car. There were a lot of people in the laneway, with missiles flying, pinning us down. I managed to identify a few of the cohorts but wasn't too concerned at the time about making an arrest. Arresting people now wouldn't be a smart move. As I ducked down below the shelf of the door, the rear passenger window of one of the police cars shattered with an explosion of glass.

I looked around and saw some of the other police sheltered behind the cars. I knew how they were feeling. I peered through the driver's window again to see if there was any sign of the deluge abating. I could see my friend from earlier throw a projectile at the police car I was hiding behind. It was like he knew I was there. This tirade continued for what seemed like an eternity before I saw two officers standing behind a police van at a nearby intersection, out of harm's way, holding riot shields and helmets. When the onslaught began to slow, some of us ran to the van and donned protective gear. When we were covered, we walked in a line towards the police vehicles with our shields held strong. The barrage of projectiles had all but stopped, and for a few moments there was an eerie silence. A stand-off between the aggressors in the laneway and the police in the street ensued.

When the all clear was given, some of the trapped officers climbed into the remains of their war-torn police cars and drove them slowly from the area. My freed colleagues and I began walking backwards to the top of Eveleigh Street as a few final missiles landed at our feet. Once out of harm's way, we retreated to the safety of our cars. I looked back where we had come from and it was like a warzone, and I could still hear the sound of smashing glass. Angry jeers followed us as we left the area, and sounds of rebellion echoed through the streets.

On the way back to the police station, I noticed that a highway patrol car had wrapped itself around a telegraph pole at the top of the Block as it was speeding to our aide. The crumpled wreck felt somehow symbolic of what we had been through. Luckily no one was seriously injured during the riots, the HWP officer was okay, and we were able to identify the main instigators of the episode.

It was a redoubtable experience that has longed stayed with me, and I relive it every Australia Day. The troublemakers whom I identified were later charged and called before the Court. Three out of the five offenders I had identified were convicted and sentenced. The other two had their cases dismissed. Even after giving compelling and accurate evidence against the accused persons and being 100 percent certain of their identities, the Judge concluded that in his opinion I could not be absolutely sure, given the circumstances. Although we didn't know it at the time, it was the end of an historic episode in the history of Redfern, the last time such calamity and chaos scarred the celebrations of our national day.

## In The Line Of Duty

Undoubtedly one of the saddest moments in the career of a police officer is when a colleague is killed in the 'line of duty.' It is the ultimate sacrifice that an officer can make, and it is a moment that touches the hearts and souls of every officer around the state, the country and even the world. That's what makes policing so special; you feel like you are part of a big international family. We all share a special bond that unites us in our fight to achieve justice and stability, and we can empathise when things don't always turn out the way they should. Even though there have been times when I could have become a member of this band of 'fallen comrades,' I have not been witness to such a tragic event. I have, however, been on duty when the call of "officer down" has been broadcast across the police radio.

It was towards the end of a typically long shift when I received a phone call from a victim of a domestic complaint I was following up on. Her brother, whom I was chasing in connection with warrants, firearms and other serious offences, was interstate and due to return to Sydney later that week. But what she had to say changed the course of my investigation, my night and my life, because it meant I would be at work when an officer was killed in the line of duty. The victim managed to blurt out that the suspect had booked an early flight and was landing in Sydney in about one hour's time. It caught me off-guard. I wasn't prepared and was actually working on orders for an undercover operation to nab him when she rang. After some quick thinking and re-planning I managed to get the Supervisor to authorise some overtime and found an available Senior Constable to assist me.

By the time I was on my way to Sydney Airport under lights and sirens, the plane was pulling into the terminal. I raced in and found the gate where the passengers would be disembarking from the plane. I arrived just in time as the door opened. I stood, partially concealed behind the door, and waited anxiously. As passengers disembarked, I received many curious looks and glances, even from the suspect. I had to look twice, and so did he. Upon realising who I was and that I was waiting for him, he tried to make a run for it. Barging through the passengers, I tackled the felon to the ground and survived a brief struggle as the other passengers walked around and even over us. Once he was handcuffed we took him to the luggage bay to collect his bags where we uncovered a shortened firearm and other illegal paraphernalia. Don't ask me how it managed to get through airport security from wherever he came from, but luckily he didn't get the chance to use it. I placed him under arrest, read him his rights and conveyed him to Redfern Police Station to be formally interviewed and charged.

And then it happened. As I was walking into the charge room I heard a broadcast on the police radio that stopped me in my tracks. I remember hearing the three beeps to signify a Signal One.

BEEP – BEEP – then a pause – BEEEEP!!

This means that an officer is in serious trouble and needs urgent assistance. As the information filtered in about two off-duty police officers being stabbed in the neighbouring suburb, Ultimo, I began to feel sick inside. It was hard to believe it was happening, and so close. I just stood there feeling confused and embarrassed about being too busy to go and assist a colleague. I didn't know the police involved, but they were part of our policing family, and when one of them is hurting, so are you. I wanted to let my bloke go even though I had worked so hard to get him in the dock where he belonged. It felt like what I was doing was so trivial.

It wasn't long before it was confirmed that the two victims of the stabbing were police officers who had become embroiled in a confrontation while returning home from a club. I looked around in stunned silence and could see the pain on the faces of the police in the station but had to continue charging my man in the dock. It was chaos on the radio for what seemed like a lifetime, and I found it hard to concentrate. And in the end it was a lifetime. A short time later the Police Radio announced that as a result of his injuries from the stab wounds, Constable Peter Forsythe had lost his brave fight for life.

It was one of the saddest moments of my life and my career. A soul-wrenching feeling consumed me. I was sad for Forsythe, then for his colleague. Sad for his family, both personal and professional, that this type of violence was used against officers who endeavoured to uphold the law and protect other people and property. But it also reminded me that one of the things that attracted me to the police was the element of danger that would be ever present.

I wear the badge on my sleeve with pride, knowing what it stands for and understanding it may require risking my life to protect the safety of others. I know now, after nearly sixteen years as an officer, that it is often the minor incidents that can escalate into life-threatening situations, such as people acting suspicious, house alarms and crowd control duties. You can never afford to become complacent when attending any sort of job. Thousands of police, past and present, such as myself, have been involved in situations where their lives are put at risk. We are a family of professionals willing to take that step outside our comfort zones if it means helping others and upholding the law.

At the end of the day, we all want to go home safe, but some police, by chance, fate or destiny, pay the ultimate price for freedom. They are true heroes and are symbols of what our service and our country stand for.

## SHOTS FIRED

It was July 1998 and one of my first shifts with a new Probationer. He was very excitable and keen as a Mallee bull. We had only just started our shift when we received a call about a possible break and enter in progress at Alexandria. Apparently, an employee of the service station had turned up to work and seen someone using an oxyacetylene torch in the back office where the safe was kept. It sounded simple enough, but nothing ever is in this job. We were one of the first cars on the scene but couldn't see anyone inside the shop. We made a quick canvass of the area but assumed that the offender had already left.

My partner and I returned to our police car and made a quick patrol, heading south along an adjoining street. I knew the area well, so I was aware that there was a laneway that joined the two parallel streets either side of the service station. I approached the laneway cautiously and turned into it. Halfway along was another narrow laneway that led up towards the back of the service station, so I turned right into it. I immediately wondered why I had done that, as it was such a bad officer survival decision because it eliminated the possibility of a quick retreat if required. So I reversed out of the laneway and began to head towards the parallel street.

As I did, I caught a glimpse of a white car screaming along the road about fifteen metres in front of me. Seconds later, a call came over the police radio: "Shots fired. Shots fired."

I recognised the voice of an officer who was at the service station, so I accelerated along the laneway, around the block and into the service station. I found the senior officer who had made the call, drew my firearm and rushed to his assistance. It was soon clear that the shots fired had actually come from his gun. I spoke to the police involved and they told me that they had found the offender in a vehicle near the service station. As they tried to stop him, the offender reversed his car and knocked over the junior officer, causing him to roll over the boot and fall onto the ground. The senior officer discharged a number of shots at and into the vehicle as it sped away down the street. Not surprisingly, it was the same white vehicle I had seen screaming down the road only seconds before I heard the call over the radio.

They found the stolen car abandoned in a nearby street with the suspect nowhere in sight. It was riddled with bullet holes. The officer had fired four times, one of which would have blown the driver's head off if he hadn't ducked. It seemed that the driver had lost control of the car trying to get away and smashed into parked cars on one of the streets, and then just left it there, fleeing for his life.

I later discovered that if I had looked right when I turned left to go around the block after hearing the police radio call I would have seen the white car careening down the road. I was so annoyed. I was also alarmed and relieved at the same time, as the penny dropped. If I hadn't driven into the narrow laneway I would have pulled out in front of or even behind the stolen car, directly in the line of fire of the other officer. The whole incident could have ended more seriously, but thanks to a slip in concentration on my behalf I avoided being shot or shot at. Someone was watching over my partner and me that day. And as far as I'm aware the crook is still on the run and I bet it was the last servo he ever broke into…well, in Redfern anyway.

## Not My Gun

A couple of weeks later, I was working down the Block with an experienced Senior Constable. It was a very busy time of year and the weather wasn't helping things much. It seemed the hotter the weather, the more alcohol was consumed and the more restless the locals became. We were making a foot patrol of the area, which surprisingly was fairly uncommon. The number of attacks on police were on the increase, but we couldn't afford to take a backward step, otherwise we would not only lose the limited respect and control that we had but also any advantage we had secured through hard frontline policing.

As we were walking along Eveleigh Lane, we spotted some of our local crooks running into the back of an abandoned house. They were well-known robbery and property theft offenders in their late teens and were a 'hot item' amongst the local community. They were carrying a couple of shopping bags, which aroused our suspicion. We chose to continue our patrol and see what we could discover.

Eveleigh Lane is best described as a gauntlet. It is possible to fit a vehicle down there, but there was no guarantee that if you drove down, you or the vehicle would reach the other end in one piece, or at all. The laneway was full of locals drinking and yelling abuse at us. It was nothing unusual. Lawfully, we were entitled to be there, despite their constant grievances. We were patrolling streets within the boundaries of NSW. That in itself made us targets of their intense hatred towards our uniform and presence.

As we walked around the laneway we could hear our 'love birds' rustling through some bags in an abandoned house.

The girl said, "Open it up. The coppers are coming."

This just seemed to pique our interest. We weren't afraid to get involved, and this was our chance. As we walked past the back of the house, the two offenders came into the backyard. My partner and I walked towards them as the male ran along the laneway, seeking refuge far away. As we spoke to the female, I could see that she was holding a number of new T-shirts in bags. We questioned her about them and she became abusive towards us, but we had enough suspicion to believe the shirts were 'hot,' so we arrested her for having stolen clothing. That didn't go down too well.

She pushed my offsider in the chest and began running for the back door of the house, screaming, "Leave me alone."

We grabbed hold of her as she attempted to squeeze through the door. As she began waving her arms and body about violently, I knew things were about to get seriously out of hand. By this time, the backyard of the house was filling with locals yelling their disapproval at us. And then the inevitable happened. A shower of bricks and bottles began spraying over our heads and smashing at our feet. Deja vu? I heard one whistle passed my head and smash on the wall not too far away.

I grabbed my portable and called, "Redfern 80 urgent. Eveleigh Lane." When I was working on the truck and heard those words it used to send shivers up my spine. Everyone knew that if someone called urgent from the Block, they definitely needed help. At least backup was never too far away.

The young woman continued to thrash her body about like a shark in shallow water. She lunged for the back door and yelled, "Help me, help me. Open the door."

As if at her command, the back door opened and a sea of arms reached out and tried to pull her to safety. This wasn't supposed to happen. Either we would all be dragged in through the door or she would get away. My partner and I just looked at each other and knew we had to do something fast.

We had shards of glass smashing at our feet and bricks whizzing over our heads, so we grabbed her by the arms and just yanked her from the doorway and slammed the door shut. The locals began to surround us and yelled at us to let her go, but we weren't going to let that happen. The girl continued to scream so we tried to calm her down, but this just seemed to aggravate her more.

I again called for assistance, as the matter was getting way out of hand. "Redfern 80. We need urgent assistance right now, Eveleigh Lane."

It came over the radio twice as a Signal One. Cars were coming from everywhere. I saw the girl move towards my right-hand side, which at first I couldn't understand. She was moving away from her best point of escape closer to me. My adrenaline was pumping but I was too busy to feel just how afraid I was.

I felt a tug on my gun. I didn't know who it was, but I knew it wasn't good. As I felt my gun lifting from its holster I turned to see the young woman pulling it up with her hands. It was all happening in slow motion. The noise and chaos of the background seemed to be silenced by this distraction.

She threatened me, saying, "I'm gonna get ya gun. I'm gonna get ya gun."

I was terrified. I knew that if she was able to just get her finger on the trigger there was nothing stopping her from firing at me. She was wired like a caged animal and was willing to do anything to escape. That was clear. I grabbed hold of her arm and forced her body against the wall. The impact jolted her hand free of my gun, which thankfully fell back into its holster. I could only dread what would have happened if it had fallen onto the ground.

I didn't have time to secure my firearm, so I forced the right side of my body up against the girl and pinned her to the wall. She continued to struggle and lash out at us with the vocal support of her extended community. It seemed like forever until assistance arrived, but when they did the crowd dispersed more quickly than they had appeared.

We restrained and handcuffed the young offender and led her safely from the area without further incident. I clipped my gun back into its holster and thanked the Almighty God for looking out for me. In the end we had prevailed, which was reassuring, but it had been too close for comfort. It's amazing how thin the line can be sometimes between a good outcome and a tragedy. We could have been set upon by the crowd, hit by the projectiles or even shot with our own guns. Thanks to fate and courage, and a lot of back up, we managed to survive.

The offender remained uncooperative back at the station and declined to be interviewed. She was charged with assaulting and resisting police, attempting to steal my firearm and being in possession of stolen clothing. The matter went to Court and she ended up serving a few months in gaol for her trouble.

## Birthday Pursuit

It was December 28th and I couldn't believe that I had to work on my twenty-fifth birthday. But it was bearable because Rachael and I were working together. Most of the times we worked on the same car crew it was fine. Occasionally, it was difficult and a challenge. Despite the odd lovers' quarrel we were able to share some extraordinary experiences. Normally I am hungry for action, but maybe because of the occasion, I was starving for it, much to the chagrin of my beautiful offsider. The first half of the shift was flat out. With heaps of minor crime reports, we didn't even have time for a dinner break. But as the night grew longer, the workload started to slow. So did our police truck. I don't remember what actually went kaput in it, but it wasn't going too far. Through some creative negotiation skills I managed to swap the ratty old truck for a fully marked sedan. Now I knew I was in heaven because it meant I could go hunting for stolen cars! But despite valiant attempts and relentless patrols around the area, we remained starved for action.

As the late night turned into early morning, Rachael was getting tired and hungry, so I took her to the finest restaurant I could find in the middle of the night on short notice and with a limited budget — half-price McDonald's at Stanmore. It wasn't haute cuisine, but it was all that was available at that time of the morning. We drove back to the station for a feed and for Rachael to take a catnap. I couldn't sleep, and because I couldn't stand doing nothing I went out patrolling with her 'buddy.' We were out for about an hour with no success, so we retreated to the sanctuary of the police station.

When I got back, Rachael was in a panic thinking that something big had happened and that she had slept through it all. After stringing her along for a bit and making the most of her guilt, I managed to alleviate her concerns and convince her to come on a late-night sortie with me. As she chewed on what was left of her bitterly cold french fries, my ears pricked as a message was broadcast over the police radio. It was a report of a black Celica that had just been stolen from a neighbouring patrol following a break-in. I didn't take much notice after that; I just got into the car and went hunting.

I drove down the main street of Redfern, took a right at the intersection of Cleveland Street and pulled up to the traffic lights. As I did, I saw a dark-coloured sports car drive into the turning lane on the opposite side of the road, facing towards me. There were only three other cars on that side of the road and the lighting wasn't good, but I had a very strong gut feeling that it could be the stolen Celica I had just heard about over the police radio.

"Surely not; it couldn't be that easy," I thought.

I pointed to the sports car and said to Rachael, "That car's stolen."

She looked at me and replied, "Oh shit."

The sports car turned onto Cleveland Street and headed in an easterly direction away from us. I still couldn't confirm the registration but was sure it was the stolen Celica. As it made a sudden right turn towards Redfern along a darkened alley, the driver extinguished the vehicle's headlights. Rachael jolted upright in her seat at the realisation that I wasn't joking. I darted down the laneway as Rachael notified the Police Radio that we had located the stolen Celica and were in pursuit. I activated the warning lights and sirens of the police car as we sped through the back streets at a frantic pace. I was gaining ground in my mighty Holden sedan, but it was obvious by the way the offender was driving that he knew what he was doing and that he had a good knowledge of the area.

As we headed into Waterloo, which has a number of high-rise buildings, we were joined by other policing units. We made several laps of one of the high-rises and weaved in and out of the laneways. The radio operator called for a marked highway patrol car to assist, but Rachael was doing an excellent job. She was calm and calling the locations and conditions clearly, which made it easier to concentrate on my driving. We were a good team, and that night we were going to prove it.

We drove around Redfern at speeds of up to 100km/hr in a residential area. If it had been daytime, the pursuit surely would have been terminated, but luckily that night things were quiet. As we headed back out to Waterloo we circled the same high-rise building again, so close to the Celica that we often lost sight of the number plate. When the radio operator asked how close we were and heard our response, he rightly advised us to drop back a little, which in hindsight was a good decision.

Whilst pursuing on the outskirts of Waterloo, the Celica came to a sudden stop and the driver's door opened. I maintained a safe distance, took off my seatbelt and had one foot out the door ready to continue the pursuit on foot when his door slammed shut and he sped off into the darkness. I sat down and stuck to his tail. The highway patrol car was having trouble catching up and complimented us on our "excellent job."

The pursuit kept going around and around. We tried setting up roadblocks with little success as the driver kept slipping past. He was so desperate to escape that he even tried playing chicken with the caged trucks. The Highway car soon caught up, and I pulled aside to let it take over. It was neck and neck. We, the stolen Celica and the highway car were all within the space of just over three car lengths.

The pursuit went back out onto Cleveland Street, an open stretch of road. The Celica hit about 120km/hr heading back towards Redfern with the highway car not too far behind. As we crossed the intersection where I had first noticed the Celica, it began to slow instinctively. I reacted and slammed my foot on the brake, which wasn't a smart thing to do (in hindsight), but I was able to correct the slide and saw the Celica drive into, of all places, the Block.

I headed into Eveleigh Street, which was abandoned at the time. All of a sudden, the night sky filled with the sounds of sirens and flashing red and blue lights. It wasn't too long before the locals came out to see what the raucous was about. The Celica drove around and around the Block, so many times that we began to get in each other's way. Then, at a speed of about 100km/hr, the Celica scooted down a narrow laneway you would have trouble negotiating in the daytime at a reasonable speed. As the driver re-entered the block, the radio operator must have been reading our minds, as he broadcast that we were not to set up roadblocks to catch him.

Because there were so many police cars with headlights and flashing beacons zipping everywhere, we momentarily lost sight of the car. So rather than keep chasing my tail, and everyone else's, I found a position on the eastern side of Eveleigh Street and waited for an update on his location. Just as I did so I saw the dark figure of the stolen car zooming towards me from behind without headlights. The thought did cross my mind to pull out in front and ram the car off the road, like the American police are trained to do, but I remembered the direction of the DOI and didn't want to lose my licence.

Moreover, there was no information as to whether the offender was armed or not, and this wasn't the best place or time to have an accident in a police car. So we waited until it drove past and commenced chasing it again around the block with the highway car directly behind.

It headed north along a parallel street and at speed made an attempt to run the gauntlet of Eveleigh Lane, but instead it got wedged between the walls and fences on either side. The driver fled the car and ran into a row of nearby houses as the highway officers and I followed close behind. But being the middle of the night and in an area where there is minimal street lighting, it was too dark and there were just too many unknowns, like who else might have been hiding and waiting for us, or whether the floors were safe or strong enough to walk on.

We did our best and searched the area as thoroughly as we could in the circumstances, but without success. Just as it seemed that the driver had managed to escape, the Supervisor searched the stolen car; sitting on the driver's floor was his wallet with all his details, name, address and even a photograph. So even though we didn't have the body, we had the next best thing: his identity. The car was dragged from the laneway and towed away, where it was searched. The stolen items were recovered and returned to the owner. We all left the area somewhat disappointed, but revved up and wanting more action.

Sometime later, I learned that the owner of the stolen car was actually standing on his porch in Surry Hills listening to the pursuit while reporting the theft to the police. Even though he was grateful for the recovery of his car, there wasn't much left to salvage.

What a birthday present!

I heard that one of the highway officers commented afterwards that it was one of the best pursuits that he had been involved in for a long time. It just goes to show that you never know what will happen on your birthday. Rachael managed to find my present that she had tossed in the back seat when the pursuit started and pulled me down from the clouds long enough for me to open it. It was a beautiful surprise and an unforgettable birthday. The police did catch up with the crook, and he was subsequently charged and convicted.

## Chapter Five:
# The Voir Dire

One of the aspects of police work that a lot of people don't understand is that arresting the criminals is not the end of the story. There is a never-ending stream of paperwork and procedures to follow in order to see the offender through the justice system. Depending on the type of matter for which the offender has been charged, they might be appearing before a Magistrate or facing a full Court hearing before a Judge and Jury. This, of course, will determine how long the matter will take to be finalised. In some instances, it can be years between the initial arrest and subsequent Court appearance, as was the case with the Black Market Murders. The offenders were caught in 1997, but it wasn't until May 1999 that the trial process finally started.

Due to our involvement in the arrest and charging of one of the murderers, Adamson, and in the identification of the other, Doyle, my partner and I would be integral to the process, which would hopefully result in a conviction. I had been concerned since the arrest that the Fetts might seek some sort of retribution against my family or me or my partner's family because of the part we played. But thankfully no such incidents arose.

After the lengthy jury selection, and before the trial commenced, the Defence argued that some of the evidence that the Prosecution were relying upon was inadmissible, therefore requiring a Court process referred to as a 'voir dire.' This is best described in layman's terms as a trial within a trial where the Prosecution and Defence argue points of law relating to the relevance and admissibility of evidence before tying up jurors for months. One of the Crime Agency Detectives told me that I would be required as a key witness. Without such testimony, vital evidence linking the accused to the club, the Porsche, the firearms and the medical evidence would be inadmissible and jeopardise the outcome of the case. It was a lot of pressure on me as a junior Constable, but I made sure I knew my statement and listened to the pursuit tape over and over so it was fresh in my mind at the time of giving evidence. By this time I had come to terms with the initial shock following the arrest, but as the trial drew nearer I began having similar feelings of panic.

I knew that one of the central points of argument for the Defence was going to be the validity of the arrest. They would argue that the arrest was unlawful and so any evidence gathered as a result of that alleged unlawful action was inadmissible and irrelevant. Luckily, one thing I am confident of is my knowledge and understanding of police powers, and I was certain that my actions were lawful and justified. I asked a Sergeant at work for advice about the incident and what to expect in Court, but that was the wrong move. She made me feel like crap, telling me that my arrest was unlawful. To hear that on the morning of the voir dire was devastating and made me doubt my actions and myself. She had to be wrong.

Because my offsider and I were unaware of the shooting murders at the time of detection, pursuit and arrest, we had to rely on our reasonable cause and observations that they were up to no good. I held that I had the lawful power to stop, search and detain these men to investigate my suspicions by virtue of Section 357E (a) of the Crimes Act 40/1900, which states:

"A member of the police force may stop, search and detain: Any person whom he reasonably suspects of having or conveying any thing stolen or otherwise unlawfully obtained or any thing used or intended to be used in the commission of an indictable offence."

Based on my observations at the scene, I strongly believed that I had "reasonable cause to suspect" that Adamson was in possession of something illegal that may have been or was used in the commission of an indictable offence (an indictable offence is another way of saying a serious offence, like robbery, sexual assault, drug supply and homicide). He was running out of a nightclub, in the early afternoon, in hot weather, wearing a trench coat in which he was concealing something. He also stopped running when he saw the police car and got into a high-performance vehicle without removing his hand from his coat. That screams reasonable cause to me. Although I believed that he might have been concealing a gun inside his coat, it was not something I expected to be confronted with in suburban Sydney.

When the Porsche started weaving in and out of traffic at high speed and kept going when we pursued, my reasonable cause was strengthened. (Just the fact that he was a passenger in the car during the pursuit is not reasonable cause. It's not even an offence, unless the vehicle is stolen.)

At the time when I stopped Adamson and held him against the wall, I was exercising my statutory powers according to this Section. Because Adamson pushed off the wall and ran away from us whilst we were attempting to exercise our stop, search and detain powers, he committed the offence of resisting police.

Section 546C (Resist Police) of the Crimes Act 40/1900 states: "Any person who resists or hinders or incites any person to assault, resist or hinder a member of the police force in the execution of his duty shall be liable on conviction by a stipendiary magistrate to imprisonment for twelve months or to a fine of ten penalty units, or both."

My beliefs that I had acted professionally and lawfully were further justified after I consulted the Butterworths law journal. The moment Adamson pushed off the wall and began running away from my partner was the moment when the 'resisting' took place. By this action, Adamson prevented me and my partner from executing our duties and from searching him based on our observations and reasonable cause. He was resisting our efforts to search him by running away and attempting to escape.

I had stopped and detained Adamson under Section 357E with the intent of searching him. Therefore, his liberty had been removed and he was not free to leave. I was satisfied that I had established reasonable cause to execute my duties based on my observations and the events immediately prior to this instant. I left Adamson with my partner, still under the lawful detention of Section 357E, to determine the whereabouts of the driver of the Porsche. I had walked no more than a few metres away and was absent from Adamson for no more than a few seconds when he ran.

After reading Butterworths and speaking to a Prosecutor, I felt vindicated in my actions and chose to ignore the advice of the Sergeant. On my way to the Sydney District Court with the Crime Agency Detectives, I went over my evidence again in my mind. After the initial scare, I was confident within myself again, as I had given evidence before a Judge and Jury previously. The thought that the case somewhat hinged on my evidence did buzz around my head a little, but it gave me the edge I needed.

When we arrived, I noticed some of Adamson's bikie friends had turned up to the Court, and it wasn't long before I learnt that the case had been moved to the secure Court because of recent bomb threats. I spent some time before entering the Courtroom reading my statement and collecting my thoughts. When it was time for me to give evidence, I strode to the witness box. Both Adamson and Doyle were seated in the middle of the Court behind the Defence barristers, guarded by two security guards. Directly opposite was the barrister from the DPP whom I had previously met with following the arrest. He was a friendly man who possessed the wisdom of experience. I had a lot of faith in him and hoped that he would be there to back me up or object if the need arose.

The Defence barrister for Adamson was a large Mediterranean man with a thick moustache who was loud and very confident. He looked like the type who ate inexperienced Constables for breakfast and used their batons to pick his teeth. I wasn't scared…much!

Those who know me know that sometimes I have the tendency to speak too fast, particularly when I'm nervous, but luckily I got through reading my statement without too many dramas. Then the barrage began. For the next few hours, the Defence drilled me on every aspect of my statement, which of course was his job. He even drew importance out of the most irrelevant detail just to confuse me.

He was very intimidating, and I wasn't overly confident when I came out. Even though on the day of the shooting I had tried to dot all my i's and cross all my t's, I had slipped up. All of the mistakes were vital to proving reasonable cause and confirming that the arrest was lawful. My first mistake that the Defence hounded me about was when the shooting was first broadcast. I was asked why I hadn't informed the Police Radio that I had seen Adamson and Doyle run from the scene of the shooting, as this was the alleged location where I had seen them get into the Porsche and chased them through parts of Sydney, where they threw the murder weapons into the street. My only response was something like, "I don't know. Inexperience."

He was right. It was no justification or excuse, but I had only been out of the Academy a little over twelve months at the time of the incident. It was vital information that I should have passed on. But at the time everything was happening so fast it was hard to keep up and to believe it was really happening. I have learnt from it, though. Following that incident I always make sure I tell the radio as much information as I can, just to be sure. Next time the end result may not be the same, and I don't like making the same mistakes twice.

After that battle ended, then came the next onslaught. I was challenged about the actual arrest and the powers I had used. I didn't have too many problems in this area, but the barrister was tricky. Just as I was starting to feel at ease, I was ambushed with questions relating to the contemporaneous notes I had made on the paper at the charge room. I couldn't see anything wrong with them. I had made notes soon after the time of the incident, which my partner co-signed, and then used those notes to make a formal statement. Wrong answer. There was nothing wrong with making the notes, just the fact that I hadn't offered them to Adamson at any time to read or sign. Big mistake!

Sometimes in our legal system it feels like the defendants have more rights than a perfect score in a spelling test. It hadn't crossed my mind at the time to offer it to him. He was being treated by the ambulance, which again is no excuse. To make matters worse, there was no date on the paper, a fact the Defence quickly gobbled up, accusing me of falsifying the document and making it all up. Good try, but I don't operate like that. I just tell it how it is. Then the question was raised as to why I hadn't transferred these notes into my official police notebook. Oops again. "I didn't have time!" I was so engrossed in helping with the investigation I just didn't do it. My saving grace was the fact that I had made the statement on the day of the incident and it could be clearly seen that the notes were used as a guide in preparing my statement. Phew!

I had been so confident for the past eighteen months since the arrest that I had done everything right and that the Defence would have nothing to persecute me about. But reality hit with a resounding thud. And with it came my pride and my sense of accomplishment. Once I finished giving evidence, the Defence sought leave from the Judge to have the matter dismissed because of no 'prima facie' case being established.

This test is performed when the Prosecution's evidence is taken at its highest (or strongest) and the Court considers that the accused might be responsible for the crime. This is based on the 'balance of probabilities' test rather than the 'beyond reasonable doubt' test, which is the next level if the matter progresses to a hearing or trial.

I was devastated. The judge adjourned for lunch and I honestly thought I had let everyone down and that the matter would be dismissed. All of my efforts to know and learn my powers and my statement had been fruitless. Nothing could have prepared me for that. I was embarrassed and ashamed. I headed straight for the door and hid around the corner of the Court. I tried not to show how much it affected me, but I was so disappointed that the tears came anyway. The lead Detective saw me struggling and offered some constructive, yet kind, words of wisdom. He'd been there and done it all before. His talk sort of helped, but I just wanted to go home. At that moment, the Defence barrister came around the corner and saw me reeling from the experience, which just added insult to injury. He gets paid big money to destroy evidence and fact in the Courtroom, and I have to admit that he was in his element that day. I went back to the station and took the rest of the day off.

On my next shift, I was called in to see the Crime Manager, who sat me down and closed the door. He was a very senior, experienced, 'old-school' style Detective who didn't know the meaning of fear or failure. I knew what this was about, and I felt about an inch tall. I had shown 'unpolice-like behaviour' and was going to be punished. He wasn't very supportive, just negative and condemning. But he hadn't been there, and it was really hard for me. I was told "not to be silly," which just made me very defensive. It was obvious that I wasn't coping too well and that I should have been offered the opportunity to speak to a counsellor or anyone independent who was willing to listen. But that didn't happen.

Thankfully, a few days later I received a phone call from the Detective, who told me we had been successful in the voir dire. The judge believed that we had reasonable cause to stop and search Adamson and that there was enough evidence to suggest Adamson and Doyle had a case to answer. I was so relieved. It was like being on a roller coaster. And to make my day even better, the Judge actually complimented me on my excellent evidence and stated that I was a very credible witness.

Although the first hurdle had been cleared successfully, the actual trial was still several months away, so I headed back to the mean streets of Redfern and continued my duties, armed with the knowledge that what I did was right but still remembering what I had done wrong.

## Chapter Six:
## Signal One

Earlier in 1999, I made the decision to switch from the mundanity of general duties to the lure of more proactive police work. Our station had established a new unit made up of plain-clothes officers who targeted 'hot spot' crime areas. It was known as the Target Team but affectionately referred to as 'the Funky Squad.' I saw it as an opportunity to concentrate on one particular aspect of policing rather than continuing to chase my tail working on the truck. I was getting a lot of arrests on general duties, but together with the never-ending list of jobs I attended to, it just made the mountains of paperwork insurmountable.

During this time, I developed a new persona in my methods of policing. I enjoyed the anonymity of plain-clothes work and being able to work closely with the Detectives, but at the same time I missed the respect that being in uniform commanded.

After a while, we were channelled into performing a lot of shifts in uniform as part of a policy of 'high visibility policing' (HVP). This is what was commonly referred to as 'showing the flag.' Police presence was seen to be a vital key to deterring crime in the area, and by having frontline officers in plain-clothes, there was a perception that police numbers on the streets were lacking, which upset local community members. So most of my work was back in uniform, which kind of defeated the whole purpose of the squad.

One of the guys in the unit, Morgs, was a good friend of mine. We had worked together at Gosford for a short time before we both ended up at Redfern. He was hardworking and loved to get involved, just like me. We held each other in high esteem and worked together often enough to be able to know what the other was thinking without expressing it in words. On this day, our friendship and understanding was challenged and stretched to its limits, with almost fatal consequences.

It is very meaningful to be able to connect with another officer on a level that you feel you could trust them with your life. It's also very important in an area like Redfern to know someone is watching your back. I knew that Morgs was someone I trusted and could rely on without question. Such a bond was soon to be tested.

It was late afternoon on June 1st, 1999 when Morgs and I were patrolling the Block. It was a cesspool of violence and crime and a smorgasbord of wanted and active offenders. I prided myself on my knowledge of the offenders and crooks in the area. Remarkably, I couldn't remember too much about a conversation I may have had just minutes earlier, but point someone out in a crowd and more often than not I could tell you their name and what they were known or wanted for.

As we were driving around the streets in a marked sedan, I saw a young Aboriginal man in the rear of one of the houses backing onto Eveleigh Lane. I had prior dealings with him and knew that he was wanted in relation to a number of outstanding warrants for robbery and other violent offences. Morgs and I looked at each other and knew what was going to happen next. Luckily, there weren't very many people in the laneway, which made the opportunity tactically perfect for a rapid and incident-free arrest. Or so we thought.

I informed the Police Radio that we had identified a person in Eveleigh Lane who was wanted for robbery offences, and we requested that other police cars in the area start making their way to our location just in case we needed some assistance. As we circled the Block and back into Eveleigh Street I could see that the young person was still in the laneway. He appeared to be avoiding eye contact with us. As I drove into an adjacent street, I stopped the police car behind a large electricity container. Morgs and I jumped out of the car and began running towards the youth. I notified Police Radio that we were attempting to pursue the offender and requested further cars. The young person ran into one of the rear yards through the back door of a house and slammed the door shut, with us in close pursuit.

(According to statutory legislation and Police Service guidelines for police powers of entry, we have the authority to enter a premises to arrest a felon who is wanted on a warrant and who is inside the premises. In this instance, my partner and I were in 'immediate and continuous' foot pursuit of the offender; we knew he had outstanding warrants and had just seen him running through the back door, which gave us entry without consent.)

My partner kicked in the door and sent it flying off the hinges. I ran in close behind to see a number of people in the living room area. We dodged our way into the front room of the house, where we saw the young man hiding beside a mattress.

Morgs and I ran towards him, and he began yelling at us — "Get away. Fucking leave me alone" — as he held a length of wood and waved his arms and legs about in a violent manner. We grabbed him by the arms and dragged him onto the mattress on the floor.

I said, "You are under arrest; stay still."

The young man continued to thrash about and scream loudly, when a misguided punch from the youth hit Morgs in the arm. Within moments, about twenty Aboriginal males and females came into the front room where we were struggling with the young person.

He yelled out, "Help me. Get them away."

The crowd became enraged at Morgs and I, and started shouting abuse, trying to grab the offender from our custody. They were like a wall of retribution. Condemnation was etched on their faces and their eyes burned with anger. I looked at Morgs and knew what he was thinking — we were in trouble. Because we had run in through the back door after the male, we had no idea which house we were in, so when we called for assistance we couldn't give an exact location. We were having so much trouble restraining the young person and were in danger of being seriously assaulted by the marauding crowd. The fact that Morgs and I were well known to the local community for our involvement in arresting wanted criminals didn't help the situation. I could feel the intensity of their hatred.

I continued to struggle with the young man on the mattress, who was growing increasingly violent, as Morgs got to his feet and confronted the angry mob.

"Get back," he shouted. "Get back."

The crowd was oblivious to his directions and continued to yell and taunt us. To them, we were the enemy and were trespassing, despite what the young person had done. They were protecting their own like a pack of wolves. Morgs ran for the front door to seek urgent assistance but was prevented by the horde blocking his way. They weren't going to let us out without a fight, and I was terrified. I didn't have time to think about it; I just did what I had to do. I was still having trouble restraining the offender, and the room was spinning, blurred by the intensity of the situation, as the mob edged closer to intervene. It was hard to watch the young man and the crowd at the same time. I had to rely on Morgs and vice versa.

I reached for my portable and while pinning the youth down with one arm made the call: "Redfern 45, Signal One. We need assistance now!"

As I did so, the young person bit into my right forearm, causing excruciating pain. Despite this, I was fearful of pulling my arm from his mouth. He was a known drug user, which put him at a high risk of having a communicable disease such as Hepatitis C, so I didn't want the skin to be torn, which would make me susceptible to infection. I looked around, reached for a lamp that was on a nearby table and smashed it over the young person's head. That did the job! He released my arm from his jaws, sprang from the bed and began running towards the back door. I quickly recovered and thrust him against the wall.

He yelled intently, "Help me. Get them off me."

The crowd became more vocal, and two Aboriginal women grabbed the young man by the arms and began pulling him away from me. He was still holding the stick in his left hand, and I was conscious that he would use it against me if he only realised that it was in his hand. Thankfully he was as caught up and as wired as we were. It was like I was fighting a losing battle with the women and the young person.

Just then, Morgs drew his capsicum spray (OC spray) from its holster and pointed it at the riotous crowd.

He said, "Get back or I will spray you. Get back."

Thanks to his quick thinking, the women withdrew, and I wrestled the young man onto the mattress with Morgs' assistance. He continued to thrust his arms and legs about and was able to escape from my hold a few times, but only momentarily. It was like a never-ending tug-of-war.

At that moment, my 'friend' from the Australia Day Riots came forward and said, "Let them be; they've got him."

And just like Moses parting the Red Sea, the crowd dispersed and a wave of police came crashing through the front door. I had never been so relieved. The young man continued to struggle, even though the room was full of police and it was apparent he had no chance of escape. We pinned him onto the mattress and handcuffed him for our protection and so that he couldn't escape again. He was led to the police caged truck parked outside and conveyed to the police station.

Once we arrived at the station, we had a chance to reflect and take stock of our injuries. Apart from the bite mark on my forearm, which was swollen, bruised and bleeding, I had come out physically alright. Morgs noticed a small puncture wound on his arm, which we believed might have come from a 'needlestick' during the struggle, as the front room was riddled with discarded syringes.

Rachael was also working that shift and was at the other end of the patrol when the incident occurred. When she heard my call for assistance, the police truck she was working in broke down, which only heightened her anxiety and fear for our safety. But she was a great support. She took Morgs and I to the hospital, where we were treated and had blood samples taken. It was the scariest moment of my life. But it didn't hit me all at once.

The next day I managed to crawl out of bed in the morning and travel to work, like I normally do, but once I got there I fell apart. I was struggling with being back at work so soon after the incident. The flashbacks were overwhelming. My hands were shaking, my heart was pounding and I couldn't fight back the tears. I couldn't let anyone see me like this. I had to get myself under control, but the thought of putting on my uniform and heading back out on the streets was terrifying. I was falling apart.

I locked myself into an office and put my feelings onto paper:

### *"I Thought That I Would Die"*

*I just couldn't go to sleep*
*Thinking about last night,*
*Of all the things that could have been*
*And the things that were done right.*

*I thought about the fear*
*Of being bitten by a 'crim,'*
*Of how my life changed right then*
*All because of him*

I thought about my partner
Who was with me through it all?
About the 'needlestick' he got
Entangled in the brawl

I thought about the fear
Being trapped inside that room,
Surrounded by the prejudice
Violence entombed

I thought about the risks we took
Relying on each other,
Putting our lives on the line
Trusting one another

I thought about the feeling
Of being trapped just like a dog,
Of calling for assistance
Fucking "SIGNAL ONE"

I thought that I was dead
My partner, alone and I,
I could not see me getting out
I thought that I would die

I thought about the tests
The shots to stop the pain
And what I'd do if I could
Just do it all again

Of how it felt to be safe
Absent from the threat,
To find some time to contemplate
To think, to cry, regret

But I thought about so much more
Of what was real to me,
About my world, my everything
What meant most to me

I thought about the job
And the promises that I made,
Of all the chances that I take
For the money I get paid

## Chapter Six: Signal One

*I thought about my life*
*'Bout my family and my friends,*
*About what price I'd have to pay*
*For 'justice' in the end*

*I thought about my girls*
*My 'Poohbear' and my 'T,'*
*If I would ever hold them close*
*Or would there be no me*

*About my everything*
*The pain I caused that day,*
*To myself, my mates*
*But mostly my fiancée*

*Shivers to the bone*
*Crying from within,*
*Hoping that I am OK*
*Crumbling within*

*I'm sorry for the pain*
*And worry that I caused,*
*You are my world, my every dream*
*And forever I am yours*

*And to my mates, my colleagues*
*Who came crashing through that door,*
*You saved my life I owe you heaps*
*And love you so much more*

*I took a chance I almost died*
*For what I thought was right,*
*But in this job it's do or die*
*I hope I sleep tonight*

*So all that's left is history*
*Memories inside,*
*I swear to God I was so scared*
*"I thought that I would die."*

***Judy. 2.6.99***

Even thinking about it now makes my heart race and my chest feel tight, and it brings tears to my eyes. I was devastated by what I had been through, and the Police Service offered no support or counselling to Morgs or me. Morgs had taken the day off because of the possible needlestick injury, which is understandable, but I thought I was strong enough to make it through. I was wrong. I walked into the Supervisor's office, broke down in tears and went home. It was a long trip, but I knew that at the other end Rachael would be waiting for me.

Days went by, and I heard nothing from work. I kept in contact with Morgs because he understood what I was feeling. It all got too much for me and I thought about quitting more than once. Rachael finally had enough and contacted the Police Welfare Branch, which referred Morgs and me to a psychologist in Gosford. We went a few times and kept in contact. But as time went on, it got harder and harder to talk about. After six weeks I began to shut it out and just tried to move on.

It was a very confronting time for me. I was used to being in control of my life, and for one of the first times, I wasn't. I wasn't sleeping, and when I could I would wake up screaming from my nightmares, covered in sweat. I was drinking way too much and locking myself away from any contact with the outside world. I didn't answer the phone, didn't shower or eat properly. I was snapping at my daughter over trivial things and crying uncontrollably for no apparent reason. The incident almost cost me not only my life, but also my relationship. Rachael was deeply affected by what had happened, exacerbated by her inability to come to our assistance at the time. She was going through her own personal nightmare while at the same time consoling me and keeping me from falling over the edge.

We had to wait months for the blood test results, so I was apprehensive about going near Rachael or my daughter, just in case. It was traumatising. I submitted a report to the presiding Magistrate requesting that a blood sample be taken from the offender. He was an intravenous drug user, which placed him in the high-risk category, and if I could establish that he was suffering from any diseases and eliminate those, my concerns would be allayed faster. But my request was declined and I was forced to wait the full term. Luckily, the results were negative and I was able to return to some sort of normality in my life. But the stress and uncertainty of not knowing whether I had a communicable disease or not had already taken its toll.

And despite all of the conflict between the police and the Aboriginal community over the years, the brave youth who stepped in was able to overlook the past and the prejudice. I strongly believe that what he did that day saved our lives. I saw him a few months after the incident and thanked him. Like a true hero, he just shrugged his shoulders and went on his way. I will never forget and will always be grateful.

## Chapter Seven:
# The Trial

I was on leave for about six weeks following the 'Signal One' episode. During that time I underwent counselling and did some serious soul searching to decide whether I had a future in the Police Service. It was during this period that the Black Market Murders trial began. I was still feeling a bit shaky about things from my last experience in Court, but the lads from Crime Agencies were very confident about the case. I was a little nervous, but after the grilling I had received in the voir dire, I was more prepared for the onslaught. Just prior to the start of the trial, Doyle made an application to the NSW Supreme Court to have a separate trial for Adamson so the evidence against his co-accused wouldn't taint his case. Wisely, this application was dismissed, which saved a lot of time and money and meant not having to give the same evidence in two different trials.

Some of the families of the slain Vaders OMCG were there, which added a sense of humanity to it all. I hadn't actually seen the crime scene or any photos of the bodies up to that point, nor had I dealt with any of the victims' families or witnesses, so I had been divorced from the worst of it. It was humbling to see that despite the stereotypical images of OMCGs, they really are people like you and me, with families who love them. I got to speak to the mother and sister of one of the victims. They were so warm and grateful, and it was a very sobering experience.

When it was time for me to give evidence, I took a deep breath and entered the lion's den. It was packed, and the jury sat intently as I walked to the witness box. I read my statement onto the record and for the next few hours went through a barrage of questioning similar to the one I had faced in the voir dire.

But this time I was more prepared with the thought, *If I can survive it once, then I can survive it again.*

I was able to read my statement to the Court and Jury because I had made it soon after the incident. Although I knew what was in it and had replayed the incident in my head a thousand times, it was a relief not to have to try to remember every little detail. Then it started. It was like round two of a title fight, where the reward would be freedom for the crooks. But I stood my ground and answered the questions honestly, already aware of what I had and hadn't done right from giving evidence in the voir dire. I remember turning to the jury when I answered questions so they could see I was telling the truth and so I didn't feel intimidated by having to look at Adamson and Doyle, who were seated directly behind their legal team in the dock area.

I was feeling pretty confident about the evidence I had given when we stopped for lunch. My spirits were lifted even higher when I saw Rachael and Teagan standing outside the Court, waiting for me. It was a good dose of reality that I had something to look forward to after giving evidence. They had come down from the Central Coast for moral support, and it meant the world to me. We had a brief lunch and a chat about things—nothing to do with my evidence, of course—to take my mind off the trial. When I went back in after the adjournment they sat in the back of the Court next to all the bikies.

The vicious Defence barrister looked at me and whispered, "Is that your family?"

I nervously nodded yes, which surprisingly put a look of terror on his face and made me feel more relaxed. It was as if he felt guilty about hammering me in front of my family. Maybe he was human after all?

When I finished giving my evidence, I felt pretty good about the whole ordeal. No tears of anguish, just a big sigh of relief. I had fulfilled my obligations. The rest was up to the big-money barristers and justice itself. We headed back to the police station and then went home. I tried to keep up to date with the trial, but it dragged on for months, and it became too much with my work and family commitments to attend Court on every occasion.

In October of that year, I was driving to the shops when I heard on the radio a story about some murderers being convicted in a Sydney Supreme Court. It had to be them. And it was. I couldn't believe it.

Both Adamson and Doyle had been found guilty of three counts of murder and one count of attempted murder. Although I was a bit annoyed about not being told that the jury had reached a verdict, as I had been waiting for this day for years, the disappointment only lasted for a few seconds. We had won! After years of waiting and days of giving evidence, it was over and justice had been served. I learnt later that Adamson had spat the dummy at the Judge and been charged with contempt of Court—not that it made any difference to his sentence.

I went to the sentencing in November with Rachael. It was a big occasion. There were lots of people there, and it was hard to tell whose side they were on because they were wearing suits, with their hair slicked back and no 'colours' on display. We went inside and the Judge gave his address to the Court. I was sitting at the end of a row of seats near the only entrance/exit door when one of the lawyers from the DPP came up to me and whispered that if either Adamson or Doyle tried to escape, I had to intervene. I thought, *Well, isn't that why we're here in the first place?*

And then came the crowning moment we had all been waiting for. The judge sentenced Adamson and Doyle to thirty-three years in jail for each of the murders, to be served concurrently. This meant that the sentence for each murder commenced at the date of each accused's arrest, totalling thirty-three years for all three victims, with a non-parole period of twenty-eight years. We all wanted to scream with joy but walked outside and quietly congratulated one another instead.

The Crown Prosecutor and the Detective Inspector in charge of the Homicide section came over and congratulated me on my efforts. My offsider wasn't at the sentencing, which was a shame. It really meant a lot to have some recognition for doing a good job; it made all the anxiety and risk worthwhile. And it was a big relief. Although we still don't have a notation on our service records that reflects it ever happened, I know deep down that we made a difference. Praise should be given to my partner for her involvement in the matter and to the Detectives from Homicide and Crime Scene, who worked tirelessly through the investigation and Court proceedings to help secure the conviction. After the pleasantries had ended, it was time to go home and get on with our lives.

However, that wasn't the end of the matter. In 2001, both convicted men appealed to the Court of Criminal Appeal on a technicality, claiming that the murders were not part of a 'joint criminal enterprise' (that the accused reached an understanding or arrangement amounting to an agreement between them that they will commit a crime — can be implied by circumstances of case or expressed between parties), and were granted a retrial.

Following three mistrials within a week, the matter was finally heard in February 2003, and a jury of their peers, after four days of intense deliberations, again convicted both males. They were re-sentenced on October 30th, 2003 to the original period of imprisonment, the judge citing the fact that neither of the accused showed any sign of remorse or contrition. Despite their best efforts, the prosecution were unable to secure a 'life term' for Adamson and Doyle, but it was nevertheless a virtuous result. Although they both tried to appeal the conviction again in 2005, the NSW Criminal Court of Appeal quickly dismissed the application. Thankfully, that was the last time the matter was mentioned before any Court.

---

Shortly after my experience at the original Court case, my leave was up and I returned to work. I felt back on track. As the saying goes, 'Whatever doesn't kill you makes you stronger,' and after all, I had survived this far.

By this time, Rachael and I had been engaged for two years, and our bond was growing stronger and deeper. In October 1999, Teagan's birth mother moved back to NSW, close to where we lived, after years in Queensland. Rachael and I had been travelling up there every couple of weeks just to see her for a few hours, and it was wonderful to have her close again. In November, Rachael and I were married in a beautiful ceremony on the Central Coast. The day was made even more special by having Teagan there as our flower girl.

Our relationship as father and daughter improved as we enjoyed regular contact over the following months. In April 2000, she came into our care full-time. Rachael and I were overwhelmed by a sense of responsibility and fulfilment. We had never really thought it would be possible to have her on a permanent basis, but we embraced the change with open hearts. We had an instant family that, despite some initial teething problems, united us and helped us grow stronger.

For the rest of the year, I was able to avoid any major confrontation or critical incident. I still managed to keep up my high arrest rate but decided to change the way I operated. *Work smarter, not harder.* I decided to out-think the crooks rather than outrunning or out-muscling them. I even began enjoying work again.

## Chapter Eight:
# Field Intelligence

After twelve months in the Target Team, I decided it was time for a change. I spoke to a Sergeant in the Intelligence Office and expressed my interest in becoming a Field Intelligence Officer. Their role was to perform regular patrols around 'hot spots' and provide intelligence relating to active and wanted offenders within the Command. They would also liaise with other specialist groups, including the Detectives, Target Team and other Local Area Commands. I was confident with my overall knowledge of wanted and active offenders in the area and the main crime hot spots and believed that I could make a big difference to policing in this position.

Personally, I believe that the Intelligence office is the core of the police station because it is responsible for relaying information to frontline police and other external agencies about where crime is happening and who is responsible. I spent a lot of time working in and out of the office and enjoyed free range on my duties. I became comfortable in my position and provided incentive and encouragement to police within the Command. But I still managed to get involved in high-risk incidents even then.

In September 2000, I got involved in something that could have ended up a lot differently than it did. Because I lived so far away from work, I sometimes caught the train, which gave me a chance to catch up on some much-needed sleep.

As I hadn't heard the news before leaving home and it was too early for the newspaper, I didn't know that there had been a minor train derailment at Redfern that morning. When I got off the train, I saw a crowd of people gathered at the top of Eveleigh Street, which in itself wasn't a good sign. There were people standing on boxes looking over the wall onto the tracks and photographers hoping for a piece of momentary brilliance. It took a while to click, but when I realised that they were looking at the aftermath of the derailment, I went to have a gander.

As I walked towards Eveleigh Street in my stylish tracksuit pants and shirt, I heard a woman screaming. At the top of Eveleigh Street, I saw an Aboriginal man struggling with a young blonde woman. The man was attempting to pull the woman's handbag away and she was screaming for someone to help her, but no one did. The photographers clicked away as the offender snatched the bag and ran for safety down the Block. I couldn't believe it.

I instinctively began chasing the offender into Eveleigh Street. I got most of the way into the Block when I realised where I was and what I was doing. This wasn't the best place to be without any appointments or assistance. I quickly saw the error of my ways and ran back to the railway station. I saw the young girl still on the ground in the foetal position, embarrassed and in shock. I helped her to her feet and identified myself. I spoke to the police inside the railway station and went for a walk with them down the Block into Eveleigh Lane to try to identify the offender, but no luck. I took the young girl back to the police station, where I took her statement and later drove her home. She had heard about how dangerous the area was but said she had felt safe because of all the people around, yet no one went to her aide.

I made contact with one of the photographers from the Daily Telegraph who was there, and he sent through the photo of the offender he had taken at the time of the incident. It was perfect, showing his clothing, facial appearance, the stolen handbag under his arm and the dishevelled victim slumped on the ground. It was front-page news in the Daily Telegraph the next day, which is why I refer to him as the 'Telegraph Bandit.'

I took over the investigation because of my involvement, but after weeks of investigation I wasn't any closer to identifying the crook. That was until I arrested another man for an unrelated matter with whom I had a good rapport. I showed him the photograph and he positively identified the crook for me. Because of that information I was able to confirm his identity, and he was arrested days later in Kempsey, for this and fifteen other serious offences. In the interview he admitted to all of the crimes, including the one I had seen, and even confessed to a few others. He didn't spend much time in gaol but never returned to Redfern. Well, not that I was aware of.

## (aka) Brocky

He was young, he was slick and he liked to drive really fast. He was known as 'Peter Brock' to his friends and was well known to the local police. Unlike the former living legend of racing, this impersonator was a criminal, a young Aboriginal boy who thought he was smart and untouchable. On the racetrack, given the opportunity, he probably would have done alright. The only problem was that the cars he drove were stolen, other people's possessions. They were items of convenience and sport to him. His favourite car was the Hyundai Excel. Apparently, every night he was zooming through the darkness in someone else's vehicle. But on this day, in our area, during our shift, his luck ran out.

I was working with Frosty, who was a competent and enthusiastic Constable. We had worked a lot of shifts together while I was relieving as Intelligence Supervisor over the Olympic period. He was my right-hand man, and we spent hours patrolling the streets of the command, leaving no stone unturned. We made it our business to find out who was out and about and what they were doing. Frosty knew 'Peter' as well as I did and knew too well what he was capable of.

On this particular day we had just arrested a male for drug supply in the Block area. Some other police offered to take over the charging process because we were searching for an offender wanted for a number of armed robbery offences on taxis. When we received a message to return to the station to see the acting Commander, we thought we were in trouble for something, which wasn't unusual. We were both very proactive officers who liked to police in our own unique—but very legal, of course—way. Thankfully we hadn't done anything wrong and the boss just wanted us to visit an address in Waterloo in relation to some visiting dignitaries. It sounded easy enough, so off we went.

About 100 metres from the station, we saw a white Hyundai Excel turning towards us. We both looked at the driver and said simultaneously, "It's him" (aka Peter Brock).

By the time we had driven 180 degrees around the roundabout there was already quite a distance between the Excel and our unmarked Ford. I got the registration number, stuck the revolving beacon on the roof, activated the sirens and informed the Police Radio that we were in pursuit.

Brocky drove around the Waterloo area at about 20km/hr over the posted speed limit. It was early in the morning, so there weren't too many cars on the road. And because he was a local boy he knew all the lanes and hidey-holes in the area, which would be best described as a rabbit warren. It would have been easy to escape, and he was quick, but Frosty did very well keeping him in sight. The radio operator asked us if we were aware of the driver's identity. We confirmed we were. As 'Peter Brock' drove on the wrong side of the road around a roundabout and accelerated away, the radio operator directed us to terminate the pursuit.

The Excel fishtailed into a narrow laneway and a marked sedan pulled in behind him, initiating another pursuit. The Excel drove onto the main street of Redfern across two lanes of traffic and proceeded through a red light at the next intersection. Police followed the Excel into a laneway, where it travelled against the flow of traffic, when the radio operator terminated the pursuit for the second time. The radio operator decided that because we knew the identity of the driver there was no need to engage in a pursuit with the vehicle.

In hindsight, it was both a good and a bad thing that we had told the Police Radio who the driver was. Bad because we weren't allowed to chase it, but good because when the matter went to Court we had made a record over the police radio as to the identity of the driver. I had made a mistake with the Black Market murders in 1997 by not giving enough information to the radio operator. I wasn't going to make the same error again.

We followed the Excel into Waterloo, where we lost sight of it. After a moment, a City East highway car spotted it heading north in Redfern towards Cleveland Street. He also initiated a pursuit of the car, much to the irritation of the radio operator. She wasn't impressed. The pursuit lasted only a few seconds before it was terminated for a third time. The highway patrol car continued to follow the Excel into the more affluent area of Surry Hills to the north, as it ran through numerous stop signs and red lights.

Because I had a general knowledge of the Surry Hills area and was monitoring the radio transmissions, I had an idea of the Excel's location. We drove into Belvoir Street, which is separated from Devonshire Street by a park popular with local families. When I heard that the vehicle was last seen driving into the grounds of the park, I feared the worst. I looked through the trees and saw the contour of the white Excel heading south towards us. There were about twenty small kids and adults in the park who were forced to run for safety as the driver fishtailed and swerved over the grass. Frosty stopped the car and we both ran to the southern side of the park, standing on the footpath.

I could see the Excel approaching and raised my right hand and shouted, "Stop. Police."

He continued to tear across the park and I began to fear for my own safety. There was no way out except through me. I drew my service revolver from its holster and pointed it in the direction of the Excel.

I shouted, "Police stop. Police stop."

The driver looked at me and turned the front of the car in my direction. He accelerated towards me, so I raised my firearm to the level of his head and shouted, "Stop; police. Or I will shoot."

I was hyped on adrenaline. This was the first time I had threatened to shoot anyone in the line of duty. I had drawn my firearm for building searches in the past, but this was intense. I had my finger poised on the trigger to shoot as he accelerated faster towards me.

But at that second, I remembered something I had heard on the radio on my way to work that morning. One week prior to this incident a police officer had fatally shot the driver of a stolen car in the City. It was alleged that the driver was reaching for something under his seat. That morning it was announced that the police officer had been charged with murder. It was enough to make me think two, three and even four times and distracted me long enough to allow the Excel to ram through a line of trees directly in front of me.

He was doing about 70km/hr when he became airborne towards me. I didn't have time to react. The impact of the car hitting the trees uprooted one, which knocked me on the side of my head and shoulder. I thought 'Peter Brock' was going to run me down, so I jumped out of the way. The passenger side of his getaway car narrowly missed me by only a few inches. I was lucky.

As the car sped onto the footpath, it collided with a white sedan parked nearby and rebounded onto the front of a marked police car that was attempting to block his escape. But he was good. He corrected the vehicle and began speeding off down the street. By this time I had picked myself up off the ground and decided to chase the car on foot with my firearm in my hand. I knew I had no chance, but I was hoping that the accident damage would slow him down or he would lose control again.

I jumped back in the police car with Frosty and we headed back towards Redfern. We didn't know where the car was or where to look, but as we approached the intersection of Cleveland Street we could see a tower of water about thirty feet high spraying from the ground. In the middle of the fountain a white car was stalled. It wasn't the Excel but the police car that had been rammed just moments earlier. Apparently the collision with the Excel caused the steering to fail on the police car, and when the officer tried to turn a corner he lost control and rammed an underground water hydrant. Thankfully the officer wasn't hurt.

A message was then broadcast that the Excel was seen entering Castlereagh Lane and the driver seen jumping a nearby fence. This was a laneway synonymous with violence, threats against police and large-scale drug supply. It was a good place to hide, and 'Peter' was a known associate of the area. A perimeter was quickly established and a ground search was made. Moments later, an officer from Redfern who had firsthand knowledge of the young person saw him leave a house that backed onto the laneway. He tried to walk away like nothing was wrong, but he was quickly arrested.

Frosty and I made our way to where the officer was and confirmed that 'Peter Brock' was in custody. To say he wasn't too happy to see us would be understating the obvious. I think he was surprised more than anything. His trail of destruction had come to an end, but the adrenaline was still surging through me. My hands were shaking and I kept thinking about what would have happened if I had decided to shoot.

He was conveyed to the charge room at the Sydney Police Centre, where he declined to be interviewed. He was charged with a number of serious offences, including assault police, use offensive weapon (vehicle) to avoid arrest, dangerous driving and vehicle theft. Despite all of his moves and fluky escapes, this time his luck had finally run out. He was refused bail and spent the night in the lock-up.

After all the formal procedures had been completed I reflected on what had happened. I was shaken and felt like I had put myself in the uncomfortable position of playing God, which was unsettling. I know that we are trained to use our firearm when the need arises, but it doesn't make the decision to shoot or take someone's life any easier. It's even harder wondering whether you will be supported by the NSW Police Service or hung out to dry.

I had to make a *split second* decision whether or not to shoot, and if I hadn't heard the news on the radio about the officer being charged with murder, I am certain I would have pulled the trigger. I was in immediate danger of being killed or seriously injured, which entitled me to use my firearm for self-defence. I can remember looking through the sights of my firearm as I pointed it at the driver. In that moment, the decision of whether to pull the trigger or not was mine alone. Being in the position to decide whether to kill another person, whether I was justified in the circumstances and whether I would be supported, was scary. I was unsettled by what had happened and had trouble processing it even though I had survived and was alive to tell the story. But it wasn't over yet, not for Brocky.

A few weeks later, after the Court had released him on conditional bail, he absconded to Queensland, where he went on a rampage. He got involved in a high-speed pursuit with the cops up there and rammed their cars to get away, but only managed to get himself caught again. However, they handcuffed him and left him in the back of the police car — alone. Being resourceful, he found a baton, smashed the window, ran off into the darkness and wasn't seen for some time.

When the Queensland police finally caught up with him, he served time there and was extradited to Sydney. My matters went to Court and he was convicted of the offences and sentenced to nine months' imprisonment. He served only two months. That's justice for you. Frosty told me later that he honestly thought I was going to shoot.

All he could say was, "Oh shit."

We never did manage to get to the address in Waterloo for the boss, but I'm sure he understood. The legend and reputation of 'Peter Brock' had been foiled, and I am certain that he was very lucky not to be lying in his grave, officially retired. I was lucky that I wasn't there, as well.

Oh, a few days later Frosty and I arrested the taxi robber who was running rampant holding knives to the throats of cab drivers around the area. He tried to hide in an alcove and conceal the weapon, but his violent crime spree had come to an end.

## City East Rampage

At the same time Sydney was celebrating the 2000 Olympic Games and the armed assailant was robbing taxis, there was another one-man crime tornado causing havoc all over the City East and Sydney Metropolitan areas. Over a period of about six weeks he had committed no fewer than seventy offences, including robbery, vehicle theft and stealing. He had been very busy, and just by chance I managed to come across the case just as his reign of terror commenced.

During this period, there were some big changes in my life, both personally and professionally. Rachael discovered that she was pregnant with our first child, which was amazing and also meant that she could get a compassionate transfer closer to home at Tuggerah Lakes LAC on the Central Coast because she was so sick and wasn't allowed to travel. It was a great relief to get her away from the mean streets of Redfern. She had been such an amazing support for me. I was having enough 'excitement' for the two of us anyway.

I also started relieving as the Intelligence Supervisor, where I was responsible for coordinating and informing police within the Redfern LAC of when and where crime was happening and which offenders were wanted for committing offences, as well as relaying daily crime statistics to the City East Region intelligence office. It meant a lot to me because I enjoyed the responsibility the role demanded and the work that it involved. At that stage of my career I was interested in crime statistics and wanted to promote good police work within the command. Despite the heavy workload, I always made time to get out on the streets and see who was out and about. That way I could update the troops more accurately.

On one occasion, in the space of two shifts I recovered two stolen Commodores in a street a short distance away from the Block. They had been used in robbery and bag snatch offences in the inner City and surrounding areas just prior to being dumped. This ignited an interest to delve deeper into the incidents. I returned to the station and let my brain and fingers do the walking. Although I love chasing crooks, one of my strengths is analysis, which entails looking at an issue or incident, considering the contributing factors and linking incidents of similar description or method.

As I was looking through the incidents involving the stolen vehicles, I uncovered a common thread. The offender, described as a well-dressed, dark-skinned male, would wait near the entry to service stations until the owners of the vehicles went inside to pay for their petrol. The unsuspecting owners would leave the doors to their cars unlocked and sometimes even leave the keys in the ignition, which provided the opportunity for the offender to jump in and drive off before the owners could react.

Over the next few days the number of similar incidents increased. We even had a few occur in our patrol. After each offence the cars would be dumped in or around the Block area. This sounded alarm bells and meant that the offender was seeking refuge there or possibly lived nearby. I passed on a lot of my information and discoveries to the Robbery Unit. I had worked with these officers, and they knew a lot about everything, especially crooks within the area. They were very popular amongst the local police and were officers I looked up to.

As part of my analysis, I obtained a copy of a surveillance tape from the service station at Ashfield, where the man had committed his first offence. The image of the offender was fairly clear. I had an idea who he was, so I took the videotape and offender photograph and showed it to a Detective, who immediately rejected my identification. So, relying on his knowledge, I kept on looking. I took the videotape to the Shell service station in Waterloo, where we watched it on their video screen. I called the guys from the Robbery Unit to see if they could help. It was just as well I did, as they identified the offender as the same person in the photograph I had shown to the Detective. I knew I was right. Now we were getting somewhere. We had enough evidence to charge him for a couple of offences and began intensifying the investigation into the other matters. I took the tape to the Crime Scene Unit, where they made a still photograph of the image of the offender so that it could be used as identification evidence.

One morning, I heard that a stolen car was being used in robbery offences in the City East Region. So, with the assistance of plainclothes police, a perimeter was set up around the Block area. I knew that if it was the offender he would be heading to the Block before too long. A short time later the stolen car was seen entering a laneway in the vicinity of the Block, and the Detectives became involved in a brief high-speed car pursuit. They lost sight of the vehicle in Chippendale and I managed to quickly pick up his trail. I only missed by a few seconds, but that was enough for him to escape. We found the car later abandoned in Ultimo, which again heightened our suspicion that he was local.

Considering our plan of attack had failed, it was unlikely that he would dump his cars near the Block anymore, so it was time to think smart. We made enquiries into the background of the suspect and discovered that he lived at an Ultimo address, near where the last vehicle had been dumped. But when we went to the listed location, it didn't exist. We contacted the suspect's mother by telephone and 'pretended' to be a worker from the Probation Service. It was very convincing, and we were able to find out the correct address. After a bumpy start, everything was falling into place. As we drove past the house in plain clothes and an unmarked police car, we saw the suspect walk around the corner and through the front door. We couldn't believe our luck. We parked away from the house but stayed close enough to watch.

Just as we decided to pounce, the suspect walked out of the house and was joined by a female and a small child. It was too risky to confront him with others around. I got out of the car and followed them across the park. I kept in contact with my partners by way of portable radio. They headed up towards Star City Casino but stopped to have a heated discussion. The suspect turned and started walking away from the woman, which was great, but he was walking towards me, which wasn't. I thought my cover was blown, but he just kept going past me. I followed him back towards Redfern. He crossed the road and began looking around as he approached a service station. I became very suspicious and began running towards the servo. As I walked into the driveway of the servo I couldn't see him anywhere, but I knew he had to be around. This was his scene.

As I walked past the mechanic's garage, I turned to my right and saw him sitting in the driver's seat of a gold Mazda 626. He looked at me and accelerated harshly. I pulled out my police badge and called on him to stop, but he drove right at me and I was forced to jump for safety. I was lucky that the car stalled just before where I was standing, otherwise I would have become a hood ornament and another crime statistic. He restarted the vehicle and sped out onto the road but had more trouble with the car. It kept jerking and spluttering, which was probably why it was in getting fixed, so I saw my chance. The Detectives manoeuvred their car in front of the suspect, but he was able to slip around them, coughing and stalling down a laneway.

I pulled out my firearm, ran to the driver's window and said, "Police; get out of the car."

He just looked at me and accelerated down the laneway with me chasing on foot. The Detectives chased after him as he disappeared into the distance.

Before too long, both cars were out of sight, and because I didn't have a radio I couldn't hear where they were headed. I felt a bit disappointed that my involvement had ended so soon and slowly made my way back to the service station. As I rounded the corner, I couldn't believe my eyes. Instead of driving away from the City, the suspect had driven the wrong way up a one-way street and rammed cars and other vehicles to get back to the Block. His luck ran out when he got wedged between some cars and a bus and scampered into a car repairer. The Detectives chased him into the repair shop and tackled him to the ground with some help from an eager employee. He was restrained and handcuffed so he couldn't escape.

It was over. After weeks of planning and surveillance, all our hard work had paid off. I had spent many nights sleeping at the station underneath the desk in the Detective office, staying up late analysing the evidence and linking him to offences around the region. We spent the rest of that night and into the early hours of the morning charging the offender with about forty serious offences. But it didn't stop there. Now that he was in custody we had to secure the brief and speak to witnesses and victims to ensure their testimony.

It was a great feeling. I was very focused on this target, and I felt justified when he was sitting in the dock. It was a great privilege to work with the Detectives from the Robbery Unit. They took me under their wing, and for that I am grateful. I learned a lot about teamwork and investigation and am happy to report that the offender was convicted on all matters and sentenced to a long term in prison. This was one of my proudest moments and one of my greatest achievements in the Police Service thus far.

## Chapter Nine:
# Loose Cannon

After twelve months in the Intelligence office, I was 'rotated' back downstairs to general duties in February 2001. It wasn't because I hadn't been doing a good job, but because I was, according to the Crime Manager, a 'loose cannon' due to the dangerous and irresponsible way I apparently executed my duties. Considering I had been pretty much office-bound for a year, I was very proud of still being ranked in the top ten of arresting officers in the station for the year 2000, including three of Redfern and City East Region's biggest criminals. Plus, I was still able to ensure that I had a briefing prepared for each shift and that the officers were kept up to date with wanted and active offenders in the area. Besides, if the 'management' truly thought I was such a loose cannon, the last place they should have put me was back on the streets full-time. If only they could have seen what was about to unfold.

I started back on general duties with a team of junior police. I was looking forward to the challenge and believed I could have a positive impact on them. Most of my early shifts I worked with a new Probationer, Marty. He was young, keen and fresh out of the Academy. I really enjoyed working with fresh recruits because it gave me the opportunity to pass on some of my experience. Plus, they were so enthusiastic — unlike some of the senior officers, who were more renowned for avoiding hard work. I had a feeling that Marty and I would be very busy over the next few weeks and months, and I was right.

One day shift I was working by myself as Supervisor and cruising around the Chippendale area when I saw two young Aboriginals hiding in a laneway. I stopped the car and approached them. Instantly they became aggressive towards me, and I had a feeling they may have been up to no good. I recognised the boy as a young bloke who had spent time in gaol for a number of serious robberies. He must have only just been released. I didn't know his girlfriend but managed to get her name before they both ran off. I went back to the station and submitted an intelligence report so that other police would be aware that they were around. I had a gut feeling that it wouldn't be the last time I would come across these two.

Over the next few weeks, the number of bag snatches and armed robberies increased around the Eveleigh Street area. I patrolled a lot around the railway station and kept a lookout for them. I made notes about where they were, who they were with and what they were wearing. It wasn't long before there were reports of bag snatches involving a young guy and girl, and the description, even the clothing, matched them perfectly. The only problem was that we couldn't catch them. They would hide in the alcoves and dungeons of the abandoned houses and wait until it was safe to come out. There were more cockatoos in the Block then at feeding time at the zoo.

It reached a stage where they were getting out of hand. They were already on bail for stealing offences, which was intended to deter future offending behaviour, but it didn't mean anything to these two recidivists. I managed to arrest them once for a breach of bail before their rampage began. They were refused bail but released by the Courts the following day. Each time I saw them in breach of their night-time curfew I would make a note and list them as wanted in the police system. The young girl was picked up by City Central Police and arrested for the breach of bail. But one Sergeant criticised me for being too 'trivial' and released the girl without charge (if only he could have seen what consequences that would have).

The number of offences being committed was growing at a ridiculous rate, so I coordinated with two other police from the Target Team to focus on capturing these offenders during our shift. They were very good operators whom I knew I could rely on. One evening while patrolling around the Block, I saw the two crooks seeking solace in the laneway. Marty and I made regular patrols of the area, but it was impossible to be everywhere. If we were up the top, they went out down the bottom. If we had cars at top and bottom they went out the side. We didn't have the resources at night to keep constant surveillance on them as well as perform our normal duties.

At about 8.30 p.m., we met up with the Target Team at the bottom of the laneway to discuss a strategy. They had started to drive away when I saw the shadow of a male running along Eveleigh Street towards our truck. I couldn't believe it. The young man's ears must have been burning. It was him. He was holding a knife and carrying a wallet in his hand. The girl and a blonde man were running behind him. They both stopped, but the one I was after kept running between the back of our police truck and the Target Team sedan into Eveleigh Lane. If he had only been a few seconds earlier we all would have been ready to pounce.

Instinctively I jumped from the driver's seat of the truck and gave chase.

I called, "Redfern 45 foot pursuit, Eveleigh Lane."

As I ran up the lane, I could see it was crowded and that it wasn't going to be an easy chase. Usually the laneway was empty, but not tonight. There must have been about eighty people lining the sides of the lane. I was literally running the gauntlet. I thought to myself, *This is not good.* I wanted to stop, but something kept me going. One of the locals I knew stepped out in front of me.

I yelled "Don't even think about it" and pushed him out of the way.

I saw the crook run into the backyard of a house, so I rounded the corner and caught him out of the corner of my eye. He was hiding up against a corrugated iron fence with the knife in his hand. I grabbed hold of his arm, but he was slippery. He didn't have a shirt on and the sweat made it difficult to get a firm hold.

So I picked him up and dragged him into the laneway, where he shouted, "Help me. Get him off me."

By this time I had him pinned on the ground, face-first. He was still holding the knife in his hand and I was conscious that he might intend to use it if he got the chance. He was viciously throwing his arms and body about, but I wasn't letting go. I had him now.

But before I could start rejoicing, I was grabbed from behind and pulled off the man. He stood up and glared at me. I couldn't move. He lifted the knife threateningly and I waited for him to slide it through my skin, but instead he began punching into me about the body and head. With each blow, I waited to feel the cold blade of the knife. I couldn't believe he wasn't doing it. I was petrified. I thought I was going to die.

I had my arms pinned to my side as the man continued punching into me. Then I was thrown to the ground and surrounded by about twenty people who began hitting and kicking me. I tried to shield myself with my arms, but there were too many of them.

I was still holding my radio and desperately called, "Redfern 45, Signal One, Eveleigh Lane."

I was also worried about being stuck with or rolling onto one of the discarded syringes that littered the laneway.

Amidst the pounding blows, I looked up and saw the man run down the laneway. Almost at the same time, my assailants eased off and the crowd dispersed. I managed to get to my feet and run down the laneway, where I saw the Target Team officers involved in a mighty squabble with the bloke who had grabbed me from behind and pinned me to the ground. There were fists flying and shirts getting ripped. They released a spurt of OC spray, which sent the crowd scattering. We managed to restrain the man as the Block filled with the echoes of wailing sirens and blue and red beacons. It was like music to my ears. I informed the Police Radio that I was alright and that the one I had been after had gotten away.

I went back to the station, where I was treated by ambulance officers for bruising, swelling and grazing to my face and body. I reflected on what I had done and what could have happened. I had been lucky this time and I knew it. My only thoughts at the time had been to get the man I was after. I wasn't going to let anyone or anything stop me from achieving this. It was the thrill of the chase. One on one. If it weren't for the man's helpers intervening, the outcome would have been a lot different. But it could also have been different in a more serious way. All the young offender had to do was lunge that knife into me and I could have been killed. I hadn't been issued with any OC spray at the time and could only rely on my physical strength or firearm. I wasn't going to use a gun down there if I could avoid it.

The bloke we had arrested told me at the station that he only grabbed me because he didn't know I was a police officer, even though I was dressed in full police uniform and appointments at the time and called my office while making the arrest. I don't know how he could have been confused, besides being an absolute idiot.

I didn't know what had happened to my Probationer partner. I had left him sitting in the passenger seat of the truck when I ran up the lane. It probably wasn't a good example to be showing, but there comes a time when you have to believe in your partner's abilities. I found out later that he had arrested the blonde man, but when he heard me call Signal One, he let him go to come and help. I am very appreciative of him and the guys from the Target Team. They were there for me when it mattered and they saved my life. The following morning Marty and I arrested the blonde man for numerous armed robberies, vehicle thefts and break-ins, so the night had not been a total loss. But I had let it happen again. I had put my safety at risk for the achievement of my goals. People kept asking me why I did it.

I could only reply, "I was doing my job."

To me, the job is important, and there are times when you must put your life on the line to protect the safety of others and enforce the law you swore to uphold. This man was dangerous and if let loose to run on the streets could have ended up killing someone. At the time it felt like the right thing to do. And I survived, again. The man I was after was arrested a few weeks later in Eveleigh Lane and put up a bit of a battle. The police were pelted with bricks and bottles but managed to arrest him.

Frosty said, "It was one of the toughest fights he'd ever had."

In July 2003, the fleeing felon was convicted by a jury of his peers for these and other serious armed robbery incidents and sentenced to six and a half years imprisonment. He probably served just over three years, but a good result nonetheless!

## Hire Car

A few weeks after the Eveleigh Lane incident I was working with Marty again and cruising around the Block doing the usual patrol, looking for 'customers.' We had been assigned that area for the first half of the shift and were keen to get some lock-ups. I enjoyed working with Marty because he was keen to learn and had a good head on his shoulders, despite his age and lack of experience. As we drove around the back streets looking for something to happen, we came across a luxurious hire car doing a three-point turn. I didn't think anything of it to begin with, other than that it was a bad place to make such a manoeuvre — in such a long vehicle, in the narrowest street in the area.

Once he finally made the turn, we followed him along the street, only because he now happened to be travelling in the same direction as us. There was nothing out of the ordinary about the vehicle until the driver of the hire car planted his foot, fishtailed around the corner and sped off up the street. I think it caught both of us completely off-guard. I activated the lights and sirens of the police truck, but by that time he was scooting away. There was no way we could catch up.

By the time we turned the corner, the hire car was headed for a roundabout with a garden bed in the middle some 100 metres away. I was watching and waiting for the brake lights to come on, but he just floored it. He hit the roundabout and the garden bed at an impressive speed. The hire car became airborne as sparks ignited from the undercarriage while the car flew through the air, drifted to the left and headed to the front of a hotel that was packed with patrons, both inside and outside, on the footpath. The car landed on a garden strip at the front of the hotel. The impact of the collision caused both front tyres to explode before the car swerved over the road and rammed parked cars onto the footpath.

It was all happening so fast. As we came through the roundabout I saw the driver of the hire car run along the footpath back towards us. I stopped the police truck and with the lights and sirens still activated took off after him. I was pleased to see my partner running alongside of me with his portable radio, because I had forgotten mine. We chased the driver of the car, who was in his twenties and of solid build.

I yelled out, "Stop; police. Get on the ground."

But he kept running in circles, doing what he could to get away. But he wasn't scared. Marty and I tackled the driver to the ground, but he just pushed us off like we were feathers. He ran back down towards the roundabout and I shouted, "Get on the ground."

He turned back and ran towards me, so I tackled him against the wall of the building, but he just bounced off and kept running. I knew something wasn't right. He didn't look all that strong, so he had to be 'raging' on some drug or stimulant. I ran him down again and somehow managed to grab hold of him and pin him on the ground as he continued to struggle viciously. He moved his head down towards my forearm and shouted, "I've got AIDS. I'm going to bite you."

That was enough for me. He opened his mouth and moved closer to my arm. I'd been bitten before and didn't want it to happen again, especially if he was claiming to have AIDS. So I let go of him and he ran off. I wanted to arrest him but I was afraid that he would bite me. I didn't know whether or not he had AIDS, but he said he did, and that was enough for me to believe it. But I also had a job to do. Who knows what he would do if we didn't detain him. I chased after him again and tackled him onto the road. He began waving his arms and legs about like he was having a fit.

He threatened me again: "I've got AIDS and I'll bite you."

But this time I didn't let go. I held him down to move my arms away from his head, but he managed to push me away. I was getting tired and my arms were aching from the adrenaline. I was hoping he would give in, but he kept running. He didn't get too far before I tackled him to the ground for a third time. I pinned him chest-first to the road and we struggled. I ripped his shirt off while trying to put him into a wristlock. But he was too strong.

I kept yelling, "Get on the ground, get on the ground."

He just kept lifting his body off the road like he was doing push-ups. Pushing my entire 100 kg bulky frame onto him just didn't seem to make any difference. Marty jumped on his legs and tried to hold him down.

I looked at Marty and said, "Spray him. Spray him."

He drew his OC spray and pointed it at the man, demanding, "Stop struggling or I will spray you."

It just seemed to motivate the driver more to get away. He kept pushing off the ground and I was really getting worried. I was tired and didn't know how much longer I could hold on. When I heard some sirens approaching, I could see an end in sight, but I almost died when I saw them drive straight past.

I said to Marty, "Call urgent."

He informed the radio of our location and the need for urgent assistance. Within seconds, the cavalry arrived. A number of officers helped restrain the driver, who was still struggling wildly on the road. With five of us pinning him down, we were able to handcuff him and lead him back to the truck.

Once we were sure the fleeing felon was securely locked away, Marty and I walked back down to survey the carnage. It was like a warzone. People from the hotel and nearby residents had flooded onto the streets to take photos and catch a glimpse of the scene. I congratulated Marty on a good effort. The Supervisor came down and wasn't impressed. He criticised me for pursuing the vehicle, even though I hadn't. He offered no support. I felt terrible. I had just been involved in a lengthy and violent struggle with an offender and was tired and sore, but all he could do was wave his baton of authority.

We got the details of the owners of the cars and made a sketch of the scene. Apart from the cars littered on the footpath, the driver had left an indentation in the road surface that went for over forty metres. That just demonstrates the speed he was travelling at during the time of the incident. It took us a while to clean up, and then we returned to the station. The driver was taken to hospital after suffering minor injuries during the arrest. I received some lacerations to my hands, elbows and knees and had my wristwatch broken during the struggle. Other police also came into contact with the driver's blood but were not otherwise injured. I pulled Marty aside and asked why he hadn't used the spray, and he confidently and justifiably explained that if he had, he may have contaminated me and the incident may have gotten completely out of control. It was a very good decision, although I didn't think so at the time.

Once the driver returned from hospital, it took us a while to establish his identity. We eventually worked out that he was a boxer trained by a famous boxing legend. He admitted to taking amphetamines, which explained his superhuman strength. We were spoken to by the Duty Officer about the incident but not formally debriefed. We charged the crook with various traffic matters, driving a stolen motor vehicle and resisting arrest.

## Burning Saab

On Mother's Day, May 2001, my second daughter, Keely Anne, was born. Strangely enough, about ten months earlier, whilst executing a search warrant in inner-city Waterloo, I 'handled' what I thought to be an imitation African artifact only to learn that it was supposedly a fertility pole. Although I didn't believe it at the time, I quickly threw it to the ground and washed my hands. I guess it may have just been coincidental. Nevertheless, she was a very precious and welcome addition to the family, and I took a couple of weeks off so I could help her settle into the world before I returned to the fray. Rachael hoped that being a new father would mean I would become more cautious at work and not take so many risks. Initially I was more careful, but I soon slipped back into my old ways. It was just part of the job for me, and the way I did my job, like putting my uniform on each shift.

It was a couple of days before my eldest daughter's seventh birthday in June when I was at work on night shift with a new Probationer who had just transferred to Redfern from the country. She was enthusiastic and only weeks away from graduating as a Constable. We'd already had two arrests and a foot pursuit in the shift and were looking for our third. Towards the end of our shift we got lucky.

We were driving around the Block when I saw a car in one of the side streets with its headlights on high beam. As we approached, it sped off down the street. I managed to get the registration of the car and identify it as a white Saab. My partner checked with Police Radio while I attempted to see where it went. From the driver's reaction when he saw our police truck, the location and the time of night, there was a good chance that the car was stolen. Police Radio soon confirmed this and found that it had been involved in a number of recent armed robbery offences. Bingo! As we turned into a street at the bottom of the Block, I caught a glimpse of the Saab driving across an intersection and out of view, so I headed in that direction. I knew I wasn't allowed to pursue the Saab because it would breach the Safe Driver Policy and I would lose my police driving certification, so I didn't attempt to stop or catch up to it. I just monitored where it was going.

The caged truck was a category-three vehicle, which could only engage in a pursuit when no other higher-category vehicle was available, which there wasn't. Unfortunately, there had been a number of incidents in the region during which caged trucks had rolled during a pursuit or urgent duty due to the imbalance the caged area caused under high speed. This meant that pursuing in a caged truck was out of the question.

As I came over the rise into Darlington I saw the Saab turn left near the university some 200 metres away. It accelerated over a speed hump, causing the undercarriage to spark. My partner informed the Police Radio of our location and requested that a marked police sedan (a category-one vehicle) be expedited to our location to stop the vehicle. The Saab made a sudden left turn into a side street, causing the rear of the vehicle to swerve over the road. By the time I turned the corner, the Saab was at the other end of the street turning left. I didn't expect to see it again, but as I reached the end of the road and turned left, the Saab reappeared in front of us, sliding all over the place. There were skid marks on the road that indicated that the driver had probably lost control and made a 180-degree turn to end up back in front of us. More good luck than good management!

We informed the Police Radio of our location as the Saab turned harshly into the street, causing the rear end to slide out and collide with a number of parked cars. The driver was able to correct the vehicle and accelerated through a red light at the intersection with Cleveland Street. We stopped at the intersection for the red light and watched the Saab accelerate into the distance.

Once the lights turned green, we saw the Saab collide with a roundabout and slide over the road. It accelerated away towards Broadway and then headed back towards Redfern. We kept informing the Police Radio of our location as we continued to monitor the Saab's location. It wasn't too difficult to keep him in our sights because he was driving slowly and swerving over the road. My guess was that he was probably affected by drugs or alcohol because of where we first saw him.

At one stage, the vehicle was on the wrong side of the road and hard up against the gutter. I wasn't sure if the driver was still on board, but as we turned the corner he accelerated and lost control again. By this time the vehicle had spun around and was facing us.

The driver of the Saab looked directly at me and accelerated towards us. I swerved to avoid a collision, but he hit the driver's side of the police vehicle, buckling the driver's front guard. My partner informed the radio that the stolen vehicle had just rammed us and where it was headed. We saw the Saab turning wildly towards the university.

My instincts told me that he was headed for the Block, considering that was where he first came under notice. We still didn't have the assistance of a marked sedan or any other car at that stage, but we soon saw a marked police truck with its warning lights activated heading towards the Saab. The car swerved into the path of the oncoming police truck, causing it to brake suddenly and change direction. This also caused the Saab to slow down considerably, allowing us to get within a few metres.

But the driver accelerated away from us again and headed towards the Block. As he attempted to make a right-hand turn onto Caroline Street, he slid across the road, mounted the footpath with an explosion of sparks and rammed the front of a house. I jumped from the police car and ran towards the Saab as my partner notified the radio. As I approached I could see flames licking the front and undercarriage of the Saab. The driver was still trapped inside. My first thoughts were for his wellbeing.

I ran to the driver's door and attempted to open it, but it was jammed. I yelled at him to open the door, but he leant forward and gripped the steering wheel. I asked again but he wouldn't budge. I could see the flames under the car and didn't want to hang around too long. I had no choice. I raised my left leg and kicked in the driver's window. There was an explosion of glass as my foot followed through, hitting the driver in the face.

I leant through the window and shouted, "Get out, the car is on fire. Get out."

He struggled with me and held the steering wheel tighter. I tore his hands from the wheel and dragged him through the window, struggling and swearing. My partner and other police helped me restrain him on the ground, away from danger. He began complaining that we had ripped his shirt and lost one of his shoes. At least he wasn't seriously hurt. Just to make sure, we checked that he had no injuries and handcuffed him so he couldn't escape. The Fire Brigade arrived a short time later and extinguished the fire. It was a mess, and the driver was very lucky to be alive.

The driver was taken to the police station, where he was placed in the charge room. The ambulance was there but the driver refused to be treated. Instead, my partner and I were taken to hospital. As a result of dragging the driver from the burning car, I had sustained a severe strain to my lower back and could barely walk, and my partner had received a laceration and swelling to her knee during the struggle to restrain him.

After about an hour at the hospital we returned to the station with some pain relief and continued our enquiries. We managed to establish the driver's identity and locate a number of stolen items within the vehicle, as well as a knife believed to have been used in an armed robbery. During this time I was called into the Supervisor's office and told by the Duty Officer that I was a "fucking idiot." He criticised me for pursuing the Saab and breaching the Safe Driving Policy. I was adamant that I had done nothing wrong and that I had just risked my life to save the offender, but that didn't seem to matter. I hoped he would at least speak to my partner before taking any disciplinary action.

The driver was charged with various offences including dangerous driving, vehicle theft, armed robbery and break and enters. By the end of the twenty-hour shift, I was exhausted, suffering backache, and I barely coped with the drive home.

I took a couple of weeks off work for treatment for my back. But when I returned the dust still hadn't settled over the incident and I was informed that I had been breached for contravening the Safe Driving Policy. I was so angry, especially since my partner hadn't been spoken to before the decision was made. I had done everything in my power not to flout the policy. I had at no time activated the warning lights and sirens of the police vehicle, hadn't called pursuit and at no stage attempted to stop the stolen vehicle. It was only by chance that we were able to keep up with the Saab. The offender was a shocking driver. Just when we thought he was gone, he would spin out on the footpath or appear right back in front of us again. I don't know how many times we lost sight of the Saab throughout the incident. I wanted to arrest him, but I wasn't willing to breach Police Service regulations to achieve this. What would have been the point in that?

A few weeks later I received an official file from the safe driving panel about my punishment. They had decided that my actions were contrary to the guidelines and decertified me for three months without even speaking to me. You might as well have taken away my appointments and uniform because I was paralysed without my licence. The Inspector who recommended the action against me only saw the last few seconds of the incident when the Saab collided with the wall and at no time interviewed my partner or me. I had spoken to the same Inspector at the beginning of the shift about using a marked sedan, knowing I was working in the Block area and had a high possibility of coming across a stolen car, but he refused my request, saying, "I know what you're like."

I was livid. I had a right to appeal, so I submitted a five-page report to the Commander of the School of Traffic And Mobile Policing (S.T.A.M.P) outlining the reasons why the decertification should be overturned. Little did I know that it would be years before a decision on the appeal would be reached and that another far more serious incident would impact the outcome.

## Chapter Ten:
# Waterloo Riots

Although the Block had been a contentious issue for police, the government and members of the community for thirty years, in June 2001, the spotlight deviated from this 'cistern of crime' to another highly populated Aboriginal area: Waterloo.

The area of interest (AOI) was commonly controlled by a group of teenage Aboriginal youths referred to as the 'Waterloo Boyz' and had been a festering problem for the previous two or three years. Over this time, there had been an increased level of criminal activity, ranging from property theft, anti-social behaviour and offences against people (like stealing, assaults and robbery). Police were able to contain the crime in this area with a 'front-on' approach. The use of high profile, proactive policing, regular intelligence briefings and knowledge of active offenders within the area allowed the police to have the upper hand.

From Christmas 2000 to May 2001 the number of incidents reported in this area fell significantly. On the surface it appeared the problem had been resolved. There were a number of underlying problems in Waterloo that needed to be addressed on a long-term basis. These included high welfare reliance, truancy, alcohol and drug dependency, lack of structured social activities, poor literacy levels, family breakdowns, stereotypical views of police, inadequate access to medical facilities, poor living conditions and the high arrest rate amongst indigenous people.

About 6 p.m. on June 22, police witnessed an eleven-year-old Aboriginal boy in the company of a group of juveniles attempt to rob a motorcyclist on the main strip of Waterloo. Police pursued the juveniles into an adjoining street, where one of the boys attempted to scale a fence and was allegedly injured during the subsequent arrest. As a result, the area became congested with hostile members of the Aboriginal community hurling abuse towards police. The situation quickly escalated, with police and vehicles being bombarded with bricks and bottles, causing injury to officers and damage to police vehicles.

I wasn't there when the original incident happened but started work just when things started to get ugly. It was chaos. We were used to this sort of behaviour from the Block, but not here in Waterloo. As we attended to the injured boy, members of the community and teenagers from the 'Waterloo Boyz' who were intent on revenge jostled us. There was no chance to reason or opportunity to communicate. Bricks and bottles were hurled at our heads and we were forced to make a strategic retreat from the area. A few arrests were made for minor offences, which really didn't help matters. For the rest of the afternoon we received ongoing reports of bricks and bottles being thrown at cars and buses.

About 10 p.m. that evening, the situation escalated, with Fire Brigade officers being injured while attempting to extinguish fires in the area. The youths had gone from throwing rocks at cars to burning trees in order to lure police and Fire Brigades to Waterloo. It was premeditated. We responded to the job of assisting the Fire Brigade, and as we approached we were pelted from both sides by bricks and rocks. As I arrived at the scene I looked to my right and saw a youth throw a rock that hit the police truck on the b-pillar between the front and back windows. If the rock had impacted just a few centimetres towards the front of the car, the window would have shattered in my face. It was scary and getting out of control; the youths showed no concern for the safety of others, especially us. We were targets.

But in the short term, police were confronted with approximately sixty to eighty juveniles who had blocked off a major road in Waterloo. Some of the kids were intoxicated and demonstrating violent, anti-social behaviour. These youths were uncontrollable and determined to get revenge for the alleged abuse of police powers against the eleven-year-old boy. The countless confrontations between police and the youths of the area had finally come to a head. Many police and members of the community had predicted this would happen, but the warnings were simply ignored.

The question was "What do we do now?"

Confronted by the imminent danger and threat to life and property, police established a perimeter around the riot scene, closing streets and warning residents to stay inside. Police from adjoining LACs were summoned, including a police helicopter, numerous dog squad, Highway Patrol and crowd control police (OSG personnel). In the absence of the Local Area Commander, the Duty Officer assumed control at the command post nearby. As we donned our protective gear and confronted the riotous youths standing a few blocks away, we were yelled at and goaded by them. A stand-off ensued for the next three hours while we waited for the LAC Commander to arrive from the coast. During this time, numerous television reporters, cameras and members of the community arrived. The newspapers referred to it as "Operation SAW" (Stand Around Watching). During these hours the morale of the police dwindled and the youths became bolder, taunting and making fun of the officers and continuing to hurl projectiles.

When the Commander finally arrived and spoke with a senior member of the Aboriginal community, a decision was made that they would attempt to speak to the youths to resolve the conflict. A short time later the Commander returned and police were released from their positions. The 'softly, softly' approach had ended the situation, for the moment.

The following day the Commander, members of the Aboriginal community and youths involved in the riots attended a meeting, which ended again in violence and further outbreaks of rebellion, including bricks and bottles being thrown at the Commander and representatives of the Aboriginal community.

That same night, more riots occurred in Waterloo following a stabbing and a brawl at a local club. Again, police and members of the public were injured. A number of taxi drivers were conveyed to hospital after being assaulted with bricks and bottles. Their taxis were left damaged and abandoned on the streets, as if to signify a warning of a repeat of the previous night's unrest.

Once more, police from surrounding LAC's and OSG personnel were summoned to the area, but kept away from the action, in riot gear, waiting for the signal to advance. Police vehicles were parked at the command post in a nearby street. Report after report of violence came flooding into the station. Media outlets recorded the pictures of anarchy without a police vehicle in sight, for hours. By the time police had decided what action to take, the youths had dispersed and police were again left to clean up the mess.

In the space of forty-eight hours, the reputation of Redfern Police had been destroyed; we were seen as "avoiders" who were more willing to "stand around watching" than face confrontation. It was the most embarrassing moment of my five years at Redfern. After working so hard to build respect in the community, especially after the controversy of *Cop It Sweet* during the early 1990s, in two nights it had all been for nothing. And I wasn't the only officer at Redfern who felt this way.

No one was arrested in relation to this incident. Police were 'advised' to avoid the area, like a 'no-go' zone. After that day, crime in Waterloo started to escalate, local police morale fell and officers from other areas became hesitant in assisting Redfern Police. The newspapers condemned police for their inaction, with headlines such as 'Anger as Police let kids of 10 take over street' (*Sunday Herald*, 24 June 2001, page 4). The youths were made out to be celebrities, and because they went unpunished, they believed they were 'above the law.'

In this incident, police were confronted with a violent and dangerous situation that had the attention of everyone. They lost a lot of respect and dignity. In the absence of the Commander, his representative should have made a determination based on the situation at hand. More than sufficient numbers of police were there within minutes of the situation escalating into a riot. The police were not only prepared, but also willing to place their safety at risk to ebb this violent tide of crime. Standing around for hours in full view of the public and members of the media waiting for someone to make a decision was not only embarrassing to Redfern Police and the New South Wales Police Service, but also insulting to the experience and fortitude shown by those police who were there ready. It was a step in the wrong direction to allow these kids, some as young as ten, to take control of a city street. What message is that giving them and other kids, as well as their parents and the wider community?

The option of 'contain and negotiate' was ineffective. The use of swift, firm action would have achieved a more desirable result and allowed police the opportunity to look at the long-term solution more closely. It would have sent a clear message to the instigators of the riots that police would not tolerate such actions and probably would have prevented the reoccurrence of the riots the following day and night. The incident tied up expensive and valuable police resources with a worse than negative result. To add insult to injury, being told that the area of the riots was an 'unofficial no-go zone' infuriated me and other officers.

A similar situation arose in the Block in August 1988. Twelve police were seriously injured whilst trying to arrest an offender. The article, titled 'Policing the Sydney Ghetto,' read "Rank and file police were bitterly critical of force policies which, they claimed, had been designed to avoid trouble by preventing the police from enforcing the law."

Incidents such as these are not uncommon in Redfern. Throughout the years police have learned to confront the situation whilst maintaining officer survival strategies. It appears that over time we have almost made a full circle. We went from frontline police back to frontline observers.

## Work Smart

We all had to put the Waterloo riots behind us and just get on with the job. I turned my attention back to Redfern Railway Station, where criminal activity continued. It seemed at times that I was just chasing my tail or playing a reactive part to crime in the area. I'd lock up an active offender with the misguided belief that it would reduce the amount of crime, but as soon as one was locked away, two or three more offenders would emerge from obscurity and hit the ground running.

There was one particular young bloke down at the Block who was becoming a real handful for police around Redfern and in neighbouring areas. He was very cocky and thought he was invincible, but after a while it was easy to predict his movements. He was running red-hot around the station, and because of his youth and speed it was difficult to catch him. So I literally had to out-think him.

The Redfern Railway Station had only recently improved their surveillance system on the platforms, concourse and entryway. It was manned almost permanently, so it wasn't long before I and other police developed a professional rapport with the operators. Working together seemed to reduce the amount of running around we did. They were like 'Big Brother' watching out for targets who were loitering, coming and going.

In late June, this young boy was causing havoc and at times flaunting his successes, to the embarrassment of Redfern Police. Our crime statistics for the affected areas were reflecting the impact he was having, so something needed to be done. I got together with other police on my team and we decided that it was time to mount a local operation, general duties style. July 1st was the night we would move on the boy.

The Probationer I was working with was as keen to nab this young offender as I was. And because of my decertification, she got to drive. I kept in constant contact with the CCTV operators and security at the railway and let them know who our target was. It had worked well in the preceding shifts, with this valuable assistance resulting in wanted offenders ending up behind bars. We hadn't seen the boy around the area that night but knew it wouldn't be long before he appeared. He couldn't resist. It was as much a challenge for him as it was for us. As the night wore on, I received a call from the railway staff saying that our boy was hanging around the concourse. Each time we thought about moving in to make an arrest, he disappeared into the safety of Eveleigh Street. It was getting late in the shift, and soon it would be daylight, so we all agreed that it was now or never. We only had one more opportunity. If he managed to escape this time, we wouldn't see him until the following day.

Not long after our last failed attempt, I received another call. I informed the other police in the area, who were to take up position within the Block in the event he headed for home. But this time my partner and I changed our plan. Instead of trying to covertly park beside the station and run into the railway, I got out near the top of the Block with another officer whilst my partner drove past the front of the station to give the impression that it was safe to come out—and it worked!

I walked onto the concourse area and the boy looked at me as he entered the turnstiles. We were directly next to one another, but it seemed to take a while before he recognised me in full uniform, or before I reacted. As he often did, he turned and ran towards the alternate exit to the train station. In hot pursuit, the other constable and I gave chase. By the time we got close, he had thrown himself onto the external fencing of the station, which was lined with metal spikes, and was doing his best to get away. I hadn't spent all night waiting for this opportunity to let him go, so I grabbed him by the scruff of the shirt and restrained him on the ground. With the assistance of the other constable we soon had him in a shiny pair of silver bracelets, courtesy of Redfern Police. To say he wasn't impressed was an understatement. He was taken to the cop shop and placed into the dock, where his bravado sunk as reality set in.

It was a great feeling. But my elation soon turned sour when the boy's mother arrived at the police station. She ripped into my partner and me for allegedly 'man-handling' her innocent little boy. Feeling safe in the belief that we had acted appropriately and professionally, and with CCTV footage to support our actions, we conveyed the young boy and his bellowing mother to the children's hospital for a pre-existing medical condition. We spent hours guarding the boy and being abused by his mother. But despite all the grief she caused and the noise she made, it was worth it to put her son before the Courts in the hope that he would learn his lesson.

Two years later, he still hadn't learnt, and our paths crossed when he was brought before the Court again, wearing another pair of fashionable bracelets courtesy of juvenile detention, where he was a long-term resident.

## CRAZY MAN

A few weeks later, I was on a night shift with the same female Probationary Constable from the burning Saab incident. About eight o'clock we received a call to an address in Waterloo in relation to a man wanting to confess to the murder of a child. As there were no Detectives rostered on and no other cars available, we went to the address. We were aware that the man was probably suffering from a psychiatric illness, but we had to investigate anyway. When we got to the premises, I noticed the front door was heavily secured. We tried knocking on the front door but weren't able to evoke a response, so we contacted the shift supervisor, Ray. He was very experienced and knowledgeable, and you could always rely on him to back you up.

Not long after contacting Ray, the front door of the unit opened and I saw a shabby, middle-aged man standing behind the security door. We tried to get him to open the front door, but he just stared at us.

After a short time he asked, "How do I know you're police? Show me your badge!"

Considering I was in police uniform, I didn't know how much more identification he needed, but I showed him my police badge, which seemed to help. Just as he opened the door, the Supervisor arrived.

We walked into the man's unit, where I saw a hunting knife sitting on the shelves beside the door. I began to feel uneasy and wondered whether the knife was intended for us. I alerted my offsider and the Supervisor and guided the man to a lounge on the opposite side of the room. As I spoke to the male, it became obvious that he was 'a few slices short of a full loaf.' He told us that he had stabbed a child in the elevator a few weeks ago and that he felt the need to "kill again." This information didn't do much to settle my nerves about the knife, but he remained calm and said he wanted to be arrested and placed in gaol. The Supervisor and I agreed to contact the crisis team to assist with assessing the man for a possible psychiatric illness.

We told him what we wanted to do, and initially he was agreeable, but as we led him to the front door, something seemed to snap. He pushed Ray and me out the door and tried to slam it shut on us. We kicked the door open instantly, only to find the man had armed himself with the hunting knife. Rather than contain and negotiate, instinctively we ran at him, and a struggle ensued.

We both grabbed his arm in an attempt to get him to drop the knife. He was waving his arms about and thrashing with his legs with the knife still in his clutches. Somehow we managed to disarm him, which just made him more aggressive. We wrestled with him in the lounge and onto the ground, where he was restrained and handcuffed with the assistance of other police.

He may have been scruffy, old and of slight build, but he put up a hell of a fight. We had to forcibly carry the man out of the unit, down three flights of stairs, along a narrow corridor, into an elevator and into the rear of the caged truck. My arms were aching and I felt pumped with adrenaline, which was surging through me. My mind kept flashing back to the hunting knife, and I was angry at him for what he had tried to do. It's like he had a death wish, and we were only seconds away from being his victims.

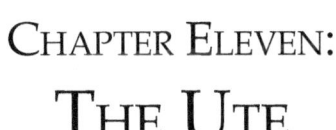

## CHAPTER ELEVEN:
# THE UTE

It was only a few weeks later when the intensity of the last five months (and probably five years) finally took its toll…

It was early Monday morning on July 30th, 2001 when I made my ritual two-hour commute south from the Central Coast to the streets of downtown Redfern. It was a journey that I had made, every shift, for the past four and a half years, and I was certainly content to do it. I mean, I loved my job, chasing crooks and fighting crime — plus I was only a few months away from being promoted to Senior Constable — but for some reason that morning I couldn't shake the feeling that it wasn't going to be a good day.

I arrived early, as always, to prepare for my shift. I changed into my uniform, wrapped my appointments belt around my waist and went to the gun safe to load my six-shot .38 calibre Smith & Wesson firearm, as I had done routinely before. I walked into the station area to sign out a portable radio, and after checking the daily roster I greeted the night shift supervisor, who looked tired from a busy night and was obviously looking forward to going home. I had been rostered to work with a Probationary Constable around Redfern Railway Station, and in particular the Block, using call-sign Redfern 45 (RF45). Although I hadn't worked with him before, I knew that he was keen and looking forward to getting out on the road.

About 8.30 a.m., at the start of peak-hour traffic in arguably the busiest city in the country, what I had earlier dreaded became my reality.

RF45: Redfern 45 urgent, I'm in the back of a stolen vehicle, Charlie Alpha Mike 0-6-2, on Cleveland Street.

Police Radio: Yeah, Redfern 45 did you say that you were in this vehicle?

RF45: I'm in the tray at the back radio; can I get some assistance quickly? North on Cleveland Street.

BEEP (audible tone)

Police Radio: Standing by further Redfern cars, any car in the vicinity, to make their way to Cleveland Street, northbound. Redfern 45 is in the rear of a confirmed outstanding vehicle, Charlie Alpha Mike 0-6-2, urgent assistance required, further Redfern cars, thanks.

Police Radio: Redfern 45, your current location and a suburb, thanks.

(silence)

Police Radio: Redfern 45, your current location thanks...

We had made regular patrols of the Block and Redfern Railway Station for about an hour when I noticed a white 4WD Ute parked in the vicinity of Eveleigh Street. Such a sight wouldn't have aroused my suspicion in some other areas of the Command, but since it was situated in a location renowned for its high levels of crime and drug activity, I suspected that the Ute was stolen. Because I hadn't seen the Ute parked there earlier in the shift or previously in the Block, I decided to confirm whether it was stolen with Police Radio, and, of course, it was.

After cruising around the Block for a short time, hoping to catch someone inside the vehicle, I noticed the same utility driving north towards us, with two males on board. I yelled at my partner to stop the truck and block the vehicle against the kerb. As the utility turned towards us I jumped out planning on making an easy arrest. I came around to the front of the Ute as it squeezed past us and drove off down the street. The driver and his male passenger glared from within.

I shouted, "Stop, stay where you are" standing only a few feet away from the driver's open window. The driver ignored me and accelerated away. The next thing I knew I was in the tray of the Ute looking back at my partner, who was looking bewildered, as we rumbled down the street. In a reflex action I instinctively grabbed the back of the Ute and flung my bulky frame into the tray. I was in, and there was no turning back.

## Chapter Eleven: The Ute

I was glad I had a portable radio and quickly scanned my surroundings to assess what options I had. The tray was about two metres wide and three metres long and had three large metal toolboxes on each side and one against the window. There was a small corridor for me to crouch in so I leant forward and called on the portable:

"Redfern 45, urgent. I am in the back of a stolen vehicle, Charlie Alpha Mike 0-6-2, on Cleveland Street."

The radio operator's tone and intensity reflected the situation. She immediately called for urgent assistance after realising that I was in fact "in the back tray of the stolen vehicle!"

> Police Radio: Standing by further Redfern cars, any car in the vicinity, to make their way to Cleveland Street, north bound, Redfern 45 is in the rear of a confirmed outstanding vehicle, Charlie Alpha Mike 0-6-2, urgent assistance required, further Redfern cars thanks.

The driver of the vehicle looked over his shoulder through the back window and seemed surprised to see me in the rear tray of the Ute. He slammed his foot on the brake and the Ute jolted forwards, throwing me onto my chest. I managed to scramble to my knees as the driver accelerated quickly for a short distance and again slammed on the brakes, forcing me against one of the toolboxes. He looked through the back window to see if I was still there, and I could see both fear and anger in his eyes. Adrenaline was pumping through my veins, but I was terrified. I was a hostage trapped in the tray of that Ute.

He accelerated across the intersection, fishtailing over the road whilst repeatedly looking over his shoulder as I banged on the window and yelled, "Stop the vehicle. Pull over."

The driver kept swerving violently across the road, making sure he covered the entire width for maximum effect. He accelerated to about 80km/hr, braking harshly as he turned down a one-way street the wrong way and accelerated again quickly. As the back of the Ute swung out, I was thrown against the toolbox to my left again, which took the wind out of me. I looked over my shoulder and couldn't see my partner, or any police, or for that matter any real chance of resolving this soon or safely. I was alone! Even the attempts by Police Radio to find out where I was were left echoing over my portable:

> Police Radio: Redfern 45, your current location and a suburb, thanks.

(silence)

Police Radio: Redfern 45, your current location, thanks...

I saw a number of oncoming cars skidding and swerving on the road as peak hour choked the streets and this guy was driving like a maniac. Luckily I was crouching down and could see through the front window as he mounted the footpath and sideswiped a parked car, giving me time to brace for the impending impact. Wham! We jolted off the kerb in a thunderous roar. He seemed to be a man on a mission, deliberately trying to run into anything he could, just like dodgem cars.

The driver looked over his shoulder yet again and I demanded, "Stop the vehicle, now!"

But his face was devoid of concern, cocooned in the safety of the cab and what felt like complete control. I sat down to give myself a lower centre of gravity with so many thoughts running through my mind: *What should I do? What have I done? How do I get out of this alive?* All I knew was that I needed to get some assistance really quickly. I held on tight, kept myself low and muttered my locations into the radio handset:

RF45: Redfern 45, we're heading towards Abercrombie Street towards Broadway.

The vehicle's speed hit triple figures without any sign of slowing. He fishtailed around the corner at the next intersection and swerved onto the wrong side of the road. I could see the malice in the driver's eyes as he glanced back at me and the car bounced off the gutter and veered towards a sedan that was innocently heading straight towards us. The look on that old man's face imitated my own fears. He swerved to avoid us as the Ute barrelled along and rammed into the side of his car, forcing its way past. The impact recoiled the Ute, sending us crashing into a number of parked cars on the opposite side of the road. I fell towards the back, landing heavily with my whole body being thrashed about.

The driver clearly had no concern for the safety of others as he continued his path of destruction. At one point he rammed into the side of a transport van, bringing us to a shuddering stop. I fell towards the front of the tray as I lost my balance and a bit of my dignity as well. I had serious fears that if this nightmare didn't end soon, he was going to kill me or someone else. I had to do something, so I drew my firearm and banged on the window with my hand whilst holding the gun.

I shouted "Stop the vehicle or I will shoot" as I pointed the barrel towards the driver's head.

The driver looked at me with contempt and reversed the vehicle suddenly. The passenger ducked, waiting for me to fire, and I almost did, but there had to be another way.

The driver sped back towards Redfern, almost mowing down people on the footpath, whilst I was crouched down and praying for divine intervention. Then, I saw a length of rope tied to the railing underneath the back window behind the passenger seat. So, with my gun in my right hand, I wrapped the rope around my left hand along with the portable and held on for my life.

As the driver fishtailed along the road I almost pleaded, "Stop the vehicle or I will shoot."

He looked at me again and continued swerving, without watching where he was going. He sideswiped a number of parked cars and then headed towards the Sydney CBD, which at that time of morning was too dangerous to even contemplate.

As the maniac accelerated through the peak-hour traffic, cars were forced to brake and swerve whilst pedestrians ran and jumped out of the way to avoid being hit.

I thumped on the window again and demanded, "Stop the fucking vehicle. Pull over, now," as if my use of coarse language and a more authoritative tone would change his attitude.

Instead, the vehicle drifted wildly across the road, squeezing past a truck, and sped through a major intersection against a red light. It was only through good luck and fortuitous fazing that there was no one travelling through the intersection at that time, otherwise things could have been a lot worse. As he hurtled around the corner he looked into his mirror again momentarily before thrashing the Ute side to side, knocking me to the tray floor.

I bounced off the toolbox and again shouted at the driver, "Stop the vehicle now."

This had been going on for way too long. The driver was too dangerous to be on the streets in peak-hour traffic, and there were too many innocent people making their way to work that could be caught up in this incident. I didn't know what to do, but I had to survive and somehow end this safely. The driver looked over his shoulder at me again and swerved over the road driving way too fast, as if encouraged by the fear that was etched onto my face.

He accelerated towards the Ultimo area, which was crowded with people and traffic. He glared at me in the mirror yet again, as if to signal his intentions. As he approached the congested Harris Street intersection, I could see so many people just going about their business, walking to work, talking to friends and colleagues, living their lives oblivious to the imminent danger.

I had to make a *split second* decision, and quickly. I thought about shooting the driver, but what would I aim for—his leg or his chest? If I shoot the dashboard, will it disable the vehicle? Could the bullet ricochet and injure an innocent bystander? Would either of these situations cause him to lose total control and kill innocent members of the public? (Although he was driving like a lunatic, at least he had control of the vehicle.) If I take the risk and choose not to shoot, that means I might be the only one killed, or I might even survive. It was a chance I had to take and ultimately live with. I just prayed that 'someone' was watching over all of us.

My fears were not allayed as he floored it through the red light and sped towards the busy pedestrian crossing. I was sure people would be killed and that I should have done something more. But, as if by divine intervention, an opening appeared in the middle of the crossing as everyone ran and jumped for cover. We hurtled along without slowing, drifting across the four lanes and towards oncoming traffic. I knew my luck was running out.

But the ride, and certainly the danger, wasn't over yet. He swung the vehicle across three lanes and towards a blind corner on the wrong side of the road, causing the tray to tilt perilously to the left. He was flying and I was struggling to hold on. It was at that precise moment that I came to the realisation that I probably wouldn't survive. Everything around me seemed to move in slow motion and began to blur, and there was a deafening silence in the air. The driver accelerated around the right-hand bend as I waited for the impact. I couldn't see what was coming, which meant he couldn't either. It was like playing Russian roulette: with every corner I didn't know what the outcome was going to be. Would we crash? Would we tip over?

The tray began to lean more towards the road and I honestly believed that momentum would make us crash for sure. I was too scared to talk. Thoughts raced through my mind about my daughters, my wife and how I had lived. The buildings and people around me lost all sense of proportion and just faded into the background. I just wanted this to end. I thought to myself that if this lunatic pulled over right now I would just walk away. I just wanted to go home and kiss my wife and kids. I didn't want to die.

We were going so fast, too fast. I looked over the edge of the tray and imagined what would happen if the Ute flipped or I fell out. My mind was filling with negative thoughts and I could only see two possible outcomes: I would kill him or he would kill me. Then thud went the tray as we regained balance and took off up the road. The driver snuck a peek at me in the mirror; with hatred in his eyes, furious that I was still onboard.

As the driver swerved in and out of traffic heading to the City, I heard that backup was heading my way. I saw a police truck racing towards us with its lights and sirens blaring. I felt a sense of relief that this would soon end. I held tightly onto the rope with my left hand and waved my firearm in the air to get the attention of the police, who, to my disappointment, drove straight past. That was it. I'd definitely had enough. I decided that it was either him or me, and it sure as hell wasn't going to be me.

The driver increased his speed as I hammered on the window, yelling "Stop the vehicle or I will shoot" and pointing my gun at him again.

He looked over his shoulder and swerved around another corner doing about 90km/hr and narrowly missing a pedestrian. If we had been only a *split second* earlier, we would have run him down and killed him for sure. It was all sheer luck. We were like a time bomb on wheels.

I wasn't going to let him murder me and deprive my family of a father and husband. So as the Ute hurtled towards a park, I decided I had to do something drastic. As the driver accelerated along the tramlines, he mounted a concrete median strip, the impact lifting me off the tray and flinging me about wildly. As the Ute hurdled over the footpath and accelerated into the park opposite Central Railway Station, it flattened a 'No Stopping' sign and slid across the wet grass.

This was my chance to end the ordeal, one way or another.

I yelled, "Stop the vehicle or I will fucking shoot you."

He looked over at me and kept driving, so I smashed the rear window with the hand that was holding my gun. An explosion of glass showered over the driver and the tray.

I pointed my gun at the driver's head and bellowed, "Pull over now or I will shoot you."

He looked over his shoulder and in an aggressively sarcastic tone said, "Alright."

But he continued to accelerate, causing the Ute to spin in circles and almost tip over, again.

I held my firearm against his head and demanded, "Stop the vehicle now. Turn off the engine."

I had to make a decision, and fast—do I shoot or not? But before I could decide, the passenger jumped out and ran across the park so fast I don't think his feet ever touched the ground. But the driver continued with his reluctance to surrender.

I thought about letting go of the rope in case the driver decided to continue his escape on foot, like his unwitting companion, when suddenly his door opened and with the Ute still fishtailing he stumbled across the grass. I jumped from the tray and gave chase towards the railway lines.

I called on my portable "Redfern 45 foot pursuit" as the fleeing felon scampered over a chest-high steel wire fence with me not too far behind, still trying to holster my firearm.

But with my gun still in my hand and my feet wet from the dewy grass, my attempt to scale the barrier and continue the pursuit failed as I lost my footing. I managed to quickly recover only to see the driver climb onto a tall concrete wall and jump down onto the street below. I considered duplicating his feat until I saw it was a drop of about ten metres and felt that my body had already been through enough. I don't know how, but he bounced back up and was off running again.

I honestly thought that despite everything I did and had gone through he was going to get away, until I saw some Detectives from Redfern chasing him into an adjacent office building. I couldn't keep going. I was completely knackered and overwhelmed with emotion. I stopped and bent down to catch my breath, all the while listening to the ensuing foot pursuit, hoping for a positive outcome. I stumbled across the road utterly exhausted, my body aching and my hands bleeding.

Then I heard Police Radio confirm that "the offender was in custody."

Great news! I told the Police Radio where I had seen the passenger run to and gave his description as best I could. It wasn't long before he was in custody as well. It was such a relief!

It was the first time I had had a chance to rest since the incident had begun about ten minutes earlier. I started to feel faint and had to sit down. There was a café nearby with some outdoor seating, so I fell into one of the chairs, reliving my ordeal over and over in my head. A couple of members of the public came up to me to see if I was okay, which was very reassuring. A lady got me some water from the café whilst a gentleman administered first aid to my cuts. By this time I really didn't feel well. The reality was overwhelming. A Detective came up to me and looked concerned. He called the ambulance to take me to hospital. My legs, ribs and lower back were aching. My hands and wrist were bleeding and swollen and my uniform was dirty from being thrown around the tray of the Ute. I thought about what I had just put myself through and wondered how I had even survived. It was all too much for me. I decided then and there that this would be my last day in 'the job.' I wanted out. I couldn't do it anymore.

It was hard to comprehend what I was thinking and feeling at that moment. The whole incident had been so overwhelming, and there was nothing I wanted more than to walk away from the career I had dreamed of having my entire life.

The ambulance arrived and treated me at the scene as members of the public and film crews turned up to have a look. I was told that I needed to go to hospital, so I left my appointments with the Detective and limped into the awaiting ambulance. The paramedics gave me some gas to help ease the pain of my injuries, but nothing could stop the deep pangs of gloom that were shooting through me. I wanted to see my wife, but she was so far away.

When I arrived at the hospital, I felt a sense of relief because I knew I couldn't come to any more harm. I stripped to my underwear and waited to be seen. The Detective and the Inspector came to the hospital to get a statement from me. It was so hard to talk about. I wanted to start the whole day again. I kept thinking, *Why did I do it? Why didn't I listen to my gut instinct that this was going to be a bad day?* But I couldn't work it out.

It was only months later, after speaking to counsellors and reflecting on what had happened, that I found an answer. It was frustration stemming from years of little support and recognition. I felt I had been punished for performing my duties in good faith and to the best of my abilities. I'd had enough. I was sick of the bureaucracy getting in the way and resolved to just do my job and get that criminal, whatever it took. As I lay in the hospital bed watching other sick people being brought in, I realised how lucky I was to be among them. Being thrown around the back of the Ute, I never thought I would make it out alive. I thought I would be scraped off the road like a bit of sticky gum. When I saw police in the hospital who I knew, I broke down in tears. It was all too much. The doctors sent me for x-rays and allowed me to go home once I was given the all clear.

My wife rang me at the hospital and told me she was on her way down to Redfern with my twin brother, Michael, and his then girlfriend (now wife, Skye) to get me. It was so good to hear her voice. I just wanted to go home. No one had contacted her about the incident and she only found out when she rang my mobile after I had been taken to hospital. One of the Detectives on the scene answered my phone, which had fallen into the tray of the Ute during the incident, and told my wife what had happened. She was panicked and not very impressed about finding out this way, especially after I had specifically instructed the Inspector to let her know what had happened.

I told her I wanted to quit, but in her amazing, reassuring way she managed to talk me out of it, for the moment. I was in so much pain. I don't know whether I was hurting more emotionally or physically. Both my shins and knees were swollen, bruised and bleeding. My left wrist was badly bruised, sprained and swollen from holding onto the rope (which I sincerely believe was the only reason I didn't fall out). I had lacerations on my right hand and fingers from punching through the window, and bruising and torn cartilage on the left side of my ribs. But apart from that I escaped physically okay, all things considered.

When I was discharged I was taken back to the police station in the back of the Supervisor's van, where I had to stand up, squeezed in between the riot shields and helmets. When I got back to the station, my colleagues applauded me like I was some sort of hero. They told me that I had been watching too many Lethal Weapon movies. It was kind of funny, but I was dirty and tired and didn't want to be there.

One of my colleagues said to me, "That was one of the bravest and one of the stupidest things that I have ever seen," and looking back I guess he was right.

I started to type my statement with my battered hands while it was fresh in my mind, but I was in too much pain—physically and emotionally. My wife and brother arrived at the station not long after. She gave me the biggest hug. It felt so good. It was precisely what I needed. Apparently the inspector from the scene decided to criticise Michael about the incident, his poor decision-making skills and his dangerous work practices, thinking he was me, not knowing he was my twin brother. Not a smart move, sir.

Then the boss walked in and started giving me a hard time.

He said to my wife, "Take him home, and when you're finished with him send him to me and give me a go."

I couldn't believe it. That's all I needed to hear after what I had just been through. Not a "job well done" or even a thank you. It certainly compounded my feelings about quitting the job and confirmed that I was nothing more than a number. If that was the sort of support I was going to get from my boss, then who needed it? I had a wife and a family who appreciated me and who I was.

Before too long, my wife packed me up and took me home. We talked a little on the way, but I just wanted to sleep, not wanting to even think about anything. She kept crying and touching me like she had almost lost me, and I guess at that moment I wasn't the only one struggling. She couldn't do this anymore, and deep down I knew I felt the same way.

The trip home was a blur, with so many images flashing through my mind, bits and pieces of everything waiting for me to unscramble them. I kept saying to myself that I wouldn't go back, couldn't go back, like I was trying to reconcile how I was feeling. When we arrived home was when I really started to fall to pieces. I got so distraught that my wife arranged for my local doctor to do a home visit because I was too afraid to leave the house.

I knew I had to do something. There were too many things to deal with. I had ignored the impacts of all the incidents of the past for far too long. It was time to make a stand, take control and not let them rule my life. It was clear that the job had changed me even though I never thought it would. In some ways the changes were good, but I recognised that I wasn't the same happy, carefree person I used to be.

Too many feelings had been bottled up, and it was time to pop the cork.

It wasn't as hard as I thought it would be to see my doctor. She had been the family physician for the past twenty years and someone I could trust. I sat down, cried like a whipped pup and admitted that I needed professional help. She was very understanding and concerned. She referred me to see a psychologist. What a revelation she turned out to be. It was so incredibly helpful and empowering to be able to speak about my feeling uncensored and without fear of reprisals from my colleagues or the management of the New South Wales Police Service.

It didn't take her too long to diagnose me with Post Traumatic Stress Disorder (PTSD). She felt that my symptoms were so severe that I needed to seek extra help from a psychiatrist (also known as a 'shrink') and consider taking anti-depressants, which I was vehemently opposed to.

It was hard at first because I had this preconceived idea about what a psychiatrist was. Hey, I knew I wasn't crazy, even though my wife and family had been trying to convince me I was for years. As far as I was concerned, I was just emotionally injured after something terribly frightening had happened at work. So I kept an open mind and focused on getting better mentally as I recovered from my physical injuries.

I remember the first time I went to see my shrink. It was an hour's drive to his office, so there was a lot of time to reflect on what I had been through and possibly change my mind about seeing him. But I knew that if I didn't go through with it then I would probably end up killing myself or losing my mind. I sat in the waiting room for my turn and felt so ashamed that I had ended up here, feeling helpless and totally overwhelmed with life. It did help being able to talk to someone independent about all of the incidents that had led to my breakdown, even though I felt so vulnerable and had tears streaming down my face. I finally found the courage to confront my feelings and start taking control of my life and what these incidents and memories meant to me.

The sessions went so well and I felt so encouraged that I began seeing both the psychologist and the psychiatrist once a week each. Slowly, a sense of ease and security returned. I continued to block out the majority of the Ute incident from the counsellors and from myself, as I was still dealing with it in my own way. Just like fitting pieces to a jigsaw puzzle.

I think the hardest thing for me to accept about the ordeal (before, during and after), apart from being ignored by my workmates (except when they wanted something), was the realisation that the driver tried to kill me. I wrote this in my statement:

"I believe that the intention of the defendant (driver) was to throw me from the tray of the stolen vehicle to avoid arrest, and in doing so cause serious or fatal injury to me. The speed and manner at which the defendant was driving caused me immediate and extreme fear for my safety.

The defendant was aware that I was a police officer and that I posed an immediate threat to his liberty. The defendant was called upon numerous times to stop the vehicle but continued to drive in a manner that was likely to cause serious or fatal injury to myself. Any reasonable person would foresee that the manner of driving of the defendant might have caused me to be thrown from the vehicle. Such an action would definitely have caused severe or fatal injury.

I also believe that if I were killed during this incident then the defendant would have been charged with murder. The intention of the defendant to avoid arrest is further highlighted by the defendant running from the vehicle in Belmore Park prior to his arrest.

I believe that if the toolboxes and length of rope were not in the tray of the vehicle at the time I would have definitely been thrown from the tray and killed. For whatever reason, I chose to jump into the tray of the vehicle I was in full uniform and lawfully exercising my duties at the time. The defendant showed very little regard for safety, that of other road users, members of the public and to the office of the New South Wales Police Service."

This was a hard thing for me to come to terms with. Being a cop is a tough and dangerous job. That is both its lure and its curse. But to come so close to being killed and walk away somewhat intact is such a humbling and frightening reality. I spoke to a Senior Constable from Redfern some months after the incident. I broke down uncontrollably when I expressed my feelings to her that the driver had attempted to kill me. She offered to speak to the Director of Public Prosecutions (DPP) about having the driver charged with attempted murder, I think more to console me than to actually achieve this aim.

It made me feel so much better to be able to tell a colleague how I was feeling without worrying about whether I would be criticised or labelled for not coping. It made a world of difference. Just the thought of the driver being charged with attempted murder made my life feel worthwhile. It made me feel like the risk I took that day in the execution of my duties actually meant something and was appreciated, that I was more than just a number. (Not surprisingly, not only did they not lay further charges, but they even withdrew the charges that related to me. Unbelievable!) Despite my best efforts to stay positive, I still wasn't coping, so on one of the many nights when I couldn't sleep I put my feelings down on paper.

<u>The Last Chance</u>

*I made a silly choice*
*That almost cost my life*
*I chose to give it all I had*
*And forgot about my wife*

*I forgot about my world*
*My family I have at home*
*About how much they all mean to me*
*And how much I love them so*

*But I did what I thought was right*
*I was just doing me bloomin' job*
*A job that gives you no respect*
*And brings you closer to God!*

*I had to make a choice*
*Of what I was to do!*
*They were crooks and doing wrong*
*And I was dressed in blue*

*I still don't know just why*
*I risked my life right then*
*Maybe I was frustrated*
*With the getting no respect*

*But I couldn't change what happened*
*I was stranded in the back*
*Wishing I were somewhere else*
*Alone and way outback*

*But what he tried to do*
*Was take my life from me*
*He tried to murder my whole world*
*And retain his liberty*

*I always thought my job*
*Was worth the ultimate price*
*But giving it all I had*
*Meant nothing to my wife*

*Cos she just wanted me safe*
*At home with the kids as well*
*I never realised what she meant*
*Until I went through hell*

*Cos when I was in the back*
*And rolling round the tray*
*I thought about nothing else*
*But would I die that day*

*And now I'm safe at home*
*My injuries all on the mend*
*What aches is not on the outside*
*But what's inside my head*

*The fact that I escaped*
*From the jaws of death again*
*Made me feel so weak inside*
*And chuck the job all in*

*It still hurts to close my eyes*
*And think about the pain*
*Of what it's like to feel okay*
*To look death right in the face*

*My friends I had at work*
*Have really let me down*
*They haven't even called to say*
*"It's quiet without you around."*

*They've forgotten about my time*
*And effort that I have spent*
*Facing crime one on one*
*And that I was there for them*

*It makes me stop and think*
*Why should I ever go back?*
*I cannot face it on the streets*
*I'd rather get the sack.*

*But I will leave when I know*
*That I am safe again*
*Where I can walk down the street*
*And see a future ahead*

*But things will never be*
*The same as they were before*
*I bear the scars of time gone by*
*And the lessons I've been taught*

*But I cannot change the past*
*I have to live with the choice I made*
*And only hope as time goes on*
*The pain will surely fade*

After I had written the poem, I couldn't quite come to putting my name or signature on it. I guess I still wasn't really ready to accept that these feelings were mine. But despite all the stigma attached to the policing image of being tough and invincible, this simple act of putting my feelings into words, onto paper, was a massive help and a leap forward for me. But I think being away from work was the toughest part.

## THE AFTERMATH

Being off work on workers compensation (or HOD: Hurt On Duty) following the incident really took its toll on me. Apart from the stigma attached to being on workers comp and being a police officer who wasn't coping, there wasn't much I was able to do besides think and reflect on what happened. For months after the incident I felt like I was living in a glass house, trapped within a constant nightmare that everyone was allowed to see and pass judgment on. I guess it is understandable to some degree because my physical injuries were healing, so there was nothing visible that people could associate with me being off work. But I was really struggling, and the decision of whether to return to work or not plagued me endlessly and was a choice I didn't want to make.

I couldn't handle the thought of going to Sydney, not even off-duty, and especially not back to work in Redfern. I had already been through too much, and everything south of the Harbour Bridge was like a trigger for all my bad memories. It was so disappointing after all the effort I had put into becoming a tough, smart and hard-working cop. I really loved the people, the experience, the challenge. I felt so disappointed while on leave because the only time I heard from my workmates, my extended family, was when they were chasing up paperwork. The lack of support from my bosses, my colleagues and the Police Service as a whole was devastating and unforgivable, and it only encouraged me to make the decision to leave. They truly let me, and my family, down.

Meanwhile, my team of 'professionals' delved into my innermost thoughts and feelings, teaching me a lot about myself and about where I wanted my life to head. As confronting as it was, I realised that my first thoughts had to be with my family. My wife and beautiful daughters were my inspiration and purpose. Without their love and support, I certainly wouldn't have had the strength or motivation to ask for help, let alone to continue to seek it. Although my relationship with my wife had been pushed to the brink of separation on several occasions since I had been off work, somehow, thankfully, we managed to find strength and the resolve to survive as a couple.

As for my future in the police, I just didn't know. Although I wanted to try to continue my policing journey, I wasn't 100 percent sure it was the right decision. I knew I had survived some close calls but didn't know when my luck would run out, and to be honest, I wasn't sure how much I had changed following the incident with the Ute. I didn't know if I had the same belief in myself or the same passion for the uniform. It may sound pretentious, but to me it was a symbol of honour, authority and respect. The inscription on our badges and sleeves read 'Culpam Poena Premit Comes,' which loosely translates to 'Justice Swiftly Follows Crime,' which is how I preferred to execute my duties. It had been my shield behind which I felt confident, safe and protected from harm.

When I had performed my duties or become involved in a serious, life-threatening incident, I had taken security in my uniform's strength and become immersed in its passion and protection. Coupled with my experience and devotion as a police officer, my uniform had been there to look out for me and keep me safe. It had been my saviour, my blue armour. Moreover, it made me feel part of a family, a sea of blue, where we were united with the common goal of making a difference and upholding the law. It was amazing to see that no matter where in NSW you worked or which duties you performed, when you saw that blue uniform, it was an invitation to say hello; a call for assistance was a 'call to arms.'

But after the Ute incident, I became afraid to wear it. I no longer respected what it stood for and couldn't stand the thought of putting it back on. There was just too much history, and I knew all the bad memories would just come flooding back. This was a hurdle I struggled with that could have prevented me from returning to the frontline, but I had to decide what was in my best interest. I could never have reconciled myself with the idea that after only five years of service, my childhood dream of forging a lengthy career as a police officer could possibly end so prematurely.

## Chapter Twelve:
# Return To Work

At the time, I didn't know that the incident involving the Ute would play such a major role in my future as a frontline cop. It was the latest notch in a series of never-ending near misses and was almost my demise. But I shouldn't sound so surprised; things at work had been brewing for a while. I just never thought it would happen to me or that I would be such a victim. To come so close to experiencing death and yet to still be alive to talk about it changed my world and opened my eyes about everything I believed in.

It was very difficult for me to come to terms with what happened to me that day. Apart from dealing with the ensuing perpetual flashbacks and thumping nightmares, I had to reconsider the direction my life was headed in and what was most important to me: my job or my family. I know it seems like an obvious choice, but I was so immersed in my job that it often had priority. Just having to think of these things was terrifying. I had always wanted to be a policeman.

But over the years I'd been taking too many risks at work and I just could not afford to do that anymore. I had too much to lose: a beautiful wife and two gorgeous girls. It's just a shame that it took such an episode for me to wake up to reality. My wife threatened to divorce me if anything like that ever happened again, and I knew she was serious. Understandably, she was scared of getting a phone call that 'this time' her husband wasn't so lucky. For some reason, she loved me and wanted our little girls to grow up to know and spend time with their daddy.

After five months, I still wasn't sure if or when I would ever go back to work. Part of me didn't want my future in the Police Service to end like this. I wanted to go on until I decided it was time for me to leave.

There was more I wanted to experience: Dog Squad, Prosecutors, and maybe one day Crime Agencies. I didn't want to end up dead on the streets with my family left to pick up the pieces, but I also didn't want to be a bumbling mess too afraid to live my own life.

I spoke to my psychiatrist in the weeks after Christmas, and he was keen to get me back to work. So was Rachael. They were encouraging but not forceful. I started writing this book during my time off after the incident with the Ute. It allowed me to place my feelings, fears and emotions on paper for me to see and analyse. My psychiatrist wanted me to finish writing my experiences before returning to work. So I did. I finished the original version of this book on December 16th, 2001.

I was due to go back to work on January 14th, 2002. My counsellors had been working with the City East rehabilitation office to get me back on the job. I was offered a spot in Lake Macquarie, which was ideal because it was close to home. It was also where I grew up, so it held a sense of familiarity for me. I knew a few police who worked there from the past, but as the time drew nearer I just couldn't do it. I put it off for another week and decided to return to full-time work more gradually than had been planned. I knew that the first step was always going to be the hardest.

My psychiatrist wanted me to take some medication because I was depressed, but I wouldn't do it. Even though there were times when I didn't think I could continue my service, it was a battle I had to win by myself. I hadn't taken any drugs since I had gone on leave, and I knew I could come through this without the assistance of any medication—just love, trust and time.

I was only due to begin working a few hours a week, but the prospect still overwhelmed me. I was having nightmares and panic attacks up to the day of my return. It was agreed to amend my return to work plan to prevent me from having any contact with the public. This didn't allow much scope with my duties, but that was fine with me.

My first day was Monday, January 21st, 2002. I was incredibly nervous but drew on my courage to get in the car and at least drive to Boolaroo, where I would meet with the Lake Macquarie Commander and the City East Rehab Officer. I left early so I would have time to turn back if I couldn't handle it. But it went alright. The boss was very supportive and understanding. One of the downsides of working in one area for so long was that I had unwittingly created stereotypes of 'police.' I hadn't had any support in Redfern towards the end of my time there and so wasn't expecting any in my new placement.

Just before I entered the station, my wife rang me and said, "I am so proud of you. You have made a very big step and I love you so much. Just think of this as a new beginning, and if you need me, I am here for you."

That was all I needed to hear. I wiped away my tears, walked into the office and spoke with the Commander. This was the first time I had been in a police station since the incident with the Ute, and it was like a whole new world. I was scared yet confident about making a go of it.

After filling in some paperwork, the City East Rehab Officer took me to Toronto, where I would be working. I felt like it was my first day on the job, nervous and scared but otherwise alright. I was also a bit worried about what everyone else would think of me, that I was like a leper with a contagious psychiatric condition. The Station Sergeant was told that I was suffering from PTSD and that I wasn't allowed to have contact with the public. It felt awkward. The Sergeant took me around the station and introduced me to the other police. It was a small station with more senior officers than in the City.

As he introduced me he said, "This is Jeff, he's on rehab and not allowed any contact with the public."

I'm not sure if he was aware of what he was doing, but I felt about an inch tall and as if I had some disease. I thought everyone was looking at me strangely, but I eventually relaxed and it seemed okay. I had a nice, quiet little office in the back of the station, where I did some practice tests for my next increment to Senior Constable, which I had been due to complete in August 2001 but for obvious reasons had missed. I passed my exam and started working on summons and warrants with an experienced Senior Constable who I had worked with in Charlestown about six years earlier. He was good value. I spent the next few weeks helping him out and trying to complete some assignments that were due. Like all police at that time, I had to complete a degree before I could be promoted to Senior Constable.

I decided to ring the DPP officer who was in charge of the matters involving the Ute and spoke to him in depth about my feelings and concerns. I couldn't understand why the driver hadn't been charged with attempted murder. I knew that that was what he had been trying to do. The officer politely informed me that even though it was my belief, the likelihood that twelve members of a jury would believe beyond a reasonable doubt that it was the driver's intention to kill me was very minimal.

In the end, the driver pleaded guilty to vehicle theft and other driving offences and was sentenced to nine months of gaol. But he got nothing for what he did to me. He wasn't even charged with the assault of a police officer. I felt robbed and insignificant. But the case had been finalised and there wasn't anything anyone could do.

As for my police driving status, the Safe Driving Panel still hadn't made up their minds more than eight months after I had been decertified. I managed to get a message from them that I had been referred for counselling, not only because of the incident with the Saab that led to the decertification, but also because of my incident with the Ute. I wasn't very impressed. I hadn't been driving a police vehicle or any vehicle in the Ute incident, so I could not see how it related to the Safe Driver Policy. But the psychology department told me that they were looking at the picture as a whole.

Overall, my reintroduction to the Police Service went a lot smoother than I first thought it would. The bosses, my colleagues and their support were reassuring. In the Central Coast and Lake Macquarie areas, there was time to take a breath if something went wrong. In the City it was a different culture. You just got on with it and didn't say a word. I began to appreciate the differences between policing in the hustle and bustle of the City and policing in the country.

Around the time I went back to work, I received a letter from my friend and crazy-man-wrestling buddy Ray that helped me enormously.

"Hey Jude,

*It is good to hear you are on the mend a little, small steps though eh. Just a little advice from the heart. This is a job and no matter how much you do or how good you do it people will always be critical, human nature you might say. You are blessed with two beautiful children and a loving and supportive wife. You in that regard are lucky. They are your life and your future, everything you do has a bearing on them also. Don't be in a hurry and do it right. Now you are slowly returning to work, who cares what people say or think. They will say what they want anyway. Worry about yourself and what you want to achieve for Jeffrey Colin Wayne Garland. People, especially in this job are judgmental and cold sometimes. Live the life how you want to and let the rest fall into place.*

*Now is the time to be positive. You have taken a massive step returning to work and you should be proud of yourself and don't be afraid to pat yourself on the back for that. We all choose our path whether directly or indirectly by our actions and thought. Be positive mate and good luck.*

*Your mate*

*Ray."*

When I first read Ray's words, they stopped me in my tracks and made me think about everything. What he said made sense. I should be proud of what I had achieved. Less than six months earlier I couldn't bear the thought of being a police officer, couldn't leave the house or socialise with friends and family and hated the person I had become. Now look at me! I had to do what was right for me and always keep in the back of my mind the fact that I had a family that loved me and needed me. Thanks Ray.

## THE FATAL

I'd been back at work for about three weeks and was feeling fairly comfortable with my return. I was settling in alright but was still unsure about my future in the job. Then one morning as I was travelling to work, fate stepped in and made the decision for me.

On this particular morning, it was wet. It had been raining for days, and I was late for a training day. It wasn't much, but I had been stuck in a back office for weeks and was looking forward to my first opportunity to mingle and associate with the other police within the Command.

As I rounded the bend on the main road towards Toronto, I was confronted with a scene that challenged my sense of belief and my professionalism. The line of traffic heading in the opposite direction had come to a complete stop over the crest of the hill, and a man was standing in the middle of the road, waving his arms.

I saw that a van had run up the back of a Ute, or at least that was what it seemed like. I didn't know what to do. I wasn't ready to deal with a situation like this. I was still trying to make myself better. As I drew nearer, I seemed to click into 'police mode' and began thinking like a policeman again. It was a strange yet reassuring feeling. I switched off my fear and decided I had to act. I stopped my car on the side of the road and went straight over to help. It was peak-hour traffic and raining heavily. I went straight to the driver of the van and could tell just by looking at him that he was dead. I grabbed a towel from a man standing beside me and placed it over the front of the van to prevent other motorists from seeing.

I went to the Ute and saw that the driver was keeled over on the front seat. Both his doors were jammed shut from the accident, but I was able to speak with him and make sure that he was alright. Some people came up to me to help, so I arranged for them to direct traffic at the top and bottom of the hill to prevent any further incidents. I jumped into the back of the van and checked the pulse of the driver, just to be certain. I was unable to find any sign of life and ran to my car for my phone. I rang 000 and informed them that I was an off-duty officer and that I needed assistance at an accident in which one of the drivers was deceased.

I couldn't believe this was happening to me. I had spent over five years in the City and never had the misfortune of investigating or responding to a fatal motor vehicle accident, and here I was, on rehab, off-duty and on my way to work when suddenly I had it thrown in my lap, regardless of how I was feeling or what I had to deal with. I guess I could have just driven off, but I had a duty of care to help, and that's what I did.

The rain continued to pour down as we waited for the ambulance and police to arrive. A member of the public who was at the scene told me that the dead man's wife was on her way. That was the last thing I needed. Before too long I saw her walk over the hill. You couldn't see the damage from behind the van, and it was obvious the man hadn't told her the bad news, so I guessed it was up to me. I walked up to her, identified myself as an officer and regretfully told her that her husband had been killed. She just keeled in half and cried hysterically.

All I could do was support her and hold her. I told her he would have died instantly and so wouldn't have suffered. I didn't know if that was the right thing to say, but if it were me I would have wanted to know if they felt any pain. I took her up to her car and spoke to the police who had arrived. Before too long, the scene was filled with red and blue lights and men running around in bright yellow raincoats, attempting to make sense of the tragedy.

As the adrenaline began to ebb away, I began to feel sick inside and alone. Even though I was surrounded by police and other emergency personnel, I felt like I didn't fit in. I wasn't protected by my 'blue armour' and so felt isolated. I tried ringing Rachael, but she wasn't answering. The Inspector on duty was very compassionate. He made sure I was alright and asked if I had attended to a fatal accident before. When I replied no, I could see that he felt for me. He offered me the services of counsellors, which took me by surprise.

After many years in the City placing my life on the line and receiving no support, here I was being offered the help I needed after three weeks in a new area. The Inspector said I could go home, but I wanted to stay. I helped as much as I could before it all became too much for me. The Inspector could see that I was upset, so he congratulated me for a good job and let me go home.

I think I cried the whole way. When I got home I fell into Rachael's arms and cried. The whole ordeal had been so traumatic, but at the same time I felt a strong sense of pride. I snuck in a glass of bourbon and lay in the bath as I recounted what had happened. She praised me for showing the fortitude to stop and help even though I was personally going through a traumatic ordeal. I wasn't much use the rest of the day. Rachael rang my psychiatrist and we had a session over the telephone. It was good to have someone independent to talk to.

I think the hardest part was when the wife had turned up and I had to give her the bad news. I had seen dead bodies before, but none that had been snatched away so violently and unexpectedly, right in front of me. I pictured myself in the same position and it scared me. But at the same time it opened something in me that I had forgotten about, something I had hidden under all my self-doubt and cynicism for the job. It was passion. I felt a burning inside me that I had lost on the back of the Ute. It was a part of me that made me proud to be a policeman and made me look forward to going to work. But at the same time it was this passion that had almost gotten me killed. I knew that from now on I had to use my passion more wisely.

I managed to go to work for the rest of the week, which was a positive thing. I spoke to my psychiatrist about improving my return to work plan to allow me to have contact with the public on a limited basis, which he agreed to. So I began working at the station and answering phones. It may not seem like much, but considering only a few weeks earlier I had been afraid of walking into a police station, afraid of looking at Utes, of putting on my uniform and seeing myself as a police officer, this was a big step forward.

I then felt ready to take the next step to see if I was ready to perform general duties again on the streets, in uniform and with full appointments. I had to go to Sydney to participate in a 'stress shoot' before this would be possible.

## STRESS SHOOT

On the morning of March 8th I got out of bed and faced the reality of having to return to the City. It was also the first time I had worn my uniform since being on the back of the Ute seven months earlier. It wasn't as scary as I first imagined. As I donned my uniform, a flood of memories came back. It was like looking at a thousand television screens with images flashing all around me.

I headed down to the City with Rachael and the kids. The trip felt very long, and Rachael did her best to keep my mind positive. The girls were going to make a day of it while I confronted my demons and took the next step on the road to recovery. They dropped me off at the police medical office and wished me well. I was nervous but quietly confident. I met with one of the counsellors and another officer who would be doing the stress shoot with me. He was a Probationer who had been stabbed in the back by a mentally ill man in the Eastern Suburbs, which reminded me of my incident with the armed crazy man and how lucky I was.

We walked down to the Sydney Police Centre, where a friend of mine, Sergeant Jason Sharp, met me to give me my appointments and lend some moral support. He was great. He was someone I admired and felt comfortable talking to about work and personal issues. He was also a bit of a larrikin, which helped ease the stress I was feeling. After a short wait, we met up with the instructors who would be taking us for the day and started getting ready.

Then it was time to hold my gun. I hadn't touched it since the previous July and I could feel all the emotions flooding back. We first practised using our weapons by loading, unloading, rendering safe and assembly. I felt comfortable, and even though it had been some time since I had last had to handle the gun this way, it didn't take too long to remember how.

We headed down to the range for target practice. That was always the fun bit about firearms training, and I did quite well. But then came the time for the 'stress shoot.' It was made up of a number of scenarios where we had to communicate with real people and determine what action we would take. This included the possibility of pointing and shooting your firearm at them, a real person. We were only using paintball bullets, but the principle was still the same. We were encouraged to treat it like a real-life scenario and told not to shoot within three metres. But it was going to be difficult. There wasn't much room to move.

We were waiting in the common room when an officer from the State Protection Group (SPG) walked in and asked, "Where are these plebs?"

I replied, "Right here."

He looked at us and said brashly, "What do you need to see a counsellor for? I have been involved in shooting incidents where I have shot at someone and even been shot at. I didn't need any counselling."

Part of me wanted to get up and kick his ass. I was angry and felt like saying, "We aren't all heroes like you. Wanker."

But I was also crushed. I thought, *What right does he have to pass judgment on us?* We were in a vulnerable position to begin with, and it certainly didn't help our preparation. I was devastated and felt guilty about being there. I was actually hoping after that comment that the officer would be involved in the scenarios so that I could shoot at him. It would have made it a lot easier!

We went down one by one into the range after being given our scenarios. Mine was a report of a man sitting outside the front of a bank acting suspiciously, so I approached and maintained good distance and communication. Without warning, the man stood up and produced a firearm. It caught me off guard. I drew my firearm and started retreating. I called on him to "put the gun down," but he kept advancing towards me. I really didn't want to shoot him and felt quite uncomfortable, so I tried to talk him out of it.

Just then, he fired once into the ground. It confused me. I didn't know whether he was firing a warning shot or whether it meant he had shot me. I probably should have returned fire, but I was conscious of being within the three-metre limit. It was so difficult, and it was also unrealistic. I was in a confined space with a chair. In real life, I wouldn't have to worry about any three-metre rule, I wouldn't be going to such a job by myself and I would have external factors to consider, such as cover and concealment, location, bystanders, time of day and radio assistance. But more importantly I was thinking about whether the Police Service would support me if I fired.

Just then, the man fired another shot into the ground. I returned fire and shot him twice in the chest. He dropped his gun and stumbled towards me. I felt a bit uncomfortable, but it was either him or me. I re-holstered my firearm, drew my baton and told him to "get on the ground."

As he continued to approach me, I hit him a few times in the primary strike zones around the knees, which knocked him to the ground. The scenario was then concluded.

The instructor who was making notes said to me, "I know where the next bullet would have gone. Right between your eyes."

Obviously, I didn't do that well. But I felt comfortable and that I had learnt from what I had done wrong. Next time I would be able to react differently.

The second scenario was along the same lines. A man who appeared to be breaking into a car with a knife confronted me. He said that it was his car and that he had locked the keys inside, but as I asked him to move away and drop the knife he became argumentative and advanced towards me. Instead of reaching for my firearm, which would have been an appropriate response, I grabbed my OC spray and threatened to spray him. He kept walking towards me and I kept walking back, which was not a good move. I did manage to convince him to drop the knife, but I allowed him to get too close. It was a little awkward, and I was aware of my mistakes. The counsellor and instructors came to me and said that I would not be doing the final scenario — that I had failed the shoot.

I was devastated. I knew there were some things I could have improved on, but I was shocked at being failed outright. The counsellor said she thought I would be 'gung-ho' but instead underreacted. We went back to her room, where I broke down in tears. She gave me the option to come back in six weeks for another go, but I just snapped. I told her that in six weeks I wouldn't feel any more comfortable shooting at someone. How could I when I didn't have access to my gun and was sitting answering telephones? I had had enough of the lack of support from the Police Service, and this was the final straw. I said I was going to resign, but the counsellor wouldn't let me, though she didn't offer any more support or extra training either. She just said she would medically discharge me as Hurt On Duty (HOD). I spat the dummy, big time, and left.

Outside, I broke down into tears. After feeling so confident about the whole shoot, I was torn apart by the result. Rachael was so proud of me for giving it a go, but I felt like I had let her down. I took the next month off work to reconsider my position in the Police Service. It was a massive step backwards. It was like starting all over again. But after some intense and deep soul searching, I did find the courage to return to work, answering phones at Morisset. I still needed time to decide what I wanted to do and wasn't going to rush into anything.

## Chapter Thirteen:
# Full Circle

On the morning of July 30th, 2002, I was scared and afraid. Exactly a year after the incident, it was as if I was reliving the whole episode again. With a flood of emotion, I burst into tears before going into work. My wife looked at me with her puppy brown eyes and knew the pain I was feeling. A simple hug from her released the anguish. I spent most of the day haunted by images of terror. To compound matters, my best friend, my dog Buddy, had died only a few days before. A log that slipped off a trolley while I was collecting wood had fallen on him. I was still feeling sad and lost, and I blamed myself for what had happened to him. But somehow I managed to make it through to the end of the day.

A few weeks later, I received a copy of the CCTV footage and the police radio tape of the incident with the Ute. My counsellors had been trying to obtain the tape for at least six months but kept hitting 'red tape.' Finally, I got fed up and made some very insistent phone calls to the officers involved in the investigation. Within three days I had a copy of both tapes delivered to me at home.

That night I sat down with Rachael, her brother Daniel and his girlfriend (now wife) Diane to watch and listen to the tapes. It was very difficult for me. I had been waiting for many months. I was nervous and afraid of what I would see and what Rachael and the others would think. We listened to the police radio tape first. What surprised me more than anything else was how the incident seemed to be over in seconds, not the ten minutes I remembered. It felt like hours trapped in the tray. You could hear the fear in my voice. Considering the circumstances, I was amazed at how calm I sounded on the tape and thought I called my locations surprising well under the conditions.

Then it came time to watch the CCTV tape. There was no sound, only moving pictures. There was only footage of part of the incident, when it passed through Ultimo and into the City. The first pictures were of the Ute coming around the blind corner into Ultimo along Harris Street. That was the scariest part of the trip for me and the point when I thought the vehicle would roll and I was going to die.

The Ute came through the City and was airborne before rumbling into the park. You could see me hanging on and pointing my firearm at the driver, yelling something angrily. As the Ute fishtailed around the park you could see the passenger jump from the spinning vehicle to run for safety and me punch through the back window with my gun. Moments later I was chasing the driver across the park, but when I reached a small fence line, I didn't have the energy to get over it. You could see how sore I was and at the same time how intent I was on catching the driver. The CCTV operator told the circulating car crews where the crook was running as I watched him jump off a ten-metre wall onto Pitt Street. The camera followed him across the road and into the building, with a Detective from Redfern in hot pursuit.

It was very emotional, watching all this, but at the same time I was at a stage where a sense of relief came over me. I had survived. For the previous twelve months I had seen this incident from the frightening reality of the tray of the Ute, and now I was looking at it from a different perspective. In a way this made it a lot easier. I could step back and regard it with the eyes of an outside observer. I had changed my neuro-association of what this incident meant to me.

The tape continued, showing slow-motion shots and close-ups of the crook, for evidentiary purposes I suppose. And then the screen went black. It was over.

Daniel said to me, "You're an idiot."

Rachael was shocked. After hearing all my stories of the event, it was just like being there for her. She gave me a big hug and said, "If you ever do that again, and survive, I will kill you myself."

## Retraining

After passing the twelve-month mark and surviving the viewing of the CCTV footage, I began to accept the fact that I might never work out on the streets again. Despite this, my confidence had been raised by the friendships I had made at the station in Morisset, and I was looking forward to my future. Before joining the service I had always wanted to work with the Police Prosecutors, and I was accepted into the Prosecutor's course for January 2003. I was still officially on the books at Redfern and needed a release from there to move on, and I was hoping that would come through before the end of the year.

In the meantime, after months of working on the phones at Morisset I was ready for a new challenge. In October, I underwent three training days at the NSW Police Academy to rebuild my confidence about getting back in uniform, holding my firearm and perhaps eventually getting back on the streets. It was the first time I had been back to the Academy since I had graduated five years earlier, but not much had changed. The session was organised at the request of me and my psychiatrist by the police psychology unit and by Sergeant Michelle Auld, who had been with Constable David Carty the night he was brutally murdered in 1997 in a Fairfield carpark. Other officers were involved in role-playing scenarios. It was a lot of fun, with some of the performances a bit too convincing and the 'actors' enjoying themselves a little too much, but it was also an important learning experience for me.

I confronted a number of different scenarios, starting with easy situations, such as taking a report of a robbery and an assault, and working up to dealing with people armed with knives and guns. I felt I handled the situations well and with confidence.

The final session was the toughest. It involved several 'simmunitions,' which is a police term referring to a simulated real-life scenario (similar to the stress shoot) in which a police officer in protective clothing plays the crook. I had to assess the situation and attempt to resolve it using whatever force I believed appropriate. I had a firearm loaded with paintballs so that I could go through the motions of drawing and pointing my firearm and then pulling the trigger if I was required to. This time, unlike the stress shoot months earlier, I used good communication, officer survival skills and cover and concealment techniques, and when the threat was imminent, I made the decision to shoot. To me, this was a more realistic environment. The other officers were impressed, and I knew I'd done the right thing and done it well. I could feel my self-confidence increasing.

Aside from completing the tasks as required, there was the camaraderie and laughter and the opportunity to talk with Michelle about her experiences. She was truly inspirational and made me feel a little guilty about my own complaints. The whole experience was incredibly worthwhile and made a big difference to me. I could see options opening for me where the path had once been closed. For the first time since the Ute incident I felt confident about getting back into uniform and back on the streets.

## WORLD CHAMPION I

When I was still in high school, I began organising charity events for homeless children and was very passionate about this cause. Throughout my time as a police officer, I redirected that passion into making a difference on the streets. As soon as I lost my footing on the frontline, I became disheartened and unfulfilled in relation to giving to others. So while I underwent my recovery at Morisset Police Station, I focused on a new goal—becoming a Guinness World Record™ holder. The aim was to raise money for charity and set a Guinness World Record™ at the same time.

In May 2002, I came up with the idea of playing the most number of golf courses within a thirty-day period. I sent a proposal to the management of Guinness World Records™ Pty Ltd in England for their approval. They responded that they would not accept this as a Guinness World Record™ attempt but would acknowledge an attempt in the category of 'Most holes of golf in seven days, using a cart,' for which no current record existed.

In order to peak community interest, I named the attempt the '1000 Hole Charity Golf World Record Challenge,' to be undertaken at Morisset Country Club in early December 2002. It seemed like a nice round number, and I thought that playing 1,000 holes would be a challenge in itself.

The guidelines were faxed out to me: abide by the normal rules of golf, play the course in order and if you lose a ball you cannot re-hit unless you have searched for five minutes.

All I had to do then was choose a charity. My youngest daughter, Keely Anne, had been born with hip dysplasia, which wasn't diagnosed until she was six months old. As a result, she went through a number of operations at John Hunter Hospital south of Newcastle. The surgeon and staff were great, so when I heard the NBN Telethon was in aid of local charities, including John Hunter Hospital, the decision to support it was an easy one.

I received a number of disbelieving looks when I told people what I was planning. Many commented, "You won't be able to do that."

I love it when people tell me I can't do something. It just gives me more incentive to prove them wrong.

My training regimen consisted of playing a few rounds of golf a day a couple of times a week, as well jogging, lifting weights and following a healthy diet. All was going along quite well until I suffered a serious leg injury while playing soccer one night in June 2002 after a careless slide tackle from a defensive player took me out close to the goals. I didn't even get a penalty! It was the first season I had played soccer since I was in high school, so I was out of practice and out of condition, but I enjoyed getting back onto the field, socialising and even scoring a few goals (just like in the old days). After I was carried off on a stretcher and conveyed to the local hospital in an ambulance, I spent the next ten weeks undergoing regular physiotherapy and appointments with my orthopaedic surgeon. I was despondent at the thought that this would seriously interfere with any chance I had of setting a Guinness World Record™ and raising money for charity.

Tests and treatment revealed that I had sustained severe bruising to the bone in my right knee and should consider myself lucky that it hadn't snapped. I was able to return to training in September 2002, only a few months before the scheduled attempt.

I found it difficult to train as well as to get publicity and sponsorship for the event so that it would be a financial success. Thankfully, my wife and friends came to my aid and were invaluable in their assistance, especially Sharpy and his wife Natalie. Although the consensus was that I had lost my mind, they played a big part in bringing the event to fruition.

I worked out that in order to play a thousand holes in seven days, I needed to play a round of golf in two hours with eight rounds a day. Most hackers like me would normally finish a round in a buggy in about four hours, so I needed to halve my time per round. It wasn't going to be easy, and club selection wasn't going to be that important. In order to save time and keep things interesting I decided I would only use my driver, three wood, pitching wedge and putter. It was going to have to be a very tactical game rather than a social one. As I was on restricted duties due to my PTSD and only working part-time a couple of times a week, I would play one hundred holes in a day just to prepare my body for the onslaught.

Once the word had spread about this mad copper and what he was trying to achieve, the response from the media was fantastic. I shot a fifteen-second commercial for NBN, which was a lot of fun. Club Car joined the party by donating a petrol golf buggy with headlights, which eased the burden of playing night golf.

About four weeks out from tee off I sent an email to Guinness World Records™ Pty Ltd just to confirm that a record hadn't been set in the category since my initial contact some months earlier. To my surprise and astonishment I was informed that the current record for 'most holes of golf in seven days, using a cart' was 1,706, set in England in 1999. I was dumbfounded. When I first made contact I was told "no records existed." I had spent the past few months training to play one thousand holes. I had a '1000 hole' logo designed for the event and had been publicising that no record existed, because that is what I had been told. When I mentioned this to the powers that be, I was informed that it was an oversight, and they apologised for any inconvenience.

What should I do? After conferring with Rachael and Sharpy I decided that I wasn't going to back down. I would play a thousand holes for charity and then keep going to break the record and take it from the 'Poms' like we had in international cricket and rugby. I had a lot of support from friends and members of the public, who agreed to help by driving me around and supervising to ensure I didn't cut corners. It was reassuring that so many people wanted to be part of it.

Because I had to squeeze in at least another 706 holes in the seven days, I had to recalculate how fast I needed to play. I couldn't believe it. I had to knock another thirty minutes off my original time and play thirteen rounds a day for twenty hours out of every twenty-four. What was I setting myself up for? The non-believers were having a field day. They didn't think I could play a thousand holes in seven days, let alone break 1,706. But I always love a challenge, and I revel in other people's doubt.

December was fast approaching. The support from the public media and the Police Media Unit was invaluable. The community was excited about what I was trying to achieve, and it helped strengthen my resolve. Training was going well and the weather forecast for the week was fine. One of my biggest concerns, apart from failing miserably, was the rain, which would have made a difficult task even harder.

On the morning of the challenge I raced up to Cessnock with my brother in-law, Daniel, to pick up the second buggy for the supervisors to drive. I was beginning to feel the pressure of the event and was so nervous I almost vomited!

Just before tee off, Assistant Commissioner Peter Parsons said a few words of support on behalf of the NSW Police to the gathering of friends and family. My eldest daughter wrote me a letter saying how proud she was of me and what I was doing, which I read out to the crowd. It made a lasting impression. At 1 p.m. on Sunday, December 1, 2002 I teed off with a straight drive down the middle of the par 4, first hole. I only had 168 hours and 1,706 holes to go. Mr Parsons agreed to be my supervisor for the first round, which was a great honour. Not only was he my boss from Redfern, but he was an officer and a person I truly admired and respected. He was very supportive when he was in command. My instructions to him were simple: drive as fast as you can and keep score.

I finished the first round in fifty-four minutes and the second in fifty-seven. My scores were not too flash-hot, but I needed to play fast, not well. It was like watching a bad game of golf in fast forward. I didn't have the time to take a practice swing or line up my shot; I just hit in the general direction of where I wanted it to go. As long as it went forward, that was progress. The other players on the course were great and let me play through. I was ahead of schedule, but there was still a long way to go. I wanted to maintain a lead because I knew that fatigue, injury and weather could be contributing factors in the days ahead.

By 8 a.m. the next morning I had played sixteen rounds of golf and needed a well-earned rest. I also managed to strain my left shin in the first few hours with the repetitive rotations of my swinging. This was slowing me down and causing pain. My physio, Brendan Clark, was awesome. He volunteered his time to massage me every evening, which kept my body from seizing up completely. I thought the biggest problem would be my back and shoulders, but they coped very well. It was my hands that felt like they had been riddled with arthritis, preventing me from fully closing them, which isn't ideal for holding a golf club.

After the first day I decided I hated night golf. It was my first attempt. It was hard to see where I was going, the glow sticks inserted through the middle of the balls kept coming out and you had to hit the ball twice as hard just to get it to go the same distance as a normal golf ball. Twice the work for the same result, and when you're playing a marathon you need to preserve your energy. We had glow sticks attached to the flags so I had an idea of where to aim and another buggy drove ahead with torches to act as spotters to maintain some sort of pace and order. It was tough.

After a four-hour break, only two of which were spent sleeping facedown on a massage table, I headed back for the start of Day Two. It was just monotonous going round and round, but the support was great. My leg was causing a lot of problems, but I just tried to block it out. The media continually updated my progress with reports from Rachael. It was time-consuming doing interviews, but it was all about raising money and awareness, and I really didn't mind the rest. I averaged thirteen rounds for days two and three with scores ranging from 99 to 132. Under the circumstances I was surprised at how well my mind and body were coping with such little sleep and such rigorous exercise.

About 1 p.m. on Day Four, December 5th, I played my 1,000[th] hole, much to the delight of family, friends and the media. I had achieved the first goal. I stopped momentarily to appease the frenzy from the small crowd and the media that had gathered and answer some questions about my progress and health. It was poignant too, because I tore a hole in my new Wilson glove, which I bought for the event, on the 1000th hole. How's that for road testing a product?

The first three days went by fairly quickly, but by the end of Day Four I began to feel dehydrated. I wasn't tired or sore, except for the shin and my hands, which were stiff from gripping the club. But thanks to the support and assistance from the local St John's Ambulance, I was back in the 'swing' of things without much delay.

As you can imagine, it was becoming quite repetitive going round and round and round. After playing four days of golf I decided to make things more interesting and adopted the 'Happy Gilmore' style of golfing. By the end of Day Five, and especially in the night, I was able to hit the ball like Happy Gilmore every shot, every hole, every round. I was hitting the ball so well I considered adopting the technique permanently if I ever played again. Cars would stop on the side of the road just to watch me play, and the other golfers would clap me as I played through. It was so surreal.

I was still on schedule, but my shin was a concern. I remember heading down the par three, fifth hole, and falling down because the pain was so extreme. I was literally hobbling after the ball. I just couldn't run anymore.

Day Six was the turning point for me and almost the end of my attempt. By 2 p.m. I had played eighty-six rounds (1,548 holes) and only needed to play ten more rounds in twenty-three hours. Considering what I had achieved in the preceding days, it was definitely achievable. So I took a rest and a shower break, which in hindsight was the worst thing I could have done. With the finish line in sight, I let my defences drop, and my body didn't take long to shut down.

After a shower I felt tired but headed back out for more golf. My mate Morgs was my supervisor, and he was worried about me. I had been averaging around an hour per round, which I thought was great, but this round was slow. By the seventeenth hole I started seeing little green men running around the fairway; I thought they would steal my golf balls and cost me time. As if that wasn't bad enough, I asked Morgs what I was doing out on a golf course and why all these people were following me. Because we had worked so much together, he knew me well enough to know there was something seriously wrong. After I finished the round I was taken to a car for some rest. I can remember crying, thinking I had let people down, but not much else. I was so physically and mentally exhausted that everything started to come crashing down around me.

The next thing I remember was being showered by Rachael and my sister-in-law and some three hours later being force-fed rehydrating tablets. I later found out that my mate who had come down to be my supervisor had physically carried me into the showers. It wasn't the part I had hoped he would play, but I was ever so grateful for his assistance. But my record attempt was in jeopardy. There was no guarantee that I would be able to play on. I didn't know whether I had suffered any injuries as a result of the exhaustion. All I knew was that I had fifteen hours to play nine rounds of golf. It was going to be close.

By 9 p.m. Rachael had me back in the buggy and swinging away as fast as I could. I managed to hit three more rounds in three and a half hours before taking a break. When I returned to the first tee at 5.20 a.m., I needed to play eighty-six holes (just under five rounds) in just over seven and a half hours to break the record. I played the next four rounds in four hours, which got me back on record pace.

By this time it was daylight on Sunday morning and my friends and family had all arrived to watch me play the fourteen holes I needed to tie the record and set a new benchmark. NBN Television hijacked a golf buggy and followed me around for the record-breaking round, which I think was the most enjoyable round of the week.

About 10.45 a.m. on Sunday, December 8$^{th}$ 2002, I finished the 15$^{th}$ hole of the 95$^{th}$ round, which was the 1,707$^{th}$ hole and the new Guinness World Record™ mark. I still can't describe the relief, excitement, pride and accomplishment I felt. It took weeks for the enormity of my achievement to sink in. The people around me had been the backbone of my endeavours, and I was so proud that they were part of it all. Without them, I am sure I wouldn't have succeeded. It was a team victory.

I had two hours to play as many holes as I could before the 1 p.m. deadline, but instead of finishing at the far end of the course we agreed to finish on the eighteenth green. At 11.45 a.m. I set off on the ninety-sixth round, and I was playing the round of my life. By the time I came to the eighteenth tee for the ninety-sixth and final time, I couldn't believe my eyes. The green was surrounded by about 150 people just waiting to see me finish. I felt this amazing feeling of success and pride that was reflected in a long drive off the tee.

As I chipped onto the green for three, the crowd screamed and clapped like I was some sort of celebrity. It made all the pain and sleep deprivation worthwhile. To my embarrassment, I three putted the hole, but it didn't matter. At 1 p.m. on Sunday, December 8$^{th}$, 2002 I had played 1,728 holes in seven days and set a new Guinness World Record™. I had achieved my goal and raised over $8,000 for the NBN Telethon. Although I would have liked to have raised more money, I was pleasantly surprised that during my 10,633 shots I only lost about twelve golf balls.

But don't think that because I had finished the challenge and achieved my goal I could relax. I was hoping that I would be able to enjoy a good three days' sleep, but in between getting up in the middle of the night looking for golf balls around the house and conducting interviews with the media, there wasn't much time for rest.

In June 2003 I received a certificate from England certifying that I was the official Guinness World Record™ holder for 'most holes of golf in seven days, using a cart.'

A few months later, Sergeant Troy Grant from Tenterfield in Northern NSW (now NSW Nationals MP member for Dubbo) contacted me.

He congratulated me and said, "I want to break your record. Can you help?"

I was shocked at first, and although I didn't say I wouldn't help, I just didn't offer any assistance. As time went on I overcame my self-indulgence and remembered why I had endeavoured to set the record in the first place. Troy was no different. He was raising money for a local boy, Ben Roberts, who had suffered serious spinal injuries following a BMX bike accident. I felt ashamed of my initial reaction and rang Troy about six weeks before his attempt to offer any assistance I could give.

It was phenomenal the amount of local, national and worldwide support Troy was receiving. It soon became clear within hours of the first day that my record wouldn't last the week. It was an honour to support him through his challenge by making sure he had everything he needed and keeping him motivated and well fed. We had it working like a well-oiled machine.

After seven days Troy completed 1,800 holes, equivalent to 100 rounds of golf, and at last count he had raised over $20,000. As with my record success, it was a community achievement. It wasn't long before harmless jibes of 'has-been' were directed at me. But I retorted that I was not a has-been, but a 'once-was.' It was an exciting moment for me to see him become the new Guinness World Record™ holder.

## Chapter Fourteen:
# Next Step

Shortly after my Guinness World Record™ success and just before Christmas 2002, I was given the welcome news that I had finally been granted a release from Redfern. It was hard to believe. After months of lobbying from my family, counsellors and close friend Sharpy, the Commander at Redfern acknowledged the benefit of letting me go. Surprisingly, it wasn't as easy to accept as I had first imagined. It was a lot more difficult to let go of the past than I thought it would be.

Even though getting away from Redfern was what I had been pushing for, it also meant an end to a lot of things for me. I had spent most of my career up to that point at Redfern and felt I was leaving behind some unfinished business.

I had had plans for the area and had been working on a proposal to form a full-time squad out of the Redfern Railway Station to confront the problems around the Block. I enjoyed the challenge of working in such an area and had things I had wanted to achieve and new recruits I had hoped to share my experience and knowledge with. Now I might never get that opportunity, and that saddened me.

I also held some bitterness about my treatment there. I felt that my particular experiences had bludgeoned many aspirations I had once held and had ended a promising frontline and investigative career that I believe had begun to take off. I felt a bit cheated. If I had received more support, especially after the incident with the Ute, I believe I could have returned to Redfern. Don't get me wrong: some of my Supervisors and the Commander, Assistant Commissioner Peter Parsons, who was at Redfern in my early years, were great to work under. The boss was supportive and approachable and made you feel important but still led with a strong fist against crime. It was only in the later years after he left and when I got involved in more incidents that things went off the rails in terms of support. I had loved working there. My police colleagues had been great to work with, and there had always been plenty of work to do. Within my first year of graduating I acknowledged that Redfern was the type of place with the type of crime that I needed to be amongst. I loved dealing with serious offences and enjoyed the challenge and thrill of being involved.

But police who bust their guts to make a difference and risk their lives selflessly need good leadership and recognition. It's no myth that Redfern is one of the most volatile areas in the state, and those who work within such areas need constant reassurance and support from management and fellow colleagues. It didn't happen that way for me.

Redfern certainly wasn't an easy place to work or learn, and it was a place where working hard wasn't acknowledged by your peers, but judged. It was very competitive, and the challenge of fitting in amongst the popular, more experienced, cliquey and strong-minded wasn't easy, especially if you weren't coping. It wasn't somewhere you could feel comfortable to speak to others about work or how you were feeling without it having an adverse effect on your reputation or career.

I certainly wasn't someone who was afraid to work hard or be proactive. It wasn't unusual that I would spend the majority of my shift out on the road, and I was always looking for something to happen. This usually meant that less motivated police would often avoid and criticise me because I was different. Apart from the gay magazine incident, I remember childish derogatory comments being written about me on the back of the door in one of the men's toilets, fake HOD forms in my pigeon hole making fun of how often I got injured and some police not wanting to work with me. It was a tempestuous initiation into the policing family, and for me it was time to move on.

## Prosecutors

Now that my sortie at Redfern had officially expired it was time to start another chapter of my policing career. In January 2003 I started the Police Prosecutors course at the Ferguson Centre, Parramatta. I had always wanted to be a Prosecutor, having loved the challenge of the law, and had long envisaged becoming a police officer and then a Prosecutor, fulfilling two dreams at once. But I still didn't have any real certainty in my working life. It was a choice for me of becoming a Prosecutor or leaving the job altogether. Embarking on this course was a whole new world to me, and I feared I wouldn't succeed. I was nervous about this next step.

There were about twenty trainees in the class with me who would spend the next nine months learning a three-year course before we were 'made' as Police Prosecutors. There was an even distribution of guys and girls, with different ages, levels of experience and backgrounds. The course was made up of ten one-week blocks at Parramatta, where we did an exam first thing every Monday morning on what we had studied the previous session (what a way to start the week), followed by lectures. Occasionally, speeches were scheduled so that we could practise talking in front of a group. Let's face it: if we couldn't talk to our classmates, what hope did we have before experienced solicitors and magistrates? The worst thing about the course was the long train trip there and back each day. One of my friends from the Police Academy was in the class, which made the endless lectures and train rides more bearable.

There was a lot to take in, but once we started doing Court work it was easier because we could apply what we had learned. I was lucky because I was posted on the Central Coast, which was heaven compared to travelling to Sydney. The Prosecutors on the coast were a very relaxed and welcoming crew, and did they love to party! The Central Coast Cluster, as it was known, was made up of Wyong, Gosford, Woy Woy and Hornsby Local and Children's Courts. The Area Prosecuting Coordinator, Neville 'Nifty' Glover, who was a famous Parramatta and Australian Rugby League legend of the 70s and 80s, was a great boss. He was very considerate towards his Prosecutors and would bend over backwards to help us out. No matter which station or Court in NSW we went to, everyone knew him and had a story to tell about him.

I remember when I first saw a Prosecutor in Court—professional, intelligent and approachable. I couldn't wait to become one. When I walked into Wyong Local Court for the first time, it was a great experience. It helped that I knew two of the Prosecutors, one from my time at Redfern and one from working at Gosford before joining the service.

One of the things I couldn't believe was the amount of paperwork they had to shuffle. On a 'list day,' when people who are charged come before the Court to plead their guilt or innocence, you can have up to two hundred matters. At Gosford, having three hundred defendants in one day wasn't anything unusual.

The first hearing I did was a traffic matter at Hornsby. The Defence solicitor in the matter was one of the Defence barristers in the Black Market Murders trial. Luckily, he didn't recognise me, otherwise he would have objected more than he did and made life a bit more difficult for me (considering I helped put his client in gaol). I didn't do too badly, but I forgot to call evidence from the officer about the speed, which for an accident involving excessive speed was a fairly important proof. I did, however, manage to get up on the negligent driving back-up offence. I spoke to the barrister after the hearing and told him who I was. He said he was disappointed that he didn't get the opportunity to cross-examine me again in the trial because I was causing problems in the strength of his client's case.

Over time, I really enjoyed working as a Prosecutor, arguing law, calling evidence and sinking my teeth into some big matters. It was a fabulous opportunity for police to specialise in the legal field. Unlike the majority of Defence solicitors, who spend five years studying at a university before they have much of an opportunity to apply their skills, we get the advantage of working in busy Courts five days a week, checking charges, prosecuting matters and arguing our legal position on a daily basis.

The biggest drawback of being a Prosecutor is the lack of preparation time you have for matters. In some areas, when you finish the hearing that you only received that morning you get ten minutes to prepare for the next one. A lot of the time I was reading the brief as I was calling evidence. It was a bit unorganised, but we managed.

Unlike Defence solicitors, who have weeks to prepare cases for their hearings, we get changed around on a daily basis between Courts. We usually only find out what hearings are on when we arrive for work that morning, and we have about an hour to read the statements, interviews and evidence. Not a perfect world, but unless we got adequate staff, that was the norm.

The types of charges depend on the location you work. They can range from minor parking matters to serious theft, even sexual assaults and dangerous driving offences causing death. On average,

Police Prosecutors 'prosecute' about 90 percent of the state's criminal charges, which is an unbelievable amount.

Apart from being so mentally demanding, it is a really good place to be. I enjoyed it, and I think a lot of my success has had to do with confidence. If you act and sound like you know what you're doing in Court, it makes such a difference. I enjoyed the challenge and diversity of matters, appearing before different Magistrates and arguing against learned and more experienced solicitors and barristers. I also enjoyed the Monday to Friday work. It provided a good quality of life that was close to home, so much so that Rachael and I purchased a house near the water and decided to extend the family.

One of the benefits of being attached to Legal Services was the opportunity to travel around the state at the Force's expense and prosecute in different Courts and towns. I've been as far west as Dubbo and Bourke, south to Wentworth and Albury on the Victorian border and up to Coffs Harbour in the north. Overall, I have now prosecuted in about thirty different Courts and in varying jurisdictions during my time as a Police Prosecutor. I even took the family to Coffs Harbour when I relieved there, and apparently they had a great time spending my travel allowance!

I have started studying law by correspondence, which is a smart move because you have on-the-job training on a daily basis. My wife wants me to hurry up and finish so she can retire early.

Another Prosecutor from the Central Coast Cluster and I were nominated as Trainee Prosecutors of the Year in 2004. Although we didn't receive the ultimate prize, it was a great honour to be recognised.

But it wasn't too long before things started turning sour, as they always seemed to when things were going well. By the end of 2005, the number of Police Prosecutors had dwindled, especially in the City Metropolitan area, due to stress and to senior Prosecutors graduating after finishing their law degree and moving into private practice. This caused waves on the Central Coast because, apparently, we had too many Prosecutors for the number of Courts in the area. It may have seemed that way on paper, but for the amount of work and the types of hearings we had, we were only just managing to cope.

But the Downing Centre, which was the busiest Court in the state, was in dire need, and that meant people had to be moved. Although I was one of the junior Prosecutors on the coast with almost four years' experience, I had a growing family, lived the farthest away from Sydney and was performing quite well. So I thought I was safe.

Just in case, I thought it would be a good time to seek approval for a six-week rotation back to general duties at Lake Macquarie. I guess I just had to prove to myself that I could be operational again if the need arose. My psychiatrist felt it was a great idea, as it had been about five years since I had been back out on the streets. Rachael was also keen for me to give it a go but still anxious that I would get up to my old tricks and take too many risks. It was something I had thought about doing for a while, as I hadn't been in uniform or carried my appointments since my retraining at the Police Academy at the end of 2002. Although I wasn't too confident, surprisingly my request was approved, and within a few weeks I joined the thin blue line of frontline policing, where I was amongst it all again.

To say that I was nervous about the decision would be a severe understatement. Of course, I was very grateful for the opportunity and was looking forward to getting back to the adrenalin-charged excitement of chasing crooks; I was just worried that I may have been setting myself up again. You know how the saying goes: 'Once bitten, twice shy.'

So, in mid-2006, after I had reordered and been handed my new uniform and appointments and gone to the armoury and been reissued with my new firearm and handcuffs, I ventured to the Morisset Police Station, where I would be working during my rotation. Most of the faces were the same as when I had returned to work in 2002. It sure made settling in a lot easier. I also found that because of my prosecuting background and study of the law and police powers, I was more confident in myself.

It was a bit hard getting used to the twelve-hour shifts and the night work. But I loved the six days off. It was like I had been missing out on so much wearing a suit and tie and working five days a week.

Overall, the six weeks went by really fast, and I honestly felt like pulling the pin on prosecuting. I was having a great time and found the passion for frontline policing that I had left in the back of the Ute some five years earlier. Not to mention it was only five minutes away from home. But all goods things must come to an end.

Of course, the workload was different to Redfern and more exciting than prosecuting. It was such a large area to cover. I even managed to last the six weeks without getting seriously injured or finding myself in the middle of a shit fight. Maybe my luck was changing.

## SHAFTED

Despite my best attempts to secure a full-time spot in uniform in the Lake Macquarie LAC, I had to make the inevitable return to prosecuting. It wasn't that I didn't like working in the Courts and arguing law — I really enjoyed it — but I missed the action and lure of the streets.

It was a few months after my return, in late 2006 when I was relieving down in Albury, that I received a phone call from one of my bosses that basically ended my prosecuting career. To put it bluntly, I was told not to worry about coming back to the Central Coast because I was now attached, full-time, to the Downing Centre in Sydney. To say I was devastated wouldn't do it justice. I was gutted.

This 'relocation' meant that a lot had to change in my life, including longer days and the reality of not being able to see my wife or kids as often. We had also bought a house just after I started in prosecuting three years earlier that was over two hours away from Sydney and had decided to extend our family because I was under the impression that my job was secure on the Coast. It was a quality of life decision. But in the end, it didn't matter. They were short-staffed in Sydney, and again I felt like a number: 30763. And it wasn't just me who got moved, but two other Prosecutors from the Coast as well. It was a hard reality, mainly because I didn't have any control over it.

When I hung up the phone, all I wanted to do was pack my bags and go home. But it was hearing day at Albury, and despite how I was feeling, the local police were relying on me to fight for them. It had been such a long day already, and I really wasn't in the mood. I rang Rachael and burst into tears as I recalled the conversation. As always, she was amazing and helped me get through the rest of the day. Luckily, most of the matters died a natural death and I didn't have to spend all day torn between my work and considering where my future lay. But it was a mind-numbingly long drive home from Albury that Friday afternoon as I tried to work out what to do.

When I returned to work the following Monday, I started my fight to have the decision overturned, stating my compassionate circumstances against the transfer. I even applied for a spot back in uniform, or at least to a Court closer to home, but my circumstances were not considered exigent or 'exceptional' enough for my appeals to be granted.

As a result, I made the move to Sydney a few weeks later. I honestly wasn't looking forward to it, but the reality was that there wasn't anything I could do. I had worked at the Downing Centre throughout my prosecuting career on the odd occasion, so I knew most of the other Prosecutors and understood how the Court worked. But it didn't make it any easier. Don't get me wrong, they were all very supportive, but I was jaded over having been made to do something against my will. I loved prosecuting, but there had to be another way.

After all of the grief I went through in Redfern and after finally being released, I now felt that I mattered only to be shafted again. I was fairly lucky in a way, though. Rachael was near the end of her pregnancy when I was transferred, so I took some time off just before the due date. As that day came and went and the days rolled on, the obstetrician booked us into the hospital.

In the early hours of Remembrance Day, November 11th, 2006, our latest beautiful daughter, Beckah Lillian, came into the world. She was a magnificent sight and as beautiful as the day is long. Again Rachael did a marvelous job. As happy as we were for our new arrival, it was also a bittersweet day for our policing family; it was also the day that another officer, Senior Constable Gordon Wilson from the adjoining Brisbane Water LAC, was struck and killed by a motor vehicle on the F3 Freeway whilst performing Highway Patrol duties. Although I didn't personally know the officer, he was still part of our extended family, and his death hit close to home.

I did manage to enjoy my time off and even relaxed a little, divorced from the anarchy at work. As I helped our new addition settle into the world as only a dad can, I learned of an opportunity to work closer to home, but it meant leaving the Prosecutors and going back to uniform. I felt that I was ready and jumped at the chance.

There were a number of general duties positions available in the Tuggerah Lakes and Brisbane Water LACs on the Central Coast, which were both within thirty minutes' travel from home. And because I lived north of both of these locations and had to travel through both of the areas to attend work in Sydney — as well as because my tenure was over at Legal Services — I was eligible to apply under the commuter transfer policy. I must admit that I was quietly confident that things would finally work out okay.

After a few weeks of negotiation with management, I was offered a lateral transfer to the Tuggerah Lakes LAC, starting in early June. I couldn't believe it. I was so relieved and very excited about the change. As it was only a couple of months away from my transfer date, I put my head down and went on as many country trips as I could just for the experience and extra money. I travelled north, west and south, visiting the circuits around Coffs Harbour, Young, Cootamundra, Bourke, Dubbo and Queanbeyan, just to name a few. I even managed to convince the hierarchy of Legal Services to release me two weeks early, before my June 17th transfer date, which I was tremendously grateful for.

Before I left prosecuting I was able to sink my teeth into one final challenging hearing. It was a child pornography matter that would take some effort to win. After days of argument and legal banter, it was adjourned to a future date for final submissions. I spent hours reviewing the evidence and researching relevant case law before I presented my written summary to the Magistrate. Unfortunately, the matter wasn't decided whilst I was a Prosecutor, as it was adjourned again, for a decision. I wasn't sure which way the Magistrate would decide, but I was happy with my efforts, so it was out of my hands.

On the day of my final shift as a Prosecutor my colleagues threw me a small going away lunch, which was much appreciated. I didn't have too much work to do, so I sat down quietly at my desk and typed out my farewell email, which read:

It is with great excitement, and a touch of sorrow, that today (Friday, June 1st, 2007) is my last day as a police prosecutor. Due to family commitments I have decided to leave Legal Services to return to the fray of frontline policing. I have been offered a merit-based position, through the Commuter Transfer process, within the Tuggerah Lakes LAC on the sunny Central Coast, starting this Sunday. Although it has been a while since I have been on the streets I am so looking forward to the opportunity, and the days off!

I have always wanted to be a police prosecutor, and throughout the last four and a half years I have achieved a lot and come to learn a lot about myself. I've had the privilege of working in around thirty different Courts throughout NSW, from Coffs Harbour to Bourke and Albury to Cootamundra. I've enjoyed thrilling victories and the inevitable defeats. But most of all I have enjoyed the privilege and the opportunity to work amongst a group of dedicated professionals (you guys). I will miss the camaraderie and sense of family, the arguments of law, in and out of the Courtroom, and the challenge of being the best you can be, beyond the criminal standard.

Although ultimately it was an easy decision to make, having to leave Legal Services was a tough choice. But with my three beautiful daughters at home, always waiting with a smile to see their dad when he eventually gets off that train, it is something that I no longer want to miss. As I am sure all parents can attest, kids grow up way too fast. And I have so much that I want to achieve in my life. I would love to return to prosecuting in years to come, when the time is right, but now I am happy to put my family first.

I also read in today's Daily Telegraph that the DPP is trying to have some child sexual assault and drug matters to be dealt with only by the Prosecutors in the Local Courts, but are concerned because we are, in their terms, "less competent." I say to them that the Police Prosecutors are the backbone of the judicial system, prosecuting over 90% of the state's criminal matters each year, and could rise to any challenge. I say, with respect, that the Police Prosecutors have the 'grunt' to argue against prominent barristers and before experienced Magistrates, without preparation and legal qualifications, which all frontline police can attest is who you want fighting in your corner. Given any challenge the Prosecutors within Legal Services will bend over backwards and are an outstanding representative of the victims and police we appear for and with.

You are all important people, individually and collectively. You should be proud of your position and the work you do on behalf of the NSW Police Force and the members of the community you swear to uphold.

I would like to take this opportunity to thank the Prosecutors within the Central Coast cluster and at the Downing Centre, in particular, for their support and friendship. I have felt part of a family amongst you and have made some life-long friends and memories over the years.

Thank you again for your friendship, and on closing, good luck and take care.

I was amazed at the responses I received, even from Prosecutors I had never met or worked with, congratulating me on my decision and wishing me the best for the future. It was very humbling! Despite the way my prosecuting career ended, I will look back fondly at the friends I made, the cases I prosecuted and the things I learned. I may even consider heading back one day!

Oh, the Magistrate convicted the accused in the child pornography hearing and sentenced him to imprisonment. It was a very good note on which to leave.

## Chapter Fifteen:
# Returning to the Front Line

Although it had been almost six years since I had been on the streets back in uniform on a full-time basis, I was quietly confident that I had made the right move. It was close to home and I knew that there were going to be way more opportunities for a promotion and to get some relieving experience. It was also easier because Tuggerah Lakes LAC is where Rachael had been working for quite some time, since she left Redfern, and because we were both stationed at The Entrance it meant that we would get to see each other more often. I also knew that she wouldn't let me get up to my old tricks and that I had to be on my best behaviour.

There were also some familiar faces from when I was fortunate enough to prosecute out of Wyong, so my transition wasn't too painful. I was merged into Team 3 with a lot of officers I didn't know too much about. Of course, I was apprehensive about fitting in and making a good impression. Because I had worked on Team 3 in Redfern, I thought it would be a good omen. Little did I know that this band of brothers (and sisters) would share experiences with me not too dissimilar from those I had already survived.

I will never forget my first shift at Tuggerah Lakes. It was the long weekend in June 2007, which has become synonymous with the storms and floods that ravaged the Central Coast, Lake Macquarie and Newcastle regions within a short period of time.

I wasn't working with my usual team when I went to work out of The Entrance Police Station that night. I had heard reports of storm damage across the Coast and listened to the whipping wind and pelting rain throughout the course of the day. But nothing could prepare me for what I would be confronted with that evening.

Even travelling to work was an experience. Visibility was very poor and reports were 'flooding' in over the commercial radio about roads being blocked and predictions of 'worse still to come.' As I drove south along the main road towards The Entrance, the roadway was bordered by raging currents of water that were spouting into the air.

As I walked into the station, the looks of relief on the faces of the day shift staff were echoed only by the pounding rain and the number of outstanding jobs. Because the weather had played such havoc with local roads, bringing down power lines and cutting off suburbs, the bread-and-butter work of police attending to jobs was not a high priority.

I was working with a junior Constable that evening who I actually went to high school with. I was senior to him in rank then, and am again now. I hadn't had much to do with him, but he seemed enthusiastic enough. Armed with our list of jobs and sexy yellow raincoats, we headed for the streets to commence an unforgettable night. The police radio was filled with reports of flooding and storm damage, to the extent that the typical tempest emergency services weren't able to cope. The deluge caused such calamity that it made attending to jobs very difficult.

Because the Tuggerah Lakes LAC surrounds an extensive body of water (Tuggerah Lakes, surprisingly enough!), there is no direct access from east to west. The only option for orbiting the area is to the extreme north or south. But on this evening the odds were definitely against us. Traffic was a nightmare, with holiday-makers leaving in droves for a dryer climate. Arterial roads were closed, and even the F3 freeway from Sydney to Newcastle was congested tighter than a carpark on pension day.

To exacerbate matters, the suburb of Tuggerah on the western side of the LAC was several metres underwater and inaccessible. This meant that to attend to a job on the western side north of Tuggerah from anywhere south meant a forty-five-minute journey around the eastern and northern extremities.

I will never forget hearing the sound of the deafening thunder as it clapped overhead or the blankets of lighting that lit up the streets like it was the middle of the day. The howling winds that uprooted trees onto houses and tore down power lines violently rocked the police truck. We, like every other officer that night, were run off our feet trying to help as many people as we could, blocking off roads and directing traffic in gale-force wind and rain.

Our neighbouring LAC, Brisbane Water (Gosford area), was just as affected. I heard a friend of mine calling urgent on the police radio when she discovered a male floating in the water, and I heard the sound of her relief when she managed to pull him to safety. Other reports streamed in: people stuck on roofs of cars with torrents of water swallowing the earth around them, police carrying the elderly and young to safety and commandeering boats to use in rescues, houses being evacuated and buses being washed away. Not even our police cars were immune to the carnage, and they succumbed to the conditions. Throughout the night several police cars were bogged and consumed by the rising waters as the officers risked their lives in an attempt to help those in need.

Ultimately, the storm and its trail of destruction were so severe that the state government declared the affected areas a natural disaster zone. Over thirty-six hours, the intense weather battered the area with cyclonic winds and torrential rain (Newcastle 300 millimetres, Central Coast 200 millimetres), causing extensive flooding. Sadly, Mother Nature's fury also claimed the lives of ten people, including a family of five who were killed when the roadway they were driving on collapsed at Somersby near Gosford. And let's not forget the Pasha Bulka ship that washed ashore on Nobby's Beach, which gained international attention.

But despite all the carnage, I will always remember that weekend for one glimmering moment of hope.

My partner and I were stranded around the north of the LAC, blocking traffic so emergency services could restore fallen power lines. The rain had stopped and the air was bitterly cold. The sky was filled with plumes of blackness, threatening to unleash its fury at any moment. I looked around and was in awe of what surrounded us. What was normally an area illuminated with street lighting was enveloped in a blanket of darkness. It was frightening how empty the area seemed, with only the flashes of lightning to brighten the solitude.

Moments later, we were relieved by council workers, which freed us to attend to more urgent matters. Heading north along the Pacific Highway at Lake Munmorah, the thunder and lightning shattered the silence as the rain exploded onto the roadway like bullets fired at close range. The headlights were almost useless amidst the dense and violent rain. It wasn't long before we were flagged down to assist with traffic so trees could be removed from the highway.

As I stood in the middle of the road, valiantly shining my torch to warn oncoming cars and consumed by rain, I approached a vehicle to speak to the driver. I noticed that the front passenger was an off-duty female officer from Tuggerah Lakes who was heavily pregnant. She told me that she had gone into labour and been redirected to Gosford Hospital due to local power failures. She was frantic, and it was at least a sixty-minute trip in these conditions. So I walked back to my offsider, who was safe and dry in the car (smart boy), and told him what was going on. We agreed that we weren't going to let anything happen to either of them.

So I grabbed the police radio and sought permission from the Duty Officer to escort the expectant mum to Gosford Hospital under lights and sirens. I knew it was a request unlikely to be granted, but because this was a life-threatening situation I wasn't going to let red tape or guidelines risk the life of this baby or the mother, whether or not she was a fellow police officer. I ran back to her car and told her that we would help.

At that moment, the heavens opened. The thunder of the rain and the roaring of the wind were only interrupted by the wailing and flashing of the police vehicle's lights and sirens. Seconds later, the Duty Officer made some enquiries with us over the phone about the situation and gave us the approval we were after. Although we would have continued anyway, it was nice to know we had their support.

Despite it being about 3.30 a.m. with the roads abandoned, as drivers were heeding the weather warnings to stay inside, the task of getting to the hospital safely and on time was riddled with danger. The lightning strikes and claps of thunder intensified as the rain pelted the windscreen horizontally, which made visibility minimal. The blustery wind pushed the car across the lanes as rivers of water ran down like sheets across the road. At times conditions were so treacherous that we were struggling at 40 kilometers per hour in a 110 kilometer per hour zone along the freeway, still under lights and sirens, with no other vehicles on the road.

It wasn't too long before we arrived at the hospital with the baby still intact. I was honestly expecting to have to pull over and deliver the baby in the back of TL25. Thankfully, my daughter had only been born seven months prior, so the experience was still relatively fresh in my mind.

We got out of the car just in time to see the expectant mother race into the emergency room (well, as fast as she could under the circumstances). The proud father-to-be thanked us both before disappearing through the doors of the hospital.

I will admit that it was rather an anti-climax that it ended there without any further outcome, but I was relieved that she had made it in time. I was hoping that it would be a boy so she could name him Jeffrey Paul after her saviours. We returned to our area with a smile on our face and pride in our hearts, knowing that despite the anarchy that had unfolded during the past twenty-four hours, something magnificent was created. We knew we had made a difference and hoped that everything would be okay. There aren't many times in this job that you can look back on and feel like you have truly made a difference. This was definitely one to remember and one we will never forget.

Later that shift, curiosity got the better of me, so I found a quiet room in the station and called the maternity ward of Gosford Hospital. I was pleased to hear that both Mum and her baby were healthy and doing well. It was great news. The nurse offered to put me through to the ward, but I didn't want to interfere.

A few weeks later an email was sent around work announcing the arrival of the new baby girl, Ella. It was nice to see that we got a mention for our efforts. I spoke to the mum a few days later, and she was extremely grateful. Apparently, as soon as she arrived at the hospital they rushed her in for an emergency caesarean because the situation was life-threatening for both the mum and the baby. They wouldn't even let her husband in. Glad to see that everything turned out perfectly. It is one of the highlights of my career and personal life so far. Very rewarding!

## ACTING SERGEANT

One of the things I have enjoyed most about being back in uniform, apart from the camaraderie, is the opportunity I have had to relieve as an acting Sergeant. At that time I had been in the police for over eleven years and believed I had been ready for this responsibility for some time.

I was only at Tuggerah Lakes LAC for a few months when I was offered the chance to relieve on my team. Of course, I jumped at the opportunity. I was a bit hesitant at first because there were other more senior officers on my team and I had only been there for a short time. It was a proud moment to be handed my Sergeant's epaulettes with the three stripes and blue pens by my Supervisors, Sergeant Gary O'Dwyer (who we called GOD) and Detective Sergeant Keith Ross. This was an opportunity I was keen to make the most of because I really wanted to win a Sergeant's position somewhere.

Before I came back to uniform I had sat a number of assessments for the chance to be eligible for a promotion to Sergeant in 2008. I successfully passed all of my exams and made it through the initial pool of 2,000 to the final group of about 300 officers for a week-long program at the Goulburn Police Academy that included more written and oral assessments, role playing and many stressful nights studying for more interviews. This pretty much guaranteed me a promotion for 2008. The only question was where in NSW it would be.

The promotion system changed in 2007 from the old style of applying for a specific location to applying for a specific rank. Once you successfully made it through the phases of the eligibility program, you would then be 'ranked' according to your performance. Positions would then be advertised and you could apply for as many locations as you wanted with the highest-ranking officer nominated for that location. The process was supposed to commence in January 2008, but due to teething problems and other issues it didn't start until August. It was quite frustrating, but exciting at the same time.

Since starting my relieving in September 2007 I had spent a lot of time as Supervisor, which gave me some good experience to use if and when I moved. I thoroughly enjoyed the opportunity and believe I learnt a lot too. Of course, I made some mistakes and was open to constructive criticism, but I also believed I made a difference in my team by being professional, supportive, and by leading by example. I certainly wasn't the typical type of Supervisor who is anchored to an office verifying events and delegating tasks (not that there is anything wrong with that). I still loved to get out on the streets amongst it all, which was probably a bit of a negative, considering the amount of paperwork a Sergeant is expected to do in a shift.

I was able to maintain a high arrest rate and loved hunting for stolen cars, not that I had much success. I also enjoyed being approached by other, sometimes more senior, officers for advice. My passion for my job and the law, which was unusual for my length of service, especially considering everything I had been through, was still burning inside me. Over the years I have developed a strong operational and legal knowledge that I was happy to share.

I also felt that because I had been through so much during my career I would be able to give back to my troops what was lacking when I needed advice and guidance. I have always tried to treat them as people and not numbers. It's a hard thing to do when you've got staff shortages, but treating them like numbers is something I will never inflict upon my colleagues.

I received some positive feedback from some of the police on my team about my performance, which was unexpected and reassuring, but also a few digs from some 'senior' police who believed I was too proactive to be a Sergeant. I guess it was a bit disappointing to hear that, but I can understand where they were coming from. Everyone performs their duties differently, but I always made sure I supported the police I was working with and tackled the endless mountains of clerical commitments that came with the role.

There are always heaps of equipment and items to check and verify and cross-reference when you're a Sergeant, especially when there are three stations within the Command — Wyong, Toukley and The Entrance — which means there is triple the paperwork. As long as there are lots of blue ticks and crosses, the bosses seem to be happy.

The Entrance was the only charging station in the area, so all custodies had to be transported there for charging and interviews, which provided some valuable experience for me. I had never worked in the custody area prior to starting at The Entrance except for a one-day course in Sydney some years ago. I think that in my first shift as Custody Manager I had eight prisoners, which was a great initiation. It can get really quiet when there are no custodies, but there is always something to check or events to verify.

Throughout my time as an acting Sergeant I think I averaged about 500 kilometres per shift when I was the mobile Supervisor in Tuggerah Lakes (TL) 14. There were times when I would rather have stayed at home and other instances when I was glad to have that responsibility. There are two incidents that come to mind that are memorable, to say the least.

## Chapter Sixteen:
# Cracneck

It was just before Christmas 2007, and it was my first shift back as a Senior Constable. My period of relieving was momentarily cut short due to budgetary restraints, which was disappointing. Here I was trying to get some valuable experience before I got transferred as a real Sergeant, probably out west somewhere, and they couldn't afford it. I was on a roll and really enjoying it.

As usual, I arrived about thirty minutes before the commencement of my shift to get ready and organised for the day. I spoke to the Supervisors coming off night work and they mentioned that they were trying to locate a local man who they believed was a high risk of suicide. Apparently, he had arrived home and found his wife in bed with another man, and he didn't react too well. The police on night shift did a magnificent job trying to locate him, including foot patrols, phone triangulation and extensive other enquiries, but without success.

I made numerous enquiries during the course of the morning with the family of the missing person, trying to obtain any further information on his whereabouts. By this time there had been no contact with the male for several hours. Although I tried calling his mobile phone, it rang a few times before going to message bank. This was sufficient, however, to try another triangulation on his phone.

In the meantime, my Probationer partner and I left the station to make some proactive patrols around the local area, just in case. I made another phone call to a family member and was told that she had just spoken to the missing person and that he had stated that he was "on a cliff and near water." Although the information was fairly general, it did narrow down the search area to three possible locations: Forrester's Beach, Norah Head or Crackneck Lookout.

After we quickly assisted a Brisbane Water vehicle with a key (sledge hammer) for an arrest at Killarney Vale, I contacted the female again. She stated that she had located his vehicle at Crackneck Lookout. I activated the lights and sirens of our police vehicle and notified Police Radio that we were responding Code Red (urgent duty) to Crackneck Lookout in relation to a possible suicide attempt. I spoke to a female Senior Constable and her partner, who were working in another police vehicle and asked if they could assist.

Within minutes we arrived at the lookout and I noticed the vehicle belonging to the missing person. I had a conversation with the female at the scene and she directed me to where the male was. I walked through the dense scrub about fifty metres from where the carpark was and saw two males sitting on the edge of the cliff. I identified one of the males as the missing person and the other as a relative who was attempting to negotiate with him.

They were both sitting above a one hundred metre drop to rocks below, surrounded by loose gravel and thick bushland. I directed my partner to return to the carpark to inform the other police of our location.

I slowly 'edged' my way towards the male and took up a position about two metres behind them, announcing my office, stating, "I am Senior Constable Garland from The Entrance Police. I am not here to arrest you. You are not in trouble. I am here to make sure that you are okay and to see if there is anything we can do for you." Despite being told to "fuck off," I was glad he didn't panic and leap off the cliff. I wasn't sure whether I was saying the right things but wanted at least to try.

I spent the next five minutes trying to establish some kind of communication with the man. He just ignored me and continued staring off into the distance, no doubt contemplating what his options were. I noticed that he appeared to be intoxicated and was drinking from an almost empty bottle of bourbon. I had a brief conversation with Police Radio asking for trained negotiators because this was out of my field of expertise.

Two other officers approached my location, but the terrain was too steep and the loose gravel made it just too dangerous, so I asked them to return to the carpark to monitor the situation.

I remember looking around to see what options were available to me, as my attempts to talk the man from the edge were failing miserably. I was very concerned about how close we all were to the cliff and the limited access to our location. I kept thinking about what I would do if he made an attempt to jump, but frankly I still had no idea, hoping it wouldn't come to that.

I moved closer to within a metre behind the man, just in case I needed to act quickly. Because he was obviously depressed and intoxicated, there was a substantial risk that he would jump. I tried talking to him for about fifteen minutes about anything just to build a rapport and take his focus off the situation. I asked him about his job and his kids and at one point noticed that he was wearing an HSV t-shirt, so as a massive Garth Tander fan, I started talking to him about V8 supercars. It wasn't something you would find in the textbooks of negotiators, but I managed to get a limited response.

Whilst talking to the man, I saw him take a number of pills. I tried to talk him out of it, but he just downed them with bourbon. His relative threw me an empty packet of anti-depressants that the man had already consumed. Mixed with the alcohol that he had been consuming, this was a deadly cocktail. The male was clearly getting more upset and began to cry. Just then, he turned towards me and threw himself backwards towards the cliff. Fearing that he would fall, I lurched forward and grabbed him by the shoulder and jumper. I was terrified that his momentum would drag us both over the cliff. It was too late for me to do anything else. I was up to my eyeballs with this guy.

I managed to dig my heels into some type of footing and tried pulling him towards me. He looked right at me and I could see the intent in his eyes. He began to struggle by pulling away from me as he slid backwards towards the cliff face. I used all of my strength to hang onto him and managed to update Police Radio of the situation.

His relative moved away and disappeared through the scrub as I wrestled with the man on my own. I was yelling and swearing at him, as I was fuckin' angry that he was willing to take me with him over the edge.

I was left holding onto the male for another fifteen minutes, pleading with him to surrender, talking about his kids and how he couldn't do this to them, especially so close to Christmas. In a moment of clarity, he managed to confide that he had a daughter with the same name as my eldest child, Teagan, and that was it for me. It became personal because of that connection, and I wasn't going to let this selfish prick make me think of his death every time I saw her. He kept saying that he had 'stuffed up' and that he wanted to die. I just held on tighter and kept him talking as much as I could.

I had already been out there with the male for over half an hour when I saw a glimmer of hope walk through the tree line behind me in the form of a Senior Constable. I knew that if there was going to be anyone out there on the cliff face helping me, it would be him. I was so relieved. He reached around my waist, secured a rope to me and attached it to his belt. But it didn't end there. The Senior Constable and I spent another ten minutes talking to the man without any indication that it would end either way.

That was until the male threw himself backwards again towards the edge with me still holding on. I thought that was it for all of us. My 'cliff buddy' was still positioned behind me so that he wouldn't provoke or scare the man, but he managed to jump around me and grab his arm. We used all of our strength and experience to wedge the male against the ground to prevent him from falling farther. This bloke was prepared to die and didn't seem to care who went with him.

We had been talking to him for about five minutes when Sergeant Ross came down the slope. I gave him my portable and asked for another rope to secure the man, as he was continuing to struggle and seemed intent on committing self-harm.

By this stage my arms and hands were aching, but after a short time, the man appeared to be beginning to calm down. Whether that was just a ploy for us to relax so he could finish the job or whether it was the alcohol and drugs kicking in or whether he was beginning to change his mind, I don't know, but we weren't going anywhere, and we were definitely not letting go.

There we were on the edge of a cliff, physically restraining this suicidal man, with absolutely nowhere to go. Up the incline with the loose gravel was not going to happen with the male in the mood he was in, and straight down just wasn't an option. We just had to wait until another alternative arrived.

Not long after, I was starting to think that I was the one going crazy when I turned to see the Commander from the neighbouring LAC coming down the hill towards us. It was the last place I thought a boss would go, but he was very hands-on and looked after his troops.

The male seemed to sense his chance. He broke free from our hold and headed for the cliff for a third and final time. This time, with the three of us, including the Commander, grabbing the man, he seemed to give up. I pulled him up onto my legs and pinned him down, with the Senior Constable and the Commander holding down his arms and legs. I so wanted just to punch the male in the head and knock him out because he could have killed me, and in hindsight, I wish I had.

For the next thirty minutes we held the male down while waiting for Ambulance Rescue to arrive with a harness to extricate him. I could feel that I had injured my left hip and leg from having the weight of the male bearing down on me for so long with my leg bent backwards underneath me, but I didn't want to risk moving in case he tried to jump again. He was very unpredictable.

When Ambulance Rescue arrived I felt so relieved. I could finally see the incident coming to a peaceful and satisfactory resolution. A junior Constable also made his way down to assist in the recovery attempt, at great personal risk to himself, considering our location. When the male was secured to a harness we were able to somewhat relax and get to our feet for the first time since the beginning of the incident. It was only then that I could feel the full extent of my injury. I couldn't bear any weight on my left leg and my hip was screaming at me. The fact that I was still on the edge of the cliff with loose gravel around me made it more frightening because I knew there was no way I could climb up the hill to safety.

The male was slowly lifted from the edge of the cliff and guided up the hill. I did my best to assist but ended up having to be helped up the hill by other police. I was so glad to get off that ledge to the safety of the carpark, which was filled with emergency vehicles and onlookers by this time.

As soon as I got to level ground I had to lie down on the grass because the pain in my left hip was so intense. I felt like such a wuss, but I was having real problems walking. I had done, or should I say, he had done, some real damage. I was helped from the ground and hobbled over to one of the ambulances that were on standby. I was very reluctant, but the Duty Officer came and directed that I go to hospital to get checked out. Before I left, the family of the man came up to me in the ambulance and thanked me. It was rewarding to see the looks of gratitude on their faces, knowing that we had made a difference.

It was also embarrassing at the same time. It seems that every time I get involved in something serious I always end up getting hurt and having to go to hospital. At least it was better than the alternative of being at the bottom of the cliff. I certainly was not looking forward to telling Rachael. On the way to the hospital I worked up the courage to send Rachael a text message saying that I had injured myself at work and was on my way to Gosford Hospital but was otherwise okay. I didn't have the guts to ring and talk to her on the phone. Luckily, she was in a major shopping centre with her mother, so she didn't blow up too much.

We hadn't driven too far when the ambulance I was travelling in pulled to the side of the road and the driver indicated that the other ambulance, which was conveying the man, was asking for urgent assistance. Luckily, it was directly behind us, so I leapt off the stretcher, burst out the back door of the ambulance and hobbled over to see what was going on. I knew a female Senior Constable was travelling in the rear of the ambulance with the man, and because I didn't have a radio, I wasn't sure if she was okay. I knew that the man was very depressed, angry and well affected by alcohol, not to mention willing to jump off a cliff to kill himself.

By the time we got to the ambulance the man was restrained and strapped to the stretcher. Although the man went ballistic again before we arrived, both the Senior Constable and her partner were in the ambulance to ensure his safety.

I was very frustrated and angry with myself and the man for what had happened. I didn't believe in suicide and at the time thought it was a coward's way out. My understanding was that at 'that' particular moment, suicide is what is most real to some people and the only possible solution they see to a problem. Having hurt myself again and risked my life in the line of duty, I was just thankful that we were all alive, and I was now very much looking forward to going home and seeing my family. I spent most of the time in the back of the ambulance thinking about the 'what ifs.'

Once we arrived at Gosford hospital, I learnt that the man had been taken into a room and was still misbehaving. I would have loved to spend a few minutes alone with him, letting him know just how I was feeling at that moment. He placed my life, and the lives of the other police, in extreme jeopardy over a woman.

I spent several hours in the hospital getting poked and prodded just to find out that I had torn muscles and ligaments in my left hip and knee and that I had strained my lower back. I sent messages to Rachael by text with updates on what had happened and how I was feeling. She was worried and annoyed, but not surprised. She was hoping that the 'glory days' of Redfern were all behind me, but within a few months of transferring back to uniform, I was doing it again. I don't know why. Perhaps I had been doing it for so long it had become second nature.

By the time I was released, the night shift had already started. One of the crews came down to the hospital to pick me up and take me back to the police station. The senior officer called me 'Superman,' which turned into 'Stupidman' by the time I had arrived home and told Rachael. Everyone kept asking why I didn't just let him jump, but I couldn't. I honestly believe that if I had done nothing and let him jump off the cliff and kill himself I would be worse off than what I was — an emotional mess and psychologically scarred. I had to make a *split second* decision, and I chose to risk my life to save his. To be candid, if I was in the same situation I would probably do it again. But don't tell Rachael, please.

I ended up being off work for four to six weeks getting physio and treatment on my hip and back. It was frustrating because the incident was just before Christmas, and my injuries meant I couldn't run around with my kids like I normally would. It spoiled the holidays, and I was angry and disappointed about that. What made matters worse was that I had to do weapons training before they would give my gun back and release me onto the streets again.

Ever since I returned to work I want to drop in to where he works and see how he is going. I don't know if that is appropriate or the right thing to do, but I guess I just want to make sure that he is making the most of his second chance at life.

Overall, it was a very intense situation, and I am glad to be alive to share it with you. We have to make *split second* decisions at times in this job. In hindsight, you may have done things differently, but in that time and place you have to react and hope that your experience and God's hand is on your side. Rachael has finally forgiven me and I have promised to behave myself — well, at least to try!

## Chapter Seventeen:
# The Entrance Channel

I think I lasted about three months before I broke that promise and got myself into trouble again. It wasn't long after I returned to work following the Crackneck incident that I was allowed to relieve as acting Sergeant again. They probably decided that if I crash tackle someone on the edge of a cliff my first shift back as a Senior Constable, it's probably better to give me more responsibility and less street time.

It was Monday, April 21$^{st}$, 2008, and I was the mobile Supervisor on TL14. It was the second night shift and would be the last opportunity I had to be acting Sergeant. The night had been fairly quiet, and I was looking forward to a busy night of paperwork. But like everything in this job, not all went according to plan.

Just after 10 p.m., I was returning to The Entrance Police Station with two hot meals of chicken carbonara when a job was called in about a car fire near the police station in Ocean Parade. All the other car crews were busy and I was close by, so I dropped the meals at the station and went down to have a look. As I approached I could see the glow of orange flames leaping from behind a block of units, with the Fire Brigade already in attendance. I ran to the rear of the premises, where I saw an early-model Ford engulfed in flames (the best kind — go Holden!). It wasn't long before the fire was under control, but the car was gutted. I spoke to some local residents, who stated that it hadn't been there long and didn't belong to anyone in the unit complex. I noted down the registration and returned to the police station to make further enquiries.

I sat in the station area to complete the police report and spoke to the owner of the burnt-out vehicle, who was mortified when she realised that her car was not where she had left it and that the car thieves had written it off.

About 10.30 p.m., Sergeant O'Dwyer said to me, "There is a white hatchback down at Memorial Park on Marine Parade that has collided with the piers. It's in the carpark. They think the driver might be drunk."

I said, "Have you got the details of the car?"

He handed me a piece of paper with the car's registration written on it. I thought it would be an easy lock-up, so I grabbed my gear and flew out of the station.

I drove to the carpark at Memorial Park on Marine Parade a few streets away. I notified Police Radio that I had arrived at that location for a possible intoxicated driver. It was a very cold night, and the only vehicle in the carpark was the small white hatchback. The carpark was well lit and the vehicle was facing away from me, towards The Entrance channel on the northern side, with the brake lights on. This told me that the driver of the vehicle was still inside the car.

As I had been trained to do when attempting to make a vehicle stop, I drove into the carpark and left a gap of a few metres between the rear of the hatchback and the front of the police car, which was parked slightly to the right to provide a 'corridor of safety.' I confirmed that the registration was the same that Sergeant O'Dwyer had written on the piece of paper.

I fumbled around for my alcometer to test the driver for alcohol. As I got out of my car I saw a young male, aged about eighteen to twenty, thin build and caucasian, wearing a dark cap and white jumper, get out of the driver's door of the vehicle. I looked at him, he looked at me and then suddenly he ran around the front of the car and sprinted towards the park along the channel.

I shouted, "Stop; police."

I really wasn't expecting it to be this difficult, and I was rather annoyed and bemused as to why he had fled, but I chased after him and in the process dropped my torch. The male staggered in a westerly direction for about twenty metres before jumping onto a sandbank and running into the water.

I thought, *You've got to be kidding*. I quickly notified Police Radio that the male had taken off and was running into the Channel, probably affected by alcohol.

I jumped onto the sand and walked towards him, as he was about ten metres away by this time, stumbling backwards and dropping into the water. I marched back to the footpath mumbling to myself, trying to locate my torch and thinking of the possible outcomes. I decided that I had to go in after him. I wasn't going to let him drown. As I took off my appointment belt and emptied my pockets onto the footpath, I was approached by a group of three females.

One of the females said, "We are the ones who called you."

Whilst talking with them I kept a watch on the man, but I realised I couldn't see where he had gone. I was concerned because I had chased him into the water and knew that if anything happened to him it would be classified as a death in custody. This whole incident was getting out of control. As far as I knew he was just a young pissed bloke who didn't want to lose his licence, which was certainly nothing worth dying for; we all make mistakes.

I heard over the police radio that other car crews were on their way, so I left my equipment with one of the females who had identified herself as a security officer. As I walked towards the water I shone my torch, but I still couldn't see the male. TL25 with two relatively experienced Constables, Denise and Shaun, was approaching as I walked into the water with my boots, shirt and cargo pants on. Don't ask me why I left my boots and socks on, but I did. I honestly believed that the water was only knee-high. However, after only entering the water a few metres I could see that the sandbar dropped off and that beyond it the water was quite deep. I was really concerned now for the male. I could not see or hear him anywhere and wondered whether he might already have succumbed to the freezing water conditions and possibly drowned due to his intoxicated state.

I returned to the carpark, where I spoke to Denise.

I said, "I've lost him. He's out in the middle. He might drown or might have already. I'm going in after him. Can you organise a police vehicle on the northern side of the water and one on the bridge? You might want to arrange for an ambulance, just in case."

I decided to re-enter the water, but not before I removed my soaked boots and socks. I commenced walking in the direction I thought he might be in until I got to the drop-off, where I stepped into the deeper water, which was now up to my chest. I trudged along the freezing waterway for about 50 metres with my arms above the water, shining the torch in an arc, when I saw a silhouette running west towards the bridge about 100 metres ahead.

Thank God, I thought.

I could hear people yelling from behind me, "There he is."

He was staggering and tripping over in the water, but appeared to be on higher ground. It was so dark and deep that I couldn't see where the shallow parts were.

I yelled out, "Denise, he's running towards the shoreline up near the park."

As she ran west towards the park, I continued walking towards the accused in chest-deep water, shining my torch on him, just so that he knew I could see him, in the hope that he would stop. He was still staggering and falling over in the water but had turned away from the shore and was heading back in towards the middle.

*Fucking idiot*, I thought.

My attitude had turned from fear, to relief, to frustration in a very short period of time. Just when I thought this situation would be resolved, it made a turn for the worse.

I said, "Mate, stay where you are. We know who you are. Let me help you."

I still had no idea who this bloke was but thought if I could convince him we knew who he was he might give up. But he ignored me and kept heading away.

I managed to find some shallow water with a sandbank, which was a tremendous relief and which I hoped would help me catch up. My cargo pants were weighing me down and my legs were aching. I tried pulling them up, but they just fell straight back down. I tried running towards him, because I wasn't getting any closer and I didn't want him to drown, but my legs felt like cement slabs and I wasn't in the best physical condition myself.

At this time, the water sunk to about three metres in depth, so walking wasn't an option. I threw myself forward and started swimming towards him. My legs felt even heavier, and to make matters worse, my torch stopped working. I kept repositioning myself in the water so that the male was in between me and the caravan park on the northern side of the channel. At least then I could see his silhouette and know where he was.

I was getting exhausted and scared absolutely shitless, both for the male and myself. Despite the intensity of the situation, everything around me suddenly went quiet and a calmness came over me. It was like I had surrendered to my fate — that I was going to die. As I treaded water I looked around me with the saltwater lapping at my face and knew I couldn't keep swimming with the torch in my hand. My pants were weighing me down and the torch was nothing more than an obstruction. I remember looking at The Entrance Bridge and thinking of my family. Seeing the faces of my beautiful wife and three magnificent daughters overwhelmed me as if it was the last time, my last living memory. It wasn't like a normal situation where I could just walk away. It was like being in the back of the Ute again. I felt trapped and alone. I was struggling in deep water, and the only way out was straight down.

But something snapped me out of it and I realised that if I was going to conserve my energy, I should get rid of the torch. I tucked it into my pants, rolled over onto my back and tried to float. I thought, *If I can't stay afloat, I am going to drown. I am so tired.*

Fatigue was going to be a serious problem, so I tried to float for a minute to catch my breath. The male was just ahead of me, but it was deep water; all I could see were his head and arms flailing about.

I whipped my arms into the water and kicked my legs as fast as I could. When I was about three-quarters of the way across the channel and struggling to stay above water, my hands brushed sand, so I knew I would be okay and able to stand up. I dragged myself onto the sandbar and stumbled to my feet. I could see that the male was still fifty metres in front of me, going under the water, and to my horror he appeared to be swimming away.

I yelled out, "Mate, come back to me. Let me help you."

I heard him call, "You're not going to lock me up."

I thought, *What is this bloke fuckin' doing?* I am trying to save his life and trying to prevent us both from drowning, and he is worried about getting locked up for drink driving.

I tried to reason with him. "I just want to help you. I don't want you to drown, and I don't want to die either."

But he didn't respond. He just kept heading for the other side, still over 100 metres away. By this time, I could see a number of persons on the northern side of the water in the grounds of a caravan park.

With my voice filled with fear I yelled out, "Help. Help. Can someone bring a boat out, please?"

I heard a male voice reply, "We don't have one. Fuck off."

I couldn't believe it.

I shouted angrily, "I am a police officer. I need a boat. Help me please."

I saw that the male had stopped swimming, so I tried to reach him once again. I kept thinking to myself, Don't drown, don't drown. Don't struggle, just let me help you.

As I got closer to him he said, "Can you help me?"

I said, in between strokes, "I'm coming, just stay there."

The male appeared to be struggling to stay above the water, as he was splashing around and bobbing up and down. That's when he snapped. As I was about to grab him and drag him back to the sandbar some twenty metres in the other direction, he turned towards me and said, "You're not fucking arresting me."

I couldn't believe it. He grabbed my shirt at the front, then without warning headbutted me fair in the head. The next thing I knew, he had both his hands on top of my head and was pushing me underwater. All I could do was try to get him off me.

The water must have been over three metres deep because I couldn't touch the sand and push myself back up. The weight of him pushing me under forced me down like a pin. While I was submerged I desperately tried to grab his arms to stop him from drowning me. I remember panicking and opening my mouth only to gulp down some seawater. I managed to grab both his wrists and force them off me. As he let go I came to the surface, vomiting up salt water and gasping for air.

Immediately I punched him hard in the face in an attempt to subdue him. For a second he stopped struggling, so I grabbed the back of his shirt around the collar and dragged him back to the sandbar.

At that moment, as I was helping him to safety, he yelled, "You just assaulted a fourteen-year-old boy. I'm going to have you charged. Help."

I snapped, "Well, if you fucking try to drown me or headbutt me again I'll fucking do it again."

I pondered, "If you are only fourteen, what are you doing driving a car? You're too young to have a licence. And you've been drinking."

As soon as we reached the sandbar I grabbed his arm and shoved it up his back in a wristlock.

He yelled, "I lost my good jumper. Fucking go and get it. Let me go."

He started pulling away from me towards the deeper water.

I said, "We're not going anywhere." It was as if this bloke wanted a confrontation in the middle of the channel. He tilted his head forwards and rammed it backwards towards me, headbutting me again. It was enough for me to lose my grip. I wrestled to regain control by grabbing both his arms behind his back and dunking his head in the water.

I said, "You're under arrest for assaulting police."

He said, "Just handcuff me then."

I said, "I don't have handcuffs. I came out here to save you."

Thankfully, he started to calm down and said to me, "If it wasn't for you, I wouldn't be alive."

I thought, *You have got to be fucking joking*.

I shook my head and said, "Well, stop fucking fighting and stand still. I'm scared too!"

I could feel the current pulling us towards the bridge and I could feel him shaking in the cold water. When I looked up I saw people running near the caravan park and yelled out again, "Help. Help. Can somebody please get a boat?"

There was nothing more I could do but hold him and hope someone would help us. I saw a number of police and ambulance vehicles with their lights and sirens crossing The Entrance Bridge. It finally felt like help had arrived and this terrible ordeal was nearly over.

The male said a couple of times, "Let's go over to where the lights are, hurry up!" motioning towards the caravan park with his head.

I said, "I just dragged you out of there. The water is too deep. We are staying here."

I wasn't going anywhere. Help was going to come to us.

I cried out, "Help. Make sure there is a police officer in the boat."

I wasn't sure if anyone could hear me, and I was a bit worried that the male might see it as a sign of fatigue or weakness and take advantage of it.

I heard someone yell out from the shore, "We can't find a boat."

I didn't know how much longer I could hold onto this young bloke. I looked over towards the caravan park, where I could see a number of police officers with torches running along the water's edge, too far up, near the bridge.

I yelled "We're out here" in desperation and waved my hand. I knew they couldn't see me, but I had to try.

"Come down to where the green lights are. We're about 100 metres out from there," I yelled.

I saw the officers running towards the cabins with the green lights, which was a relief.

The male said, "Fucking lets go towards the shore."

I surrendered, because I didn't know how much longer I could last or when they would find a boat. I said, "Okay, I will walk back slowly along the sandbank. Please don't struggle. I am here to help you."

I held the male close to my chest and started walking backwards. I was trying to feel my way with my frozen feet, but the water was getting deeper. I dejectedly moved back to where we had been standing and waited.

The accused started yelling. "Fucking let's go. I'm cold."

I said, "It's too deep."

I looked around and saw Shaun dive into the water from near the caravan park and start swimming towards us.

Then someone yelled out, "We've got a boat," and I could hear someone trying to start it.

It was an amazing feeling. Hope.

When I heard the boat start I yelled out, "Get the officer who is swimming out first."

The two males in the boat went towards Shaun and pulled him to safety inside the boat.

When the boat approached me I said, "Take him first," and lifted the male into the boat. He began yelling and swearing. I was so tired and heavy that I couldn't lift myself into the boat, so I hung onto the side and was dragged towards the shoreline. About five metres from shore I collapsed and started drifting out again when another Senior Constable, Dave, waded into the knee-high water and shouldered me to the grassy area. I was exhausted, very cold and so happy to be alive. I lay on my back and thought about everything that had just transpired. I could hear the male screaming and swearing in the background.

I yelled out, "Dave, make sure you give him a breath test."

That's all I was concerned about. It was still within the two-hour limit for a test and I wasn't sure what effect saltwater would have on a reading. I was delusional.

I heard a male voice say, "This is Shaun," and he patted my chest, happy to see me safe.

I mumbled, "It's Jeff."

He said, "Your feet are still in the water; we need to move you some more."

I felt someone grab under each of my arms and drag me along the ground towards the caravan park

I said, "I can't feel my feet," and that was the last thing I remember until I woke up in the ambulance with a paramedic staring down at me en-route to Gosford Hospital, suffering hypothermia.

My temperature at the scene rose from 27°C to 30.4°C, which is why I lost consciousness for about twenty minutes. I remember lying on the stretcher answering some questions and replaying things over in my head. I thought of my girls and felt my chest tighten as my eyes welled up with tears. I couldn't believe that after everything I had just been through I had survived — again. My right hand was aching from punching the male. It was a painful reminder of the events of the evening.

By the time I arrived at hospital, I was much warmer. The ambulance officers and the people at the caravan park did a fantastic job getting my body temperature back up to 30.4°C by stripping my uniform and wrapping me in warm blankets. Prior to this incident, I had no clear idea what hypothermia was. But afterwards I did some research, with some startling results.

Apparently, the healthy core temperature for a human body is around 37°C. Hypothermia occurs when the body's temperature falls below 35°C. Coma occurs when the body's temperature falls below 32°C. Once the brain cools to around 30°C, the structure that regulates body temperature (the hypothalamus) stops working. This is fatal without prompt treatment. Mild hypothermia (32°C to 35°C body temperature) is usually easy to treat. However, the risk of death increases as the core body temperature drops below 32°C. If core body temperature is less than 28°C, the condition is life threatening without immediate medical attention.

The Inspector from Tuggerah Lakes LAC waited with me at the hospital while I underwent some tests. No one wanted to come near me, including the doctors, because they thought I was the crook. Some of the looks I got whilst I was there were full of loathing and disdain. In hindsight, it was understandable. I had a black beanie on my head and a scruffy beard, and I was covered in blankets and looked like police were guarding me, when they were just making sure I was okay.

It was only whilst I was at the hospital that I learnt the truth about the incident and the male in the water. It turned out that he wasn't fourteen and wasn't just a drink driver. Sure he was drunk, and more than likely affected by drugs, but he was nineteen, a well-known and high-risk offender within the command who had only just been released from gaol. The hatchback he had been driving was stolen and had a cache of stolen property inside. He was taken to Wyong Hospital and was apparently going off his head, threatening police and hospital staff. He even tried to bite the nurse who was taking his blood. He made threats and boasted to police that he would only be in custody for two years and then would be free.

It put a whole new complexion on the incident. I am sure that I probably would have done the same thing in trying to rescue him had I known the full story, despite many comments that I should have let him drown. Understandably, he was refused bail and was charged with a number of serious offences.

Sergeant O'Dwyer had already rung Rachael and told her briefly what had happened. She was at home trying to contend with our baby, who had a fever of 41°C. The Inspector rang Rachael at home so I could speak to her. It went a lot better than I thought it would. I wanted to go back to work and finish my shift, but both the doctor and the Inspector had other plans. The Inspector was a great support as he waited with me at the hospital, got a bright yellow police raincoat for me to wear, as I was only in my underwear, bought me a meal and drove me home. I tramped to my front door with my heart in my mouth. Rachael answered the door and was somewhat happy to see me. We didn't talk much about what happened; I just went into the bathroom and had a very long, hot bath.

For the first few days after the incident, I didn't sleep much at all. I think I was just trying to make myself tired so that when I did go to sleep I would be too exhausted to remember or relive what happened. It was a blessing that my nephew came to stay on the Tuesday night. We stayed up all night playing PS2. It really took my mind off things.

I knew I would struggle with what happened and that I needed to talk to someone about how I was feeling. I guess it was a blessing that I had been through so much in my career because I understood that it was okay to feel the way I did and that eventually, when I had accepted what I had been through, I would come out the other side stronger and wiser.

I had nightmares and flashbacks and broke down into tears a lot. I remember a few days afterwards I was feeling alright, because I wasn't focusing on the incident, until I got a text message from a mate at work offering support. That tipped me over the edge, as nice as it was to be cared about. I went for a drive and ended up at The Entrance, standing on the bridge, looking at the channel, in tears. Despite what you might be thinking, there was nothing untoward about my decision to end up where I was. It just gave me an opportunity to see things from a different angle and perspective. I couldn't believe how wide the channel was, or how far I had swum that night. I sent a text message to Sharpy, who just happened to be working out of The Entrance at that time. He agreed to meet me and we had a long and meaningful talk about how I was feeling, which was great.

I knew I had done the right thing; I was just fed up with things like this happening to me, which of course flowed onto my family. And what that male did, and what he tried to do, was unforgivable and was playing havoc with my head. I felt so much better after talking about it. I even went to the caravan park and tracked down the people who went out of their way to help during the rescue, both in and out of the water. They were all holidaying on the coast at the time of the incident and it was so great to find them and personally say thank you. I found out so much more about what happened from their perspective whilst I was in the water and after I lost consciousness.

The guys told me they had made numerous and urgent attempts to locate a boat that could be used in the rescue. They never gave up, even though people refused to help them. When they managed to locate a boat they assisted Shaun from the water and then rescued the male and myself. On shore they assisted Dave in rendering first aid to me whilst I was unconscious and suffering from hypothermia, which prevented life-threatening complications. They were also critical in directing the ambulance officers to my location to render further first aid. They all displayed selflessness in their actions and are responsible for my quick medical recovery. They even got some video footage of the early part of the incident, which I later watched. It looked so cold and dark in the water, even on the video.

There was talk about upgrading the assault police charges to a more serious offence of attempt drowning with intent to murder, but that was soon discarded. It really fucking pissed me off when I was told that. I felt so unimportant, like a number again, 30763. I had risked my life in the execution of my duties but wasn't given support by way of appropriate charges. I refused to go back to work, and certainly wasn't going to rush back. Why should I ever help anyone again if my life is worth nothing?

So I submitted a six-page report outlining the facts, stating case law and citing legislation to support more serious offences. Don't get me wrong, I wasn't trying to seek retribution for what he did. I'm hoping that the Courts will handle that for me in the sentencing. I just believed that the charges should reflect the level of criminality.

Even though it had been less than a week, I wanted to go back to work, and I felt a bit embarrassed about having time off. So the following Monday I decided I would give it a go. I didn't sleep well the night before and was terrified about how I would cope. It wasn't a good omen, and I probably should have listened to my body.

I didn't get to work early like I usually did and sat in my car outside the police station for about ten minutes trying to work up the courage to go inside. I was okay travelling to work until I got to The Entrance

Bridge and everything came flooding back to me. I eventually went inside and saw my teammates, hugged them, cried, spoke about what happened, cried some more and locked myself in a front room to do paperwork. I tried to help with the ongoing investigations, but Denise had everything under control. It wasn't long before the bosses came and saw me and told me to go home. A few police had raised concerns about me being at work and noticed that I wasn't coping. They were very understanding and made an appointment for me to see a counsellor from the EAP the following day in Newcastle.

I had tried my best to feel normal again by confronting how I felt, but I couldn't stay at work. I did feel so much better when I left knowing that I had tried and that it was okay to feel like I did and that people understood.

It's been amazing and completely opposite to any of the incidents I was involved in at Redfern. Since this incident, I received tremendous support from police, my family and my friends. Dave, who was also really instrumental in coordinating the rescue, GOD and my teammates were in regular contact with me, showing their support, which has been an amazing relief. It has blown me out of the water the difference in the level of care I have received compared to when I was at Redfern.

I even received some emails from Senior police:

*"I just wanted to congratulate you on the arrest of [the crook] on Monday night. He is a good crook and no doubt should be locked up. The fact that you pursued him into the water shows your great commitment to the job and your bravery. You are obviously a fine officer. I hope that you recovered from the hypothermia and that you will be right to get back into it when you return to work. The Police Force needs people like you. Congratulations on a job very well done."*

*(Deputy Commissioner)*

*"I just wanted to send (a belated note) to congratulate you on the arrest of the [crook] at The Entrance on 21 April. Jeff you showed great initiative, determination and courage in effecting this arrest. Well done and congratulations – it is great to see such good work."*

*(Assistant Commissioner)*

*"Having just read the incident on significant events about your arrest of the [crook] I felt compelled to congratulate you re the same. Reading about the brave actions of Police such as yourself reinvigorates my enthusiasm for the job that we do and reminds me of what Police work is all about. Mate you did a great job arresting that bloke, well done."*

*(Crime Manager)*

Talking to the counsellor from the EAP really helped. She was very understanding and really listened. I could see in her eyes that she understood and could feel the pain I was attempting to hide. The first session was spent talking about all my other incidents, which raised their ugly heads again as soon as this one was over. After a few visits, I considered going back to work. I was not afraid to open myself up, because I know it helps. I've been diagnosed with PTSD again but have learnt to live with it before and am confident about doing it again.

Strangely enough, a few days before this incident happened I was at a lecture about critical incidents and coping with stress amongst police. My friend Katie Sewell is the coordinator of the MATES program. I believe that this is an amazing idea that encourages police to help other police deal with and cope with work-related stress. There is no one else on this planet who can truly appreciate what life is like on the streets and the things we deal with on a daily basis than your workmates, especially when other Police Forces and Departments around the world have been using a similar system for many years. It's a groundbreaking program that will hopefully break the stigma of 'unpolice-like behaviour.' At least now I have a recent, relevant and local example to identify with. Katie has been amazing in her support for me as well. She calls often and takes the time to listen, which really helps.

I can joke about it now with pretty much everyone who knows about what happened. It's like the crooks look at my nametag now think, "Jeff Garland, I've heard of you. Let's see how tough you really are!" and then go and do something stupid and dangerous, knowing I will be close behind. Rachael reckons I am like a cat with nine lives. We worked it out and estimate that this was my eighth life. I honestly believe that something simple will be my undoing, like choking on a pea.

After being off work for over three weeks, I was feeling confident about being able to get back to work. I saw my counsellor for the fourth time and we went through the rollercoaster of emotions I went through during and after the incident. It was amazing to see her write down each individual emotion I felt before, during and since the incident. It filled half an A4 page. It made me reflect on and appreciate how I had succeeded against the odds. She agreed that I was ready to return to work, so on May 19th 2008, only a month after the incident, I donned my uniform again and got back to business. It felt so good to get full clearance from my doctor to return to work. My counsellor asked me how long it had been since I had cried, and I was proud to say it had been a while. Typically, on my way home from that session I cried with excitement when I thought about returning to work.

But the weekend before I was due to return I decided — I even spoke to Rachael about it — to quit the police and be medically discharged HOD. It could have been the fact that I was being made to see the Police Medical Officer (PMO) before I was allowed to be go back on the streets. Or my mind may have just felt that it was time to move on. It was certainly adding a new perspective to going back to work. It was so unlike me, but it felt even more liberating than when I received the clearance to go back to work.

Making the judgement to stay or go was very difficult and something I struggled to make a definite decision about. Some days I couldn't wait to go back, others I never wanted anything more to do with the police and the rest I just didn't know. My mind kept bouncing between these indecisions, which made life a bit of a challenge.

When I did arrive at the police station on that Monday morning to work with my teammates, I felt angry inside and hinted that I thought it was time to move on. My mood certainly didn't improve when I was called in to the Crime Manager's office to discuss the upgrading of the charges. Of course, I got upset and cried when I spoke about how I was feeling and what I believed was the appropriate charge, but ultimately the decision was to increase the charge to assault police occasioning actual bodily harm, because of my PTSD.

I felt frustrated and really disappointed with everything. I went and saw Rachael, who was working, and cried again, because I believed he deserved more serious charges and that my life was also worth more. She was supportive as always and helped me see that it really didn't matter what he was charged with, because the most important thing was that I was still alive and he was in gaol. I can understand what she was saying now and have accepted that there is nothing else I can do.

There was some good news, though. The crook pleaded guilty to all of the charges, which meant I didn't have to relive any of the incident in the witness box. I was adamant that I would be sitting in the front row when he was sentenced. But it was a few weeks away and I had other things to focus on.

It was time to head to Sydney for the medical clearance from the PMO. I had been there before for my other incidents and wasn't that impressed in the past. But this time I was keen to give it a go. I had been wondering for days whether I should just surrender and get out while I was still alive, but I decided I really wanted to give it another try. The fact that the offender pleaded guilty, that I was able to return to work and had a lot more support than in the early part of my policing career, made the pendulum swing towards giving my career another chance.

So after answering endless questions about what had happened and how I was feeling and a 567-question computer assessment, I was given the all clear to return to full duties. I was relieved and happy and so was Rachael. I was getting sick of sitting in the station answering the telephones, although it was a lot less stressful then working out on the streets.

When I got back to the police station I found a copy of the 000 and police radio tape of the incident in my pigeon hole. I was eager to listen to what was on it to hear what was happening outside of the water, but a little hesitant in case it tipped me back over the edge. It would have been good to listen to it before I saw the PMO, but it really wasn't as bad as I thought it would be. There was a lot of confusion and extended breaks of silence, which, at times, mirrored the emptiness that I had felt in the water as the other police tried their best to resolve the situation. Just as in the incident with the Ute, it was good to get another perspective. Thanks to all of the support from my workmates, family and friends, I believed I could make a full recovery.

About two months after the incident in The Entrance Channel, I went back to work, fully operational for the first time. Although it was very uncomfortable, especially having to drive over the bridge every shift, I managed to survive. I was adamant that I was going to stay out of trouble…!

## Chapter Eighteen:
# Welcome Back

Of course, it wasn't long before I was in the thick of it again… on my first shift back. I was working with a junior Constable and a new Probationer out of The Entrance on the primary response vehicle, TL25. I tried to slow myself down and take a step back, but I think the peaceful transition back to work lasted less than two hours.

Being a Friday night, there was always the possibility of detecting a drink driver during the course of the shift. Little did I know that what started as a simple vehicle stop for a random breath test would turn into something much more.

I was driving west along the main road that connected The Entrance area and Wyong shire when I observed an old white utility driving in the opposite direction towards me. Although that was nothing unusual, my interest was piqued when the vehicle pulled to the shoulder of the road and the female passenger got out and began walking away. I turned around and pulled in behind the utility, noticing that the driver had also exited and was arguing with the female. Concerned for her welfare, I enquired whether she needed any assistance, only to be abused: "We're having a fucking domestic so fuck off. It's private."

It was quite obvious that they were both well affected by alcohol, and the driver was bleeding from an injury to his right hand. I decided to separate the parties and subject the driver to a breath test, which didn't run as smoothly as I had hoped. Not only did the male deny being intoxicated, but he stated that he wasn't driving, even though he was informed that he had been observed driving the vehicle by police and an inspection of the driver's side revealed blood on the steering wheel, keys and inside the driver's door, consistent with his injury.

After much objection, the male submitted to a breath test, which recorded a reading of 0.197, which was almost four times the legal limit. When he was informed that he was under arrest for the purpose of a breath analysis, it was on for young and old.

He became enraged and lunged towards the new Probationer, who was standing nearby. Fearing for the officer's safety, I grabbed the male's arm and said, "Move away," which he kind of did by pushing me towards a nearby railing.

We ended up wrestling over the railing and onto the ground before he was restrained against the police car and arrested for assault police. The female then decided to get involved by grabbing her partner and attempting to pull him away from us. She had to be dragged away kicking and screaming. This just aggravated the male, who began flinging his arms about in an attempt to assist his girlfriend before being physically restrained on the ground and handcuffed.

The female was still struggling with my offsiders on the ground as I attempted to put the male into the rear of the caged truck. He barged me with his shoulder and attempted to move towards the girl but was forced into the rear cage of the police vehicle.

However, as I tried to close the door, he kicked it and tried to escape. I told him that he would be sprayed with OC spray if he continued to cause trouble. Ignorant to the consequences or oblivious to my direction, he continued to kick the door and move towards the rear of the caged vehicle, trying to jump out.

I was in danger of being overpowered. I couldn't close the caged door of the truck and my two off-siders were busy with the female, so I directed the Probationer to call for urgent assistance. I removed my OC spray from its pouch. I pointed the spray at the male and warned him again to stop before deploying a one-second burst into his face, which had little effect. It was the first time in my career that I had used my OC spray. Normally I would rely on pure physical strength, but because of the situation I realised I had no choice.

The male continued to move towards the door and kick out at me. During the scuffle, I was affected by the OC spray. The male began to feel the effects of the spray and started to settle down. Within a short time another police car arrived and both offenders were restrained and conveyed to The Entrance Police Station. The Inspector just laughed at me and shook his head when I got back, calling me a 'shit magnet.'

The male and female continued to be aggressive and to swear whilst in custody, making threats, saying, "Wait till I see you in the park and you haven't got your boys — you're gone!"

Surprisingly, the male submitted to a breath analysis, which recorded a reading of 0.130. They were both charged and bailed to appear at Court. Even more surprising is that a few weeks later, I received letters from both of them apologising for their actions that night, stating how lucky they were to get pulled over, asking for forgiveness and explaining how embarrassed they were by their actions.

I honestly thought that they were going to plead not guilty and that the Court would have to decide. Of course, they were both convicted, and I'm sure their letter was taken into account at the sentencing.

## GOING OFF

I was sure the next night shift wouldn't be as 'interesting' as the last. It couldn't be! And for the first half of the shift it was business as usual, until the early hours of the morning…BEEP…BEEP—a report over police radio about a female 'going off' in a local suburb. It got called once, twice and still no one was available to acknowledge. I was working by myself as an alpha unit, so on an officer safety level it wasn't deemed appropriate for me to attend to the call, but the reports were being updated that the female had assaulted a number of people and caused damage to property.

I informed Police Radio that I would attend, Code Red, under lights and sirens, but I was still about ten minutes away and the closest back-up was about fifteen minutes off. As I drove through the empty streets with the silence of the night broken by the sound of the wailing sirens, I made the decision to put on my protective leather gloves, just in case. It turned out to be a very wise decision.

As I pulled into the street, deciding whether to wait for assistance, I was confronted with an angry and disheveled female charging towards me up the road, yelling and screaming. Her clothes were torn and tattered and covered with stains from the blood that was pouring from a wound on her hand. Because of her close proximity, I didn't have the opportunity to draw my OC spray to subdue her, so

I grabbed the arm that was bleeding, twisted it and flung her to the ground. She was strong for a petite-looking female and covered head to toe with blood—hopefully only her own. It was obvious that she had taken some form of stimulant.

As I attempted to restrain her on the ground, kicking and screaming and obviously very unhappy, further police arrived to assist me. It didn't stop her, though. She continued her violent and abusive tirade, even as the ambulance officers treated her injuries.

It took four of us to lift her off the ground and carry her to the police caged truck. It wasn't an option for her to be conveyed in the ambulance because she was a serious risk to herself and others. She continued to thrash her body about and wave her arms around, despite being badly injured and handcuffed, until finally we were able to close the door to the truck, with the sounds of her echoing thumps as she kicked and screamed.

As the female was conveyed to the hospital by police under ambulance escort, I attempted to unravel the events of the evening that had led to her arrest. I spoke to a number of neighbours, who confirmed that she was out of control, assaulting residents and punching her hand through windows and threatening to kill everyone. It wasn't your normal case of a disgruntled neighbour lashing out, but something fuelled by alcohol, drugs and possibly mental health issues.

I stayed long enough to get some brief details of the victims and witnesses and take photos of the damage before I headed to the hospital to assist the other police and ambulance staff, as it was obvious she was going to be a handful. So it wasn't too surprising when I got to the hospital and walked into the emergency area to see the female being held down by four police, a security guard and two nurses whilst the doctor attempted to sedate her. I jumped in to hold her down to give one of the nurses a break. She was incredibly strong, and the doctor thought she may have taken GHB or speed.

After several injections, the female slowly drifted off to sleep, with an appointment made for her to see the mental health specialist upon her recovery. The hospital was told that we were to be contacted once the female had been assessed and prior to her release. With their assurances, we left the hospital to resume our duties and complete our reports, only to discover that later that day she had been released without our knowledge or consent and was on the run.

It wasn't long after these incidents when I was working day shift with a new Probationer and we received a call about a drug-affected male who had locked himself in the car boot of a resident of the local caravan park. When we arrived at the scene, we were directed to the sedan by the owner and confirmed that he was still hiding inside. Not sure if he was armed or injured, we knocked on the boot to evoke some type of conscious response. No luck. As we carefully opened the boot, with my partner and I standing to each side of the car for officer safety reasons, the male burst out and lunged at me with a knife in his hand. I recoiled back to avoid the blade, only to see my novice cohort grab the male's arm holding the knife and fling him to the ground, centimetres from me. That was too close. I'm glad I decided to adhere to my training and stand at the side of the car, otherwise there would have been no time for either of us to react. After being disarmed and handcuffed, the male was conveyed to the police station for charging. Grateful for his swift thinking, I thanked my saviour for his intervention and recommended that a notation be made on his permanent record for his efforts.

## THE SENTENCING

A couple of days later, I learnt that the crook who tried to drown me in The Entrance Channel was being sentenced in July. Although it was a relief that I wouldn't have to give evidence and relive the terror of the evening and how I have felt since, there was still a bitter taste left by the fact that he should have been facing more serious charges in a Court of higher jurisdiction. I guess it will just have to be something I learn to live with.

I was adamant that I was going to be at the sentencing so I could be part of the process and hopefully get some closure. I was very nervous and apprehensive about going, but it felt like something I had to do. Luckily, the date of the sentence was during a shift when my team was working, so there were no rostering issues or problems with the Supervisors about me attending.

Compared to the calamity of the night, the Courtroom seemed almost serene as my anticipation grew for the matter to be finalised. When he was finally brought into the Courtroom from custody, a flood of memories came rushing back. I just peered at him, wondering how someone so young could be so brutal and acerbic. But I had no sympathy for him. He had made his own decisions in life and now had to suffer the consequences.

The Magistrate was cognisant of the fact that I was present in the Court, which I believed added more of a human face to the incident and reflected how serious the incident was.

As the accused sat shackled in the dock wearing his prison greens, his solicitor offered a belated apology, stating that it was an "appalling set of circumstances" following a binge of drugs and about forty alcoholic drinks, which is probably why he wasn't affected by hypothermia. Remarkably, he couldn't remember anything about the night, which just added insult to injury. He had no defence. The Magistrate in sentencing the male considered his "atrocious criminal record" and commented that his actions were "outrageous," declaring that "the police have an incredibly difficult job" and "deserve the full protection of the Court" when they are assaulted whilst executing their duties.

It was great to hear such support from the Magistrate, and I was hoping that the sentence would reflect that opinion, and to some extent it did. Overall, he was sentenced to two years and nine months' imprisonment for his actions.

I left the Court feeling satisfied that there was some form of finality to it all. A tidal wave of emotion flowed over me as I walked to my car, and I spoke to Rachael about the result. It felt like a huge burden had been shifted and an empty space left in its place, tremendous relief tinged with disappointment that maybe he should have been locked up for a long time. But it was an opportunity to try to put the incident behind me.

## WORLD CHAMPIONS II AND III

For the rest of 2008 and early in 2009 I focused my attention on planning activities that were more positive and community focused — more Guinness World Record™ events for charity: darts and cricket.

In August 2008, three of my mates — Tony Gafa, Ian Van Veen, John Goggin — and I took part in the Guinness World Record™ attempt at the Longest Dart Marathon at Erina Fair on the Central Coast to raise money for the Westpac Rescue Helicopter Service as an expression of gratitude for the tremendous service it provides to the people of New South Wales.

In February 2007, my step-sister (in-law), Amanda Butler, was involved in a serious motor vehicle accident at Warialda, near Inverell in northern NSW, that unfortunately killed two young people, seriously injuring four others. If that wasn't bad enough, while responding to the tragedy, the Westpac Rescue Helicopter crashed, but selflessly the medical staff on-board were not deterred, hitching a ride to the accident scene to assist the occupants, whilst another rescue helicopter was deployed.

Although Mandy, fourteen, died a few days later, the efforts of those on-board the Westpac Rescue Helicopter that day kept her alive long enough for her family to visit the Children's Hospital in Sydney and say their farewells.

Whilst organising the challenge, Gafa was involved in a serious motor vehicle accident himself at work that resulted in he and a passenger being airlifted to John Hunter Hospital by the Westpac Rescue Helicopter Service. Although he survived, we joked that we now had to raise double the amount of money — to pay for the flight.

Prior to our endeavours, the benchmark was twenty-five hours and thirty-four minutes set in the United Kingdom in 2007. Although we certainly weren't professional darts players, we were keen to give it our best.

Let's just say that when we started and finished, the weather was okay at best, but during the night it was cold and pouring rain. Luckily, we had set up under a canopy in the outdoor area of the shopping centre, so we were able to huddle together and keep fairly dry.

The competition between us was very close until the early hours of the morning when the quality of the darts dropped. We weren't the best players to start with, just socially competitive in Gafa's garage every chance we got. But as soon as the sun came up in the morning and the finish line was in sight, the games were close and of very high quality.

We broke the existing record around lunchtime and played almost another two hours to set a new benchmark of twenty-seven hours and twenty-two minutes, which has officially been recognised as a Guinness World Record™ and is listed in the 2010 Guinness World Record™ Book. It was very rewarding to undertake the event with such good mates and to raise money for the Westpac Rescue Helicopter

Service. The fact that we are all now Guinness World Record™ holders is just a bonus. It was a very enjoyable experience, and I'm sure that when our record inevitably falls, we will consider another challenge. But for now we will all just bask in the glory.

In October 2008, I was awarded the Rotary Club of Australia's 'Pride of Workmanship' Award for my policing and community work, which was humbling, especially because my wife, GOD and his partner tried to keep it a secret from me.

As soon as I finished that attempt, I got straight onto my latest effort in February 2009, which was the 'Cops 4 Kids World Record Cricket Challenge' at Pat Morley Oval, Bateau Bay, challenging the Guinness World Record™" for the 'Longest Cricket Marathon' to raise money for 'Central Coast Kids In Need.' At the time I contemplated the attempt, about twelve months earlier, the record was only around thirty-six hours, but by the time it was our turn, the record had exploded to fifty-five hours, held by New Zealand.

This was the biggest and hardest event I had ever organised, with two teams of NSW Police taking part to show that police care about the local communities they serve. The teams were made up of experienced cricketers to first-timers and hackers like me and ranged in rank from Constable to Superintendent. On the day of the event there was an electric atmosphere, and the local community had embraced it warmly.

Luckily, I found out before we started that a team in Newcastle had broken the record about two weeks earlier, increasing the record to around sixty-six hours. Thankfully, I had planned the attempt around sixty-eight hours, which gave us some breathing room. It really wasn't what I wanted because I know how hard it is to coordinate such an attempt, and to take the record from them within a short period was very unfortunate and certainly not planned.

Not surprisingly, the weather forecast was for rain, and it didn't disappoint. As per the dart attempt, the endeavour started under clear skies, with the hottest day on record for about twenty years, but over the course of the match we endured rain, pouring rain, gale-force winds, thunder, lightning, hail and the coldest night on record. Thankfully, the umpires agreed to play through the majority of the conditions, with the field covered in a sea of bright yellow fluorescent police raincoats. Unfortunately, Guinness World Record™ guidelines required us to stop play, and the clock, in the event of lightning.

Luckily, we only lost around fifty minutes, so we were still on-target to break the record at the scheduled finishing time.

The attempt was hard enough with fatigue and lack of sleep set to challenge us, but the torrential inclement weather added a level of difficulty and discomfort we did not expect. Injuries were a growing problem, too, with players succumbing to leg and knee problems, but they were courageous enough to continue to the end.

The batting and bowling styles were at times glorious and verging on scary as everyone tried their best. It was a great atmosphere, despite the weather and lack of sleep. I proved my lack of ability without troubling the scoreboard on more than one occasion and managed to finish the attempt with only two hours' sleep.

We broke the New Zealand and unofficial records before we somewhat cruised towards our 8 a.m. finish. According to our records, we played for about sixty-seven hours and nine minutes when we 'pulled up stumps.' There was a crowd of friends, family, police and members of the community to cheer us on as we walked off the field for the final time, successful in our mission.

I admit that I made mistakes and should have just either played or organised, not both. It was just too much work for one person. I think I was getting on people's nerves, making sure that the breaks were calculated correctly and play resumed on time, but unfortunately we had rules and guidelines to abide by, otherwise the attempt would not be valid and all of the hard effort would have been for nothing. It was a lot of pressure, but all the players, volunteers, witnesses and umpires had given up their time, so I wanted to make sure their efforts were recognised with a Guinness World Record™.

A few months after the event had finished and the paperwork had been sent to England for verification, we were informed that we were the new Guinness World Record™ holders for this category, and we were also listed in the 2010 Guinness World Record™ Book. It was a great result, and I am very proud of all the players, volunteers, sponsors and media that supported our efforts.

## Chapter Nineteen:
# It's Not Fair

Sometimes this job really sucks. There are times when you just think it is not worth the pain, frustration, nightmares and anxiety, when you just want to turn your back on the job you love and curl up in a ball and hide. For me this was one such incident.

It was the weekend before Australia Day 2009, and kids were enjoying their last few days of freedom before returning to school the following week. It was a gorgeous sunny day, with the parks and beaches filled with families celebrating.

I was rostered on the afternoon car at 3 p.m. with Paul, a Leading Senior Constable who is a top bloke and a great cop. In the eighteen months I had been at Tuggerah Lakes, I hadn't had the opportunity to work with him, and whenever I hinted that we should work together he joked that his life insurance had expired or he had other commitments. Well, at least I think he was joking!

I think that within the first ten minutes of our shift I surrendered the driving to him so that I could conduct checks on our Mobile Data Terminals (MDTs, or in-car computers) to try to find stolen cars, which I think we were both happier doing. It wasn't really a busy afternoon, so there was a chance to enjoy the scenery.

But within a few hours the festive mood of the weekend was shattered when Police Radio broadcast a job at the northern end of the LAC. It took a few minutes to sink in and to verify that it wasn't a hoax call, but I fuckin' wish it was.

A member of the community had called 000, reporting that a teenage girl had jumped off a bridge and hadn't resurfaced. It was very confusing when a similar call came in about a different location, but as soon as the operator uttered the words "they could feel one of her feet," it really hit home.

Without hesitation, we acknowledged the job and activated the lights and sirens, with other cars responding similarly. We were still in The Entrance area and some ten minutes off when the call came in, but I already started emptying my pockets and untying my shoes. I was ready and prepared to jump in the water again if that was what I had to do. It was like a switch that gets flicked, and there was no fighting it.

Within minutes, my earlier saviours from The Entrance Channel, Dave and Shaun, had arrived at the scene with another Constable named Clint. They dove into the water without hesitation and did what they could to assist in searching for the girl. They requested that the Royal Volunteer Coastguard be notified to activate a diver to be on standby at the park, just in case. As we were passing the coastguard, we decided to divert and seek assistance. Paul asked if I wanted to keep going, because he knew that I wanted to get in and search for the girl, so it was my decision. We went to the Coastguard, but no one was there.

By the time we got to the park where the bridge was, there were already a number of police and ambulances in attendance and the girl had been dragged from the water, unconscious and not breathing.

By all reports, the girl was jumping from the footbridge with friends when she didn't resurface. Surprisingly, it wasn't a location or activity considered dangerous, with kids and adults having jumped safely into the water for the past forty years without serious incident.

Because she didn't come back up, the alarm was raised, with members of the public, who were at the park spending time with their families, selflessly and bravely searching for her by diving into the deep murky waters, but without success. When Dave, Clint and Shaun arrived, they removed their appointments and shoes and without hesitation jumped into the water and took over the search. Clint continued to dive and only resurfaced to take another breath before descending again. Dave commandeered a boat in preparation for the event that she was located, which was brought to the incident sight.

After about ten minutes, the lifeless body of the girl was dragged from the water by Clint and a member of the public, who hoisted her onto the boat where an ambulance officer immediately reached over and commenced CPR. As she was taken to shore, the lifesaving treatment continued, before she was transferred into an awaiting ambulance with further paramedics assisting.

I ran from the vehicle and tried to assist where I could in identifying witnesses and those involved in the rescue. The girl's mother was understandably hysterical and needed to be restrained and sedated. Dave offered to drive the ambulance with the girl to the hospital to allow the paramedics to work on her en-route. Clint clambered into the other ambulance with the mother and drove it close behind.

Paul and I attended the hospital to check on our colleagues and the condition of the girl. Apart from being saturated and worn out from their efforts physically, they were fine. But this wasn't the type of incident you could walk away from without being affected personally or professionally.

Because I had been in situations before where things were unnaturally demanding, I took it upon myself just to make sure they were coping okay. Being the tough coppers they were, they tried to shake it off, but I offered my assistance and contacted Katie from the MATES program to let her know what had unfolded and that her assistance might be required.

A short while later, we went inside to speak to the doctors and were told that she was putting up a great fight. I knew it was going to be hard to confront, but I went into the cubicle where she was being treated. It is an image I will never forget and that has been indelibly burnt into my memory. She reminded me so much of my eldest daughter, and honestly that is all I could think of. It really hurt and was very painful, but luckily for us, the night crew would be investigating the matter.

Paul and I went back to the police station at Wyong to make enquiries in relation to another matter, only to be directed by the night Supervisor to take over the investigation. I couldn't believe it. It was hard enough being there for a short time, let alone having a prolonged involvement. I know it sounds selfish, but I could already feel that

I wasn't coping, and I should have said something to someone. I couldn't even ring Rachael because I knew I would have broken down. I had to be tough and professional. That's what cops are, isn't it?

By the time Paul and I got back to the hospital they had arranged for the Westpac Rescue Helicopter to convey her to another hospital in Newcastle for specialist treatment. She was still fighting, but the outcome still looked bleak. The girl's mum was at the hospital being treated for shock as a result of what happened, which is not surprising. I don't think any parent could endure such a reality. Her mum and grandmother kept a bedside vigil, holding her hand, talking to her and kissing her face. It was heartbreaking, but it wasn't about me. This family was in the middle of a tragedy and fighting and praying for their little angel to survive, so I needed to be strong for them as a policeman and a member of the human race.

Over the next few hours, the girl's condition deteriorated, so by the time the helicopter arrived they had an uphill battle to save her. But they were inspiring to watch in action and they never gave up. It got to the stage where they needed extra hands, so I stepped in and assisted in her treatment. It wasn't much, but at least I wasn't feeling as helpless anymore — standing around watching this innocent girl die.

Paul was awesome. He offered to be in charge of the investigation, which was a relief, because that's just the sort of bloke he was — professional and dependable. He knew I wasn't coping and was a great support.

Once the girl had stabilised again, I was able to step outside. I rang and spoke to Katie from MATES and apprised her of the situation. She could tell I wasn't coping, probably from my blubbering on the phone. I just wanted to make sure there were support services available for the family and the police involved because this was going to hit everyone hard. She arranged for the Police Chaplain to contact me, just to make sure I was okay, even though I tried to convince her otherwise.

When I finished the phone call, I went to go back inside when I was informed by a member of the public about an incident that had occurred in a nearby carpark within the hospital grounds. Reluctantly, I went around the front of the hospital to see people arguing. One of the males was aggressive and affected by alcohol. I managed to separate them only to hear the male justify himself by complaining about his niece who had just drowned. I couldn't believe it. It couldn't be the same girl. Sure, he had the right to be upset, but for it to manifest in this way was not going to help anyone. I managed to settle him down and told him that if he didn't control himself, he wouldn't be allowed in the hospital. That would be the last thing anyone needed. So after I warned security, I went back into the emergency room and updated Paul.

About four hours after the incident, it seemed that her condition was deteriorating, and her vital signs were decreasing. I must imagine it was a heart-wrenching decision by the doctors to cancel the transfer to Newcastle because she just wasn't stabilised and wouldn't have survived the flight. They were so supportive and professional when they broke the news to the mother. I stayed with the girl as the mother was comforted by family and watched as one of the pilots stood over the girl and prayed for her safe delivery to the afterlife.

The mother and grandmother came back into the room and began saying their goodbyes — not that there could ever be enough time to say what you need to say. That was too much for me. All I could think was how I would feel if it was one of my girls. I would wish the world would just open up and swallow me. I could only imagine how hard it was for them. One minute she was a bright, happy, typical teenager frolicking around with her friends, and the next she was dying in a hospital bed.

About five hours after she was brought into the emergency room, fighting with every ounce of strength she had left, the doctors turned off all the equipment that had been keeping her alive. As the minutes passed and we all silently prayed, she slipped away peacefully, a victim of tragedy eternally etched into our hearts and minds.

Throughout the day I had kept in constant contact with the guys involved in her rescue, just updating them on how she was going. Even though they had finished their shift, they were still thinking of her and no doubt wondering what could have been done differently. But ultimately there is nothing more anyone could have done. It is because of the brave and selfless actions of the police, ambulance, medical staff and members of the public that her family was able to say goodbye before she passed away. It was a traumatising incident for everyone involved, but I guess I just took it too personally.

For the next hour, Paul and I made arrangements for her body to be conveyed to the Morgue for a post-mortem examination to determine the cause of death, whilst the family was ready to release her. We instructed them that there was no rush and to take their time in saying their final goodbyes. Over the next hour, a flood of family and close friends came to pay their respects to this young life tragically cut short. It was difficult to watch, with all of the emotions floating around. I went outside and received a call from the Police Chaplain, who I spoke to briefly. I wouldn't go into the details of how I was feeling because that would mean I had to accept it was real. I gave an overview of the incident and forwarded the details of the other police involved, just so he could touch base and make sure that they were okay.

When I went inside, the mother approached Paul and me and tearfully thanked us for our support and asked us to pass on her gratitude to all of the police involved.

It was an agonisingly long shift, and it took us until finish time to get everything organised. I went home and collapsed into Rachael's arms. I think I cried all the way home. I was a mess. I couldn't stop thinking about the girl lying on the table, feeling so helpless and picturing my daughter. It was the worst feeling I have ever felt, and something that I haven't been able to forget. I know that I gave my girls the biggest hugs of their lives, especially the eldest daughter. I still get very emotional over it now.

I didn't sleep very much, and when I managed to roll out of bed I felt even worse. I knew it was happening again. I spent most of the day on the phone to the other police involved, checking on them. I went to work and struggled through the first half of the shift, but it was obvious to my teammates that I wasn't coping. It was too personal for me, and I know that I shouldn't let it affect me that way, but sometimes it is hard to divorce yourself from your surroundings.

I spoke to a few police during the night, including Dave and GOD. I felt so stupid and guilty about how I was feeling because I didn't lose a daughter; I didn't have to jump into the water to find her. I just couldn't control how overwhelming it was for me. I was taking the job too personally, and that was not a good sign.

Just after midnight I was directed to return to the station for a meeting, which I knew had to do with the way I was feeling. A short time later the chaplain arrived, and I broke down as soon as I saw him because I knew it meant I had to talk about how I was feeling and I wasn't ready to do that. We spoke for a few minutes, but I didn't let my defences down too much, just enough to reflect that I needed help and shouldn't be at work. He referred me to a specialist, and I packed my bags and went home early.

The funeral was a few days later, and some of the guys were considering going, and it was something I had always planned to do, but on the morning of the funeral I just couldn't do it. I broke down crying at work at just the thought of reliving it again, and with all of the emotion that was going to be expressed during the ceremony it would just make me feel worse. I spoke to Rachael, Sharpy and GOD, and I couldn't even talk about it with them over the phone without getting upset. It would have been a bad choice to go, so I decided to engross myself in my work.

I know it was just a freak accident and that there was nothing more anybody could have done, but it just sucks and is so frustrating that people who intentionally hurt or endanger people's lives or threaten self-harm manage to walk away and yet young, innocent people are taken away. You see it on television all the time, how people in stolen cars or young hoons crash and end up killing other people. It's not fair...especially considering the cases of the bloke on Crackneck Lookout or in The Entrance Channel that I risked my life to save...and even more so considering these...

## ATTEMPTED SUICIDE

It was a few months later when I was working with Denise out of the Toukley area in a caged truck when a message came over police radio in relation to a male who was missing and threatening self-harm. Apparently he had been charged with a sexual assault and been advised to plead guilty and serve his time, which obviously didn't go down too well. Paul was the officer taking the report and speaking to the family. As there was regular contact between the accused and his family via text message, confirming that he was serious about his threats, we were able to conduct a phone triangulation that would give us an idea of where he may be located.

Once it was discovered that he was in the vicinity of the Ourimbah State Forest, Denise and I offered to help in the search. We went out to the area, which had one main road with lots of little tracks and plenty of bushland and properties that he could hide in. The fact that it was late at night and extremely dark made the job even harder.

We searched every track and every property without success, but as he had confirmed through a conversation with his son that he was definitely in that area, we couldn't just give up. He was even boasting, taunting us that we would "never find him" and that he planned on going down with a fight.

After about an hour of searching, Paul and his offsider joined us in our endeavours, with his family close in tow. They were still in contact with the male and were certain he was close by. Denise and I ended up taking the eldest son up a dirt track that ran over a mountain where they used to ride their trail bikes. The son was ringing him to get updates on his location, but he continued to speak in riddles, elevating our concern for his mental stability. He was certain that he was still in his new Toyota Hilux and had his headlights on, which should have made it easy for us to find him as long as we were looking in the right area.

We had driven several kilometres along a rocky road when a flash of headlights came over the hill on the western side. I quickly rang Paul and asked him to return. However, I couldn't wait. The father wasn't expecting his son to be with us, but coming alone in his car with us standing off would look too suspicious and may cause him to panic and attempt self-harm. Denise and I agreed to head towards the lights and hope for the best.

As we drove up the hill and down the embankment, I put the high beams on to disorient him and disguise our vehicle, but nothing prepared us for what confronted us. There was the male sitting in the driver's seat of his vehicle with the window partially wound down. His Ute was facing directly towards us and backed up close to a tree.

The first thing I noticed was a rope tied to the towbar of his Ute, leading up over a branch about five metres off the ground and then running back towards the driver's door with the rope through the window and…around his neck. I froze. I didn't know whether to ram his truck so he couldn't go forward or strategically retreat and try to negotiate. I even considered shooting at the rope, country and western style.

Instinctively, I jumped out of the police truck, with the son close behind, and started running towards him, hoping that the sight of his son would stop him. Instead, he floored it; the engine roared loudly, but the truck didn't move. It was still in park. The son was the first to the Ute, grabbing the keys through the partially opened driver's window before the man could change gears into drive. I tried to open the door, but it was locked, so I squeezed my arm in to grab the noose from around his neck, but he was pulling away, causing the rope to tighten. I removed my torch from its carrier and started hitting his window with all my strength.

I was stunned to see the suicidal male lean towards me, look directly into my eyes and say, "Hey, don't break my window!"

I couldn't believe it. Here he was in the process of committing suicide and he was worried about me damaging his car. All I could reply was "You're joking, aren't you?"

As the male kept pulling away, I continued to belt the window until Paul's offsider went around to the passenger door. This caused the male to focus on him and lean in my direction, allowing me to reach through the window and remove the rope from around his neck. I instantly opened the driver's door and yanked the male out of the vehicle and onto the road, where Denise restrained him without too much resistance. I couldn't believe it.

I walked up to Paul and Sergeant Ross and said, "That's it. I quit."

If he hadn't had the car in park when he accelerated, he would have ripped his head off right in front of us, not to mention in front of his own son. It was clear from the empty cans of alcohol on the ground that he had been there a while and had a bit to drink. It was also certain that he had put some planning and research into the method he chose.

The male was taken to hospital for mental assessment and treatment. He also made certain admissions during the course of the evening about his alleged criminal activity, which I am sure the DPP were happy to find out about.

## I'VE HAD ENOUGH

Over the next few weeks it was becoming clear that the job was getting to me. I was working by myself one night when a job came over about a girl armed with a knife at a refuge, smashing the place up and inflicting self-harm. It was also reported that she was suffering from communicable diseases, which made any interaction with her risky. I acknowledged the job over the police radio and proceeded to the location. Dave and Paul were in the local police truck and asked that I wait for them, which I was happy to do, but when the ambulance drove straight past me and to the front door of the premises, I was concerned because they didn't have the protection of OC spray or a firearm.

By the time I got out of the car, the ambulance officers had already gone inside. I didn't have a choice, so I had to make a *split second* decision. I informed the Police Radio of the situation, only to find that they had had prior dealings with her and already had her complying with their requests to go to the hospital.

When Dave and Paul arrived, they just shook their heads in disapproval, but what was I to do? If the girl wasn't compliant and was still armed, the ambulance officers could have been in real trouble. I tried to explain the situation, but they could see an unhealthy pattern emerging of me getting involved in too many risky situations. I returned to my car with my hands shaking from the adrenaline. Situations like this were becoming far too common.

I managed to go most of the night without too much dilemma until I saw an old station wagon driving towards me along the Pacific Highway, Tuggerah. I checked the vehicle on the MDT and discovered that it was suspected to have been involved in a break and enter offence the previous evening. So I spun around, informed the Police Radio of the situation and attempted to stop the vehicle. I activated the lights, but no response. I turned on the siren, still no response. The driver just looked at me in the rear-view mirror and kept driving slowly away.

I informed Police Radio that the vehicle was refusing to stop and that I was in pursuit, albeit at a snail's pace. I managed to follow the vehicle south along the Pacific Highway, updating my locations along the way. The Duty Officer from Brisbane Water LAC, where the pursuit had entered, was ready with road spikes farther down the road, which would seemingly end this embarrassment of a pursuit.

That was until the crook got to a residential area about 5kms later, that he seemed familiar with, and accelerated harshly to about 90km/hr, cutting corners and driving on the wrong side of the road. He weaved over the road and drove around a large block before entering a unit complex, going down a hill and colliding with the front of a house. Before the vehicle had even stopped, the driver jumped out the door and ran into the darkness. I tried to keep him in sight but lost him in the rabbit-warren-like complex. We set up a perimeter and searched the area, but without success.

I was pissed that he had managed to get away. I was taking it personally and was annoyed at myself for something that was out of my control. Yet another sign that things were unravelling. After the search had been abandoned and the police had returned to their duties, I was debriefed by the Duty Officer.

The owner of the unit the car had collided with told me she had been sitting at the front window on her computer seconds before the impact. If the vehicle hadn't swerved left as the driver jumped out, there was a distinct possibility that she could have been injured. All that was left to do was get the vehicle towed and forensically examined.

Until…a neighbour next to the damaged unit came out and said that she had heard noise in her yard a short time earlier in the opposite direction to where we were searching. I think more out of a sense of public safety than anything else, Paul walked down the laneway to appease the frantic female, only to almost step on the driver, who was hiding near the fence.

"I've got him," he shouted as Dave and I went to his assistance.

I couldn't believe it. We must have searched for over thirty minutes to the east, and here he was hiding within ten metres of us to the west.

Although he didn't admit to being the driver, he was conveyed to the hospital for blood tests and then to the police station, where he was charged. Surprisingly, the vehicle was not stolen; it was registered and insured, and he was fully licensed and not affected by alcohol or drugs. He just panicked. He ended up getting bail refused and pleaded guilty to driving in a manner dangerous and failing to stop after an accident, for which he was sentenced to nine months' imprisonment.

It was a great result but another indicator that I needed a change of scenery. My relationship with my family was also seriously under threat because of the pressure I was under from being back in uniform.

## Chapter Twenty:
# The Promotion

I was proud that I had made the decision to return to uniformed work, but after the incidents I had been involved in over the previous eighteen months it was clear that I was heading down a familiar path, towards a relapse of PTSD. I needed to get out of Tuggerah Lakes. I certainly considered walking away from the police, like I had in the past, but that was a decision I didn't want to make. I loved my job and didn't want to let PTSD end my career. I wasn't ready. My saving grace was that I had been on the Sergeant's promotions list for about sixteen months, which would offer me a chance to try something different somewhere else. I hadn't really seen anything that interested me. Sure, I applied for some positions, but I wasn't offered anything.

It was becoming rather frustrating, but around this time I noticed a few Police Prosecutor positions within Legal Services (now known as the Prosecutions Command) as both Sergeant and Senior Sergeant in various locations around NSW. I thought that this would be a good opportunity to do something I enjoyed in a much safer environment and honour my thoughts of someday returning to the Courts.

I spoke to Rachael about the option of going back to work five days a week and even moving to the country if it was something we both wanted. She was very supportive and glad that I was seriously considering leaving the frontline. So I took a gamble and applied for Prosecuting Sergeant at Cessnock, Proactive Team Supervisor at Queanbeyan and Prosecuting Senior Sergeant at Coffs Harbour, Downing Centre and Parramatta Children's Court. I didn't have much hope but had to take a chance.

I took some much needed leave over the Easter holidays and was enjoying my absence from work. During that time I received a phone call that changed my life and career. It was the Promotions Unit calling to say, "Congratulations, you have been successful in your application for a position as a…Senior Sergeant at the Downing Centre."

I couldn't believe it. I had to get him to repeat it. I was so excited. I knew it meant lots of travel and working five days a week, but I was so excited about the opportunity to be a Prosecutor again. As much as I enjoyed my time on the street, I really missed the work and the challenge it offered.

At the same time I felt a bit hypocritical about kicking up such a fuss the last time I was there before heading back to uniform. But things in my life had changed. The kids were older, and life in uniform was affecting me too personally. It was an informed decision that Rachael and I had made to return, rather than just being told that I had to go. And I was one of the Supervisors down there, which really appealed to me because it meant a good balance between Court and office work. I rang Rachael, and I think she was as happy as I was, and maybe a bit proud too.

It wasn't long before word spread through the LAC about my promotion, which added a sense of reality to the situation. It was hard to believe that I had won a Senior sergeant's position, but I knew it would be a great opportunity for advancement, and I could resume my law degree in earnest. I was excited and felt more positive about the future.

My teammates and close friends threw me a farewell party at a restaurant called The Ranch north of Newcastle that has a mechanical bull and the biggest steaks I have ever seen. Although I managed to spend some time on the bull and drank copious amounts of alcohol, I woke the next morning without a hangover and with very fond memories of my time as a member of Team 3, Tuggerah Lakes LAC.

Within four weeks of receiving the news, I was officially a Senior Sergeant and attached to the Prosecutions Command. I made sure my last few shifts in uniform were spent finalising my paperwork and having some fun. I will always remember my last shift in uniform — five arrests and overtime. I was working with Chris, who was highly motivated and knowledgeable beyond his limited years of service. I hadn't had the privilege of working with him during my eighteen months, so I was really looking forward to it.

## Chapter Twenty: The Promotion

We spent the majority of the night hunting and hoping to find some excitement. In the space of about two hours we had three arrests and almost two pursuits. The first incident occurred after we followed a car from the local shopping centre believed to be driven by a suspended driver. It took off on us at a nearby roundabout and accelerated away at an estimated speed of about 140km/hr in a 70km/hr zone. It took us some time to catch up to it, and just as I was about to call a pursuit he slowed down to below the speed limit, obviously now aware of our presence. Although he admitted to speeding, he denied doing twice the legal limit, but that is something he can argue before the local Magistrate.

About half an hour later we were driving down Wilfred Barrett Drive towards The Entrance when a small red hatchback came flying around the corner, almost sideways. By the time Chris turned our car around, the driver had sought refuge in an adjoining street, but he was easy enough to find. We spoke to the driver and three other occupants of the vehicle, who admitted to being from Western Sydney and just going for a drive, albeit at 12.30 in the morning. Checks via Police Radio revealed that the driver was the holder of a learner's permit. As he didn't have a lawful supervisor, he was issued a Field Court Attendance Notice for his trouble.

Apart from his manner of driving and the occupants being a long way from home, there wasn't any reasonable cause to search the vehicle or the passengers. There was no associated intelligence linking the persons or the vehicle to criminal activity, and for all intents and purposes they appeared to be just out for a 'drive.' I guess in hindsight it was a decision that may have saved our lives.

A few weeks later I was creating the charge for the driver when I noticed that the same vehicle and occupants had been stopped by police a few hours later in the back streets of Western Sydney. It was good to see that they heeded our warning to leave the area, but I was shocked when I read what happened after the vehicle was stopped by police. Because the vehicle was acting suspiciously around an industrial area in the early hours of the morning and under cover of darkness, the police rightly attempted to search the occupants and vehicle for anything stolen or illegal in their possession.

At that time, the male who was in the rear offside of the vehicle during our stop appeared to be concealing something inside the pocket of his pants. When police attempted to search the male, he took off on foot, throwing the object into bushland. After police arrested the male, they returned to the area to locate…a loaded handgun and ammunition. Oh my God! I can only imagine what would have happened if Chris and I had decided to search them when we stopped. It could have been quite a different result. I could just imagine a shootout on my last shift. What a way to go. I rang Chris and told him the news, and he was blown away too. It just goes to prove you don't know how things can turn out. The male did admit to owning the firearm and purchasing it a few weeks earlier. Hopefully the Court will rehabilitate him.

Before the shift ended, I decided to stop one more vehicle, which I thought would have been a simple drive whilst disqualified offence, only to learn that he had outstanding warrants. He denied his identity. So by the time he was conveyed to The Entrance Police Station, entered into custody, enquiries were made to confirm his identity and the charging process was finished my shift had ended and I was on overtime. Of course, my team was not surprised when I walked into the police station with a person in custody within the last half hour of the shift. Chris was smart and went home to snuggle with his wife, and Rachael just shook her head when I eventually got home.

Overall, I really enjoyed my time on the frontline at Tuggerah Lakes and often reminisce about the good and bad times and the friends that I have made. I really do miss them.

## The Hardest Day

I was looking forward to my new career path back in prosecuting as one of the Coordinators at the Downing Centre. Although it meant I had to travel five hours to and from work, it also meant a new beginning, safe from the anarchy of the streets, where I had my own office, more responsibility and enjoyed a good balance between boring administrative tasks and sinking my teeth into complex and lengthy criminal matters.

I'd only been working in Sydney for a few months when I had to attend Court on the Central Coast. It was the day of the severity appeal in the Gosford District Court, where the crook from The Entrance Channel was attempting to have his sentence reduced for trying to drown me. I thought that there was no chance it could ever happen…but the only thing that is certain in this job is that nothing is certain. I knew that it wasn't going to be easy, but I really felt that I had to be there just to see it through.

I was very nervous about going, but at least it was at a Court where I knew the Prosecutors and they could help take my mind off it a little. Before I got to the Court, I rang the DPP and spoke to the solicitor handling the appeal. She was comforting and sounded confident about our chances. She told me that he was attempting to have the sentence overturned by claiming that he was mentally ill at the time, which was unbelievable. In my opinion, he was drunk and stoned off his head, but not mentally ill.

When I got to the Court complex, I went into the Prosecutor's office to say hello to my former colleagues before I worked up the courage to walk into the Courtroom. It was good to see some familiar faces again. I ventured over to the District Courtroom and introduced myself to the DPP officer. She sat down with me and we had a talk about what was going to happen. I couldn't believe it when she told me that the Defence were arguing that his actions in attempting to drown me were 'accidental' and done in the panic of a rescue. I was so angry. I questioned how he could raise such an issue when in the initial sentencing his instructions to his solicitor and the Magistrate were that he couldn't remember anything about what happened — and now he wanted to argue that it was unintentional and that he should be released. Not a chance!

I went through my statement with the learned DPP officer and showed that his words, "You're not fucking arresting me," and his actions, headbutting me twice and holding me underwater, were not consistent with an "accidental" action.

When she told me that I was going to be called to give evidence, it was like the earth was opening up underneath me. I had managed to avoid having to relive the memories of that night up to this point and was devastated to learn that I would have to do it before a Judge and legal professionals. I thought that I might break down, as I could feel it before I even got to Court, but I knew that if I wanted to make sure this bloke wasn't going to be released I had to take the stand.

I went outside the Courtroom and sent some text messages to GOD, Sharpy and Denise, who were as shocked as I was about what he was claiming. It was good to feel that they were still on my side even though they weren't there in person. It's not their fault. I didn't tell anyone because it had been adjourned so many times before I didn't know for certain that it would proceed.

I spent a few hours around the complex waiting for the appeal to be mentioned. Just before it was, the DPP Prosecutor took me into an office and had a chat with me about what was in my statement and how I was feeling. I tried really hard to be strong, but I could feel the emotions welling up inside. I sat in the Court and watched the crook as he was led into the dock from the cells in his prison greens, with a smirk on his face. It made the situation seem even more real.

Then came the moment of truth — I was called to give evidence. As a Prosecutor I knew that it was part of the process, but as a victim it was terrifying. I was led through my evidence as I recounted step by step what I had heard, said and felt. It was torture, like being trapped in the water again. I burst into tears when I recalled to the Judge what had happened, how cold the water was and how I thought I was never going to see my girls again. I felt quite embarrassed, but I managed to get through my evidence and verbalise what effect the incident had had upon me and how after eighteen months I was still suffering flashbacks and nightmares.

The Judge and DPP Prosecutor were very supportive, allowing me a chance to gather myself before being cross-examined. The first thing the Defence said to me was that both he and his client were sorry for what I was feeling. I was torn between swearing, laughing and throwing something at them both, but managed to just nod my head in quasi-acknowledgement.

He asked me a few more questions, attempting to save his client from returning to gaol, including why I hadn't called Polair instead of jumping in and pursuing him. After I rattled off an immediate and in-depth answer, he decided to move on. The Judge looked at me and asked if I had given this evidence in the Local Court before the initial sentencing. I looked straight into his eyes and said that I never got the opportunity because the accused had pleaded guilty. He turned to the Defence and informed him that he was issuing a 'Parker direction.' I had no idea what that meant, but the Judge stood up and left the bench and I was ushered outside.

I went into the Prosecutor's office and summarised to them what had happened. I learnt that basically what the Judge had said was that if the crook didn't withdraw his appeal then he would have his sentence increased, not decreased or dismissed. It was too good to be true. I always felt that he deserved more but was resigned to the reality that three years' imprisonment was the best I could expect.

A few minutes later I went back into Court to learn, not surprisingly, that the severity appeal had been withdrawn and that he would remain a resident of a correctional facility for another nineteen months.

## Chapter Twenty: The Promotion

It was over. It was the hardest thing that I have ever done, except for actually being in the water on that night. All the pain of giving evidence had paid off.

As Rossy later said to me, "There is no more worthy cause than crying to send a dirty scumbag to gaol."

But the tears I shed were as real as the pain of reliving the experience all over again in the witness box. It was so overwhelming, but I was relieved that there was finally an end to it. I left the Court feeling tormented inside about how I was still affected after so long and about the fact that I hadn't dealt with my other issues of the girl drowning in the lake or the attempted suicide in the mountains. I knew I needed to speak to a counsellor again.

A short time later I received a call from one of my bosses at the Downing Centre, who was very concerned about my ordeal and offered me the support of the EAP and the NSW Police Force. I knew that I wasn't coping and that I needed to confront these feelings again. I was very withdrawn, both at home and at work, and would get very overwhelmed without reason. It wouldn't take much to make me feel emotional or lose my temper. I know my wife and kids copped it more than they deserved. It didn't help that I wouldn't talk to anyone about how I was feeling because it meant I had to confront not only these new incidents, but everything from early in my career all over again. The flashbacks were the hardest to deal with, increasing in intensity over time. I started drinking again to numb the pain and barely slept, which didn't help my bad moods. I put on a lot of weight and really didn't look after myself physically. My relationship with my wife and family definitely suffered, not just because of how I was feeling and how I was treating them, but because it was like stepping onto the same rollercoaster of emotions that we had ridden for nearly a decade.

I knew that if I didn't get help, it would cost me both my marriage and my family. Everything I had been through, Rachael had vicariously suffered as well. It was tearing her apart, and I knew that she was worried about me. I cried on the way home as I kept reflecting on the incident and broke down at the sound of Rachael's voice on the phone. But it was a relief and a familiar comfort.

I knew that I had some way to go in learning how to deal with these feelings, and I knew that it was hard for a lot of police to do, but it is the best thing that anyone can do—ask for help. Whether it is a partner, family member, friend, work colleague, MATES member or a professional, one shouldn't be embarrassed. Channel your emotions into something physical like exercise or renovations. Don't abuse alcohol or drugs because it only numbs the pain. It doesn't resolve anything and usually creates new problems. If you can't find the strength or motivation, then just write it down. It has been so effective and liberating for me.

I started seeing a counsellor again because I knew it was the right thing to do. I had been through this process before, and because of what I had achieved in the past I was confident of getting through again this time. My biggest issue was that having to relive everything again made the pain and emotion feel so raw. One of the strongest flashbacks I experience is me looking at the bridge and seeing my girls' faces, believing that I was about to drown. It was a horrifying memory, so I needed to change the neuro-association that was anchored in my mind in relation to that moment, just like the incident with the Ute when after watching the CCTV footage I was no longer trapped in the tray but looking from the outside in.

I decided that I needed to look at the incident again from a different perspective from feeling trapped in the water, cold, alone, desperate and terrified. So, one sunny Sunday morning I took my family to The Entrance Channel after the girls had finished their Tae Kwon Do grading to enjoy some morning tea and hopefully break the spell.

I was uncomfortable being near the water and could feel myself starting to panic. It was harder than I thought it would be. And because I was with my kids, I didn't want them to see how it was affecting me. But having my girls by my side so excited and looking for fish and birds in the water was a good distraction. It changed the whole meaning of that location and that memory for me. I even took a photo of my daughters huddled together, smiling ear to ear, with the bridge in the background, that I can look at whenever I feel afraid. And you know what? It works. It may not be the first time for everyone, but it does help. Just changing your view or perception of something really breaks the cycle. Now when I think of the incident and have flashbacks, I may still see myself drowning in the water, but instantly my mind 'channels' to the photo of my girls and the fun time we had there and how much I am loved.

I know that there is still some way to go, but I am confident that over time, with faith and support, when I think of the incident all I will see is my girls smiling back at me.

## Special Fixture

During a Coordinators' meeting at Parramatta in March 2010, I was approached by a Senior Sergeant from Coffs Harbour who I had gone through the Police Academy with. She asked if I could spare a senior Prosecutor to assist with a special fixture (complex and lengthy) fraud case that had been set down for five days during May at Coffs Harbour. She was suffering the same staffing issues as most of the Command, and as such didn't have the time or personnel to prosecute it. Without much hesitation I offered to prosecute the matter myself, much to her delight. As I had worked at Coffs Harbour before and enjoyed the challenge of complex and lengthy matters, I thought that I would give it a go.

A few days later, a number of arch-lever folders, with the majority of the brief of evidence, were delivered to my home. What had I gotten myself into? Luckily, I could read the brief whilst on the train to and from work. It was certainly a complicated matter and highly circumstantial, with about forty witnesses and complex crime scene analysis. The accused was a local man from Coffs Harbour who, we alleged, used a homemade time-delayed incendiary device to burn down his house whilst he was travelling to Sydney to, we alleged, collect the insurance money. The Detective in charge had done a great job investigating the case and compiling the brief, but there were still some things that needed chasing up, and there wasn't much time to make those enquiries and then serve them on the Defence fourteen days before the hearing started.

We were lucky because the accused had been interviewed a few times by the investigator from the insurance company and by the police, from which I was able to highlight some inconsistencies in his versions of the story. I was confident that despite the short preparation time and long distance from the informant and crime scene I could do a good job and he would have a strong chance of a conviction.

I rang and spoke to the Detective and discussed the brief with him a couple of times over the subsequent weeks. After receiving numerous emails with extra statements and photos attached, I was confident that I was as prepared as I could be. So after a six-hour drive north in the unmarked police vehicle on the Sunday before the hearing, I went to the police station to meet up with the Detective in charge. Following a brief conversation, we drove to the crime scene a short distance away so that I could make observations first-hand rather than relying on the two-dimensional images of the photographic evidence in the brief. I'm so glad that I made the effort, as I was able to get a better understanding of the layout of the area as well as identify some crucial evidence to support our case. About an hour later we returned to the police station to confirm the availability of witnesses who would be attending Court to give evidence so that I could determine their priority. Once I sorted that out, I travelled to the same hotel where I had stayed on previous visits to the area and spent some time reading statements and interviews before going to bed.

The next morning, I felt a nervous confidence about the matter. I had done all the preparation I could, and now it was up to me to put the evidence before the Magistrate and let him decide. I drove the short distance to the police station, where I spoke with the Detective again. We were as ready as we could be. The Magistrate had also travelled a long distance from Sydney to preside over the hearing, which was being held in the District Courtroom due to the large volume of witnesses and evidence to be presented.

Before going into Court to begin the legal battle, the Detective and I had a meeting with the veteran barrister in the foyer of the police station. Although he agreed on which statements and exhibits could be tendered, the barrister quipped that our case "was the weakest circumstantial case he had ever seen" and recommended that it be withdrawn. Not a chance, my friend!

With the comments of the Defence still ringing in my ears I made my way to the adjoining Court complex to the District Court, with the Detective in tow helping to carry the voluminous files. I positioned myself and the folders of evidence at the left-hand side of the bar table with the informant sitting adjacent to me. The learned barrister and his instructing solicitor were neatly organised to my right, with their client, the accused, seated close by to provide instructions to his legal team.

As I was filing the mountains of paperwork, I noticed that there was a semi-circular metal plate under my chair, which was apparently there to allow the bar table to rotate and face the jury during the trial. I didn't think much of it because I was so focused on the case and ensuring that I prosecuted the matter to the best of my ability and didn't let anyone down. But during the course of the hearing that week, my chair would persistently get caught on the metal plate whenever I stood to call evidence, argue case law, make an objection, move in and out from the bar table or simply sit down.

Once the Magistrate had entered the Courtroom, we made our introductions and opening submissions and the case began. Although the matter had only been set down for five days and the Magistrate was eager to finish within that time, it was clear that due to the number of witnesses and the complexity of the scientific evidence and the legal arguments, that it would take much longer, so we agreed to start early and finish late.

The first day started with a visit to the crime scene by the Magistrate, Defence and Prosecution, which the Magistrate was most pleased about, as it also gave him a better perspective on the location of the incident. The remainder of the day was spent tendering statements and arguing case law, with the Defence objecting to certain parts of the Prosecution's evidence. Much to the disappointment of the learned Defence barrister, I was able to convince the Magistrate that the Prosecution's evidence was both relevant and admissible. The hearing continued in a similar vein, with the Prosecution witnesses being examined and cross-examined at length by both parties and numerous legal arguments arising and being successfully challenged.

The second and third days involved the meticulous evidence and cross-examination of the scientific expert witnesses for the Prosecution and Defence, who argued that, based on their observations, experience and independent experiments, the accused was or was not responsible for setting up the time-delay incendiary device and burning down his house. Although it took almost two days to go through the evidence of both the Crime Scene officer for the Prosecution and the forensic expert for the Defence, there was actually very little they disagreed on considering the complexity of the evidence.

Despite the criminality of the case and possible lengthy term of imprisonment the accused was facing if he was convicted, there was a lot of detailed planning involved. There was the motive (debt/insurance fraud); the construction of the incendiary device using everyday items (matches, sparklers, citronella and mosquito coils placed inside a plastic crate and shielded by sheets of corrugated iron to act as a windbreak beneath the house); the alibi (visiting his wife in Sydney); the scapegoat (the youth living down the street) and the independent witness (the elderly neighbour who drove him to the airport that afternoon).

Our case was that the accused was struggling financially, so he concocted the plan to visit his wife in Sydney under the guise of dropping off a video camera to their son; that he used household items in the construction and protection of the device so that they could argue that someone came onto his property and opportunistically used things that were lying around and that he set up the device and spoke to the neighbour the morning of the fire to arrange a lift to the airport, and just before leaving lit the mosquito coil, which ignited the other incendiary material almost seven hours later, engulfing the house in flames whilst he was hundreds of kilometres away in Sydney, asleep.

The only problem with his planning was that we had strong circumstantial evidence from phone records, statements and forensic evidence that contradicted his version that this was a 'spur-of-the-moment trip' and indicated that it was rather a premeditated and intentional act. Most important were the experiments conducted by the Crime Scene officer relating to the burn time of the mosquito coil, which was proven to be around seven hours, the same length of time between the accused leaving for the airport and the house catching on fire.

The only thing we had to do was prove it. However, the matter was almost dismissed on the third day when the Defence asked for the actual exhibits (the incendiary device) to be shown to their expert rather than just presenting the photographs. After making a few enquiries, the Detective discovered that the exhibits had accidentally been destroyed a few months after the incident and were therefore not available for inspection or production in Court. The Defence blew up and argued that a stay of proceedings be imposed because it was unfair and an abuse of process, which would prevent the matter from ever continuing. Thankfully, the Magistrate allowed both parties to research some case law before hearing any legal arguments. Following some lengthy submissions and considerations of the evidence that was available to both parties in compiling their expert statements, the Magistrate held that there was no detriment to the Defence because the evidence had already been examined by both expert witnesses before the trial and experiments conducted as a result. The objection was overruled.

By the end of the week I was hoping to have at least finished the Prosecution case, but due to more legal arguments, that certainly wasn't going to happen. As it turned out, I wouldn't get a chance to question the accused person's wife, who was a witness for the Prosecution and more than likely a hostile one. As the case progressed, each day seemed to begin and end like the day before, staying up late reading statements and interviews, reading case law, starting early in Court, lots of legal argument and chair jarring, finishing late and conferencing witnesses for the next day. I think by the end of the week I had completed sixteen hours of overtime. On Friday morning, we could only call a few witnesses due to time constraints and adjourned the hearing for another five days in October.

## The Beginning Of The End

I had often joked throughout my career that it would be something simple that would lead to my undoing, either in life or professionally, considering all of the 'near-miss' incidents that I had survived. I just never imagined that it would really happen, and certainly not in the manner in which it did.

Whilst prosecuting on the Friday morning, with my chair constantly getting caught on the metal plate near the bar table, I felt something twinge in my lower back. I didn't think that much of it at first, as I had a job to do and had been getting my chair caught all week, which I saw as more of a frustration and distraction than a risk of personal injury. Coupled with the long drive and even longer days with late nights researching and reading, carrying heavy files, repetitive standing and sitting and probable poor posture at the bar table, my back just surrendered once the stress of the week had ended and I was able to relax. But the pain didn't go away, and my movement became slow and laboured. I had trouble standing up and sitting down and knew that something was wrong. So just prior to the adjournment and after being thanked by the Magistrate for our professional conduct during the hearing I placed on the Court record that I had hurt my back and how I did it.

I couldn't believe it. I had put so much effort into the case only to finish the first week with a work-related back injury, and there was still another five days to go during which I would get a chance to cross-examine the accused and see the case through to finality. I was hoping that it was only a muscle strain that a visit to the physio or chiropractor would sort out. But I couldn't lift my books and was very stiff and sore. I even had to ask for help from the other police to carry my gear to the car. I certainly wasn't looking forward to the six-hour drive home in that condition, but before I left I notified the Senior Sergeant of the injury and how it had happened. The six-hour trip home turned into about eight or nine hours. Because of the pain, I had to stop about ten times so that I could get out and stretch and move around. I rang my physio and chiropractor to hopefully get in to see them over the weekend, but they only worked during the week, so I had to wait until Monday morning.

By the time I arrived home, I was a mere shell of my former self, walking like a decrepit old man, wincing in pain with every step. I had to let my wife unpack the car I was so bad. I went straight to bed and woke the next morning in more pain and unable to get out of bed. I was confined to my room the whole weekend and only came out on Monday to visit the doctor and physio. It was like someone was stabbing a knife into my lower back. All I wanted to do was hit it with a sledgehammer, which ironically I couldn't even lift if I had wanted to. I rang and spoke to work and told them about what had happened. I'm not sure if they were that impressed, but believing it was only a muscle strain I hoped to be back at work towards the end of the week.

My doctor was concerned about the amount of pain I was in, so he took his time to examine me and complete the relevant workers compensation certificate. The following week I had a CT scan that revealed a prolapsed disc in the L5/S1 region of my lower back, which was worse than what I had expected. By this time I had already seen my physio and chiropractor a number of times without much relief. Because of the extent of the disabling pain and no response to treatment I was referred to an orthopaedic surgeon in Newcastle believed to be the best in NSW. I showed him the scans and he confirmed one of my biggest fears — that my frontline policing career was over. It was very hard to take considering I initially thought it only a minor injury. He referred me for an MRI scan to determine the full extent of the injury and booked me into hospital for a spinal block needle to help reduce the pain.

From then on, things went from bad to worse. The results of the MRI were worse than those of the CT scan. Not only was the disc protruding in three places, but I had also ruptured the core and torn the disc. On top of that, the spinal block was a complete failure, with me ending up in more pain and more frustrated than before the procedure. I even questioned whether they had actually done it, as there was no hole or bruising where the needle 'allegedly' went in.

By this time, about six weeks after the injury, I was really struggling mentally. The only time I was leaving the house was to attend medical appointments. I was becoming a recluse and feeling very depressed and overwhelmed about my future. I became moody and snapped at my family, and because I couldn't exercise I was putting on weight.

It didn't help that only a few weeks after the incident one of the bosses from my Command rang me and said, "I don't think you hurt your back the way you say you did!"

I couldn't believe what I was hearing. I was struggling enough as it was, and the last thing I needed was to be accused of being a fraud and a liar, especially by someone I had once respected. I wasn't getting any support from my work colleagues, which didn't surprise me; they would ring under the guise of seeing how I was only to be more interested about whether I was returning to work to finish my part-heard hearings or find where some paperwork was. It was like being in Redfern all over again. It's amazing the negative effect it had.

It was obvious that I wasn't coping and was feeling very depressed that my back was going to be a lifetime problem. I didn't know whether I would be able to return to work or whether I wanted to; I was in pain all day, every day, and none of the physio, chiropractic, hydrotherapy, acupuncture, traction, massage, heat packs, medications or exercises were making much of a difference. The truth was that it was something that I had to learn to live with. I couldn't see anything positive about my future. I couldn't work frontline because of my back, and because I sustained the injury doing a 'desk job' there was little chance for me to return in that capacity either. It also meant that I couldn't do my charity work and break more Guinness World Records,™ so my options both inside and outside of work were under threat. It was extremely hard on Rachael too, who now had me to look after as well as the kids and was working full-time.

I wasn't getting much joy out of the insurance company either. I received a call from an independent investigator who wanted to interview me about the injury so the insurance company could determine whether to accept the claim. I was distraught. I had never had to provide a statement for any of my other injuries and felt it was just another kick in the face. I should have been notified about the impending call from the investigator, but the rehabilitation officer from the police had sent the email to work, even though he knew I had been off work for about two months at that stage.

The investigator came to our house to get my statement. I was feeling very overwhelmed, especially after my bosses had already told me that they didn't believe me. Luckily, Rachael was there as a support person, even though she wasn't allowed to say anything. I had to explain what happened over and over. I was getting frustrated and wanted it to end. Although they accepted the claim, it was a very difficult time waiting for their decision.

I am very pleased to say that although I wasn't able to finish off the special fixture hearing in Coffs Harbour myself, another senior Prosecutor made the sojourn. Following instructions from me and the Detective about the case and after three more days of calling evidence, the Magistrate convicted him and imposed a twelve-month suspended gaol sentence. As much as I was looking forward to interrogating the accused myself, I was very happy with the outcome and received a congratulatory call from the Detective that afternoon. Not a bad way to finish my police career, if that was to be the case.

Because I was in pain so often with very little relief, I was unable to exercise and had put on ten kilograms in the first few months, and because I received no support from anyone within the Command, I started to relapse into my PTSD. I was having flashbacks about all my other incidents and remembered the lack of support that I had received during that time. I thought, Here I go again.

It was so overwhelming. I had no direction and no foreseeable respite from the pain. I withdrew from socialising with my friends, who were all just trying to help, and couldn't identify myself as a police officer, couldn't carry my badge or go near a police station. Although I had had relapses with my PTSD before, this was by far the worst and most debilitating because I couldn't exercise or go to the gym to vent my frustration or take my mind off things.

It got to a stage where I began having suicidal thoughts, not because I wanted to die, which I am sure would have stopped the pain, but just because I wanted to start again and didn't see any other options. There were times when I just felt that I had had enough, as the pain and negative thoughts were so constant and intrusive. It was like living in a gloomy dark hole where there was no way out. It was just you and your thoughts tearing you apart, ripping away your last shreds of self-worth. And when you were feeling trapped like this, it felt like there was no other option. As far as I could comprehend,

I had no future, no control and was better off dead. Because of this I felt robbed of the man I was and not worthy of anyone's support or empathy. I just felt so helpless, and my mind was becoming divorced from reality.

Although I never made an actual attempt at taking my life, the idea did cross my mind on more than a few occasions. The most common thoughts that I had were either going into the police station, getting my firearm from the gun safe (under the guise of needing it for weapons training) and then finding somewhere to finish the job or having a final showdown with the police, committing 'suicide by cop.' But as much as I wanted to escape the pain, I knew what impact it would have on my family and the emergency services. Having to go to the location, find and identify a fellow colleague who had taken his life in such a violent manner and then investigate it and notify my next of kin or be involved in the fatal shooting/death of another officer. I couldn't do it to them, or ultimately to myself. It's not how I wanted to be remembered. But in those deep dark moments it's what felt most real. It got so bad that at one stage my wife and my psychiatrist held an intervention because they were so concerned about me.

I remember on one occasion I decided that after picking the girls up from their Guides meeting I was just going to drive off and disappear. Just before Christmas in 2010 I was sitting in my driveway after a really bad day with a million negative thoughts flooding through my head, deciding whether to go or not, when I looked up and saw my three-year-old daughter standing at her window with her hands and face pressed against the glass, pleading, "Come inside, Daddy. Please don't go," as if she knew what I was contemplating.

It literally broke my heart. I went inside and promised never to have those thoughts again. I mean, after all the incidents I had been involved in where I so vehemently intervened and risked my own life to stop other people from committing suicide, I now felt hypocritical and selfish that the thought had even crossed my mind. I had to think about the people I was leaving behind: my wife, my daughters, my friends and family, and deep down I knew that there was still so much more I wanted to achieve.

But one positive was the fact that I asked for help, which in today's society is such a rare thing, first for a male to admit that he isn't coping and second to actually reach out for help. Initially I spoke to my doctor and physio about how I was feeling, and they agreed that my depression and negative thoughts might have been interfering with my back improving because I was so tense all the time. I mean, it was also very obvious that I needed help, as I would constantly break down into tears, was withdrawn and was generally feeling glum.

When I visited psychologist Roger Peters in Newcastle in August, I explained to him that this was my sixth time with PTSD, but I learned that PTSD is an ongoing condition and that this was just another relapse. He knew straight away that returning to work was not an option and diagnosed me with PTSD, which was not connected to the back injury. Roger was an expert on police PTSD and had written numerous books about the disorder, which he gave me to read. He also wanted me to see a psychiatrist, so I contacted my previous specialist and booked in to see him. He was surprised to see me, and when I explained what had transpired since my last visit four years earlier he prescribed a course of medication, which again I declined to take, though I did agree to see him every fortnight. I had been through this process so many times before and had successfully returned to work and maintained a happy lifestyle before this incident, so I thought I could do it again.

In early September, the police family mourned the loss of another brave officer when Constable Bill Crews was killed during a shootout with a crook suspected of supplying drugs. When the Coroner confirmed that the fatal bullet was the result of 'friendly fire,' it made the loss even more devastating. I felt sad for both Constable Crews and the officer who fired the fatal shot. He was merely defending himself in a difficult, confusing and confronting situation. I couldn't believe the amount of community support that followed.

A few days later, I had a visit from the 'return-to-work' officers, who were hoping to get me to return to work. It didn't go well, with me breaking down in tears when talking about how I was going. Within the first hour they knew that I wasn't in a position to even contemplate such an action until I had at least dealt with my PTSD issues. They did tell me that they weren't going to medically discharge me because of my back, which I was happy about. They said that even if I had one arm and one leg they would put me in an office with someone else with only one arm and one leg and we could work together. As far as they were concerned, I was a number, and if I could work four hours per week then they wouldn't consider discharge. Although I appreciated their intentions, there was also no way I was going to spend the rest of my career in some hidey-hole office just to appease them and make up the numbers. It was demeaning.

It was around that same time that I received a call from the local Police Chaplain asking if I wanted to help start up a local PTSD support group on the Central Coast. I jumped at the chance because I had always wanted to help other police with PTSD who weren't coping. I mean, I did have nearly ten years' experience and was able to return to work and a normal life following each relapse…up until now.

## KARMA

In the months leading up to Christmas I was still struggling with my back pain and flashbacks, but I was trying to be more positive. I was seeing the psychiatrist every two weeks and trying to confront my demons like I had in the past. I think it really helped being part of the PTSD support group where I could speak with people who had also been long-term sufferers as well as those who were new to the condition.

In regards to my back, I had been working really hard on my exercises, had managed to lose a few kilos just by changing to a healthy eating plan and was better able to cope with the pain by the time I was referred to a pain specialist in Newcastle. I didn't know how much he could help, but I was willing to give anything a go. My first meeting was certainly confronting when I walked out feeling worse off than when I went in. It made me realise how serious my condition was when the specialist told me that I had six months for my pain to improve before he would recommend surgically removing the damaged disc and inserting a metal plate and brace into my back. Uh-uh, that wasn't going to happen. It certainly motivated me to stay positive and work harder. The new medication he gave me really helped, even though I had so many tablets a day that I rattled when I walked.

One morning just before Christmas in 2010 I heard about a fatal car accident on the Central Coast in which a male was killed and another was airlifted to hospital with critical injuries. It was the third serious accident in the area in the past week and the fifth fatality. With Christmas less than two weeks away, I really felt for the surviving families and the emergency service officers who had to attend to and clean up the carnage. Besides being assaulted at work, it was one of the worst jobs any officer could have to do and something that tends to be really hard to forget.

I was so frustrated upon hearing of the accident that I posted the following status on Facebook: "Woken to the news of the 5th fatality in our area in the last week. I know it's the silly season people but for fucks sake drive safely and think about the people you leave behind…"

I have always been passionate about road safety and try my best to lead by example, even though at times I have been a victim of road rage, with one guy tailgating me and threatening me with a spanner near the Freeway a few years ago. I didn't think much more of the accident for the next few hours until I received a call from my wife telling me that one of the people involved in the accident that morning was the same guy who tried to drown me in The Entrance Channel and that it was his brother who had died. I couldn't believe it. Rachael felt bad telling me over the phone, but she wanted me to hear it from her, worried about how I would react. I told Rachael I was okay and shrugged off any concern that she had. It was no big deal, or at least that's what I told myself.

Within a short period of time my mind started to cloud over with images of The Entrance Channel incident and how vulnerable I was. I couldn't understand how he could have been involved in the accident when he was supposed to be still in gaol. Why didn't anyone tell me he'd been released? I started to panic and had trouble settling down, so I decided to get into the car and just go for a drive. As much as I tried, I couldn't hold back my tears. I was finally starting to feel more positive when again I was dragged back into this nightmare – one step forwards and two steps back.

I didn't know at the time if it was the right decision, but I drove to the accident scene to see if I could make sense of what had happened and how I was feeling. I had driven along the same stretch of road hundreds of times whilst working in uniform and couldn't understand how it happened. I wasn't trying to justify what he did, just using the policing part of my brain to reconstruct the cause. I remember seeing photos on the Internet that showed the car torn in two after leaving the road and hitting the tree. Speed certainly had to be a factor, and possibly drugs and alcohol. I drove past the scene a number of times and even stopped, just to give my mind time to digest my thoughts and feelings. I couldn't describe the vacuum of emotions that I was experiencing.

Over the next few days I found out more and more information about the accident. I found out that despite admitting to police at the scene that he was the driver, he tried to change his story and nominate his brother as the driver when he found out that he had died. What a fuckin' lowlife piece of scum. He couldn't even take responsibility for killing his own brother. Apparently both the males had been ejected upon impact with the tree, and if you had seen the photos you would understand why, so it was up to forensic evidence to prove who was driving at the time of the accident. Last I heard, the surviving brother from the Channel incident was to have his arm amputated, and maybe even a leg. He has also been charged with the accident and faces a number of years in goal if convicted.

I know it is never nice to wish harm upon others, but when you do so many bad things to other people and you can walk away without any sense of remorse or responsibility, it's like 'street justice' when the world bites back and impacts upon their world. I was angry and frustrated about the fact that his selfish and criminal actions had resulted in the death of another person, but as the saying goes, "Karma is a great thing." Whether he feels any remorse for what he did or the Court is able to convict him, he will have to live the rest of his life knowing that he killed his own brother. It was how I chose to look at the accident rather than feeling like a victim again.

Even though it was a big shock for the events to unravel the way they did, I believe that the overall experience was quite cathartic. I began to process my feelings, and as I drove over The Entrance Channel Bridge the following day on my way to the PTSD meeting, I made a snap decision that really made me feel more in control. Noticing that the Channel was at low tide with plenty of visible sand banks, which was completely opposite to that night in April 2008, I decided to go for a walk. As I approached the Channel, I sat on the ledge looking in and contemplating my idea, before sliding down onto the sand bank with the lukewarm water lapping at my ankles. With each step I was able to erase more of the memories that had plagued me for the past eighteen months, until half an hour later I was almost in the middle and close to the bridge. My wife didn't believe me when I texted her that I was walking in The Entrance Channel. She thought I was walking along the foreshore until she drove down in the police car in uniform and saw my lone figure away in the distance. It was a long walk back to shore but a good day nonetheless, though my back didn't appreciate all the extra resistance the shallow water created and screamed at me for the rest of the afternoon.

I finally felt like I had made a big step forward. I went to the PTSD meeting, although I was late, and relayed my experience to the rest of the group. It was a great liberating feeling. I even went near The Entrance Police Station, which I had been unable to do for the past six months, when I met up with Rachael and GOD. I felt confident and positive for the first time in a long, long time. I even spoke to Rachael about going to the work Christmas party with my old teammates that weekend. It was a start, and Rachael was so proud of me. I was a bit chuffed at myself too.

When we arrived at the local pub for the Christmas party I could see that the place was 'packed to the rafters' with people having a good time. Rachael and I were met at the bar by my good friend and former teammate Dave, who ushered us away to a quiet area of the bar. It was quite strange, but when he said that the majority of the people were there to raise money for the family of the brother who died in the car accident, I could understand his concern. Rachael and I just looked at each other and laughed. I had finally worked up the courage to socialise in public with police, albeit off-duty, and I had walked into a pub that was littered with triggers.

I just looked at Dave, then at Rach, and said, "We are both victims of the same person's cruelty. I need a beer."

So armed with my positive thoughts and a schooner of Tooheys, I strode out into the courtyard and sat with the rest of the team, who looked just as uncomfortable to be there. It was just one of those coincidences that I had to deal with. I didn't know any of the people there, and as far as I knew they didn't know me. We tried to relax and enjoy the company, but Rachael and I didn't stay too long, as we were heading to carols by candlelight to meet up with the rest of our family. Despite not being prepared for such a confrontation of emotions, I reckon I handled it really well. Sometimes you just have to laugh.

## Chapter Twenty-One:
# The Decision

Like every year, the end of 2010 and beginning of 2011 was crammed with a lot of personal reflection, self-assurance and contemplation of what direction my life would go in for the ensuing calendar year. Unlike most years, New Year's Eve 2011 held the very real prospect that my future would not include life as part of the 'thin blue line,' and that was a frightening reality that I had a lot of trouble accepting. I still very much loved being a police officer and wasn't sure if I was ready to let go, despite everything I had been through. For me it was a difficult decision, but one that had to be made. By this time I had been off work for over seven months without much improvement of my physical injury and some overwhelmingly dark days psychologically.

However, I knew that the time was fast approaching for me to either risk returning back to work or risk starting a new life outside the policing family. Either way, it wasn't something I wanted to rush into. I was still in a lot of pain with my back but was feeling more positive about my PTSD, considering recent events. I didn't want to make the wrong decision, such as choosing to stay in the Force and then having another meltdown where I ended up killing myself, losing my family or locked up in some mental hospital, or leaving and then regretting never being able to go back. Considering I had managed to confront my emotions so well over the years and was able to return to work, be an effective, fully operational officer and get promoted was encouraging. But going back for the salary, rank and security wouldn't be the right reason. There certainly was a lot of soul searching, and I listened to some wise counsel from my family, friends and specialists, but I just wasn't sure.

My focus during the early part of 2011 was diverted by the wrath Mother Nature had unleashed during the devastating Queensland floods, Christchurch earthquakes and Japanese tsunami. The fact that I was unable to even volunteer my assistance physically as a concerned Australian or as part of the police contingent that was deployed made my condition more aggravating to me.

But on a positive note, I was approached by my good friend, MATES founder and social welfare guru Katie, to assist her in organising a Suicide Prevention Forum for the Central Coast in early February. She was aware of what I had gone through during my career and the fact that I had contemplated suicide. She also knew that I was passionate about 'changing the way we think' about suicide because of my personal experiences as both a bloke and a cop. It was important for me to get involved in this project, "not despite what I was going through, but because of what I was going through." Up to that point I hadn't had much contact with people or spoken about my suicidal thoughts to my friends and family, but somehow I found the courage to speak out, including being interviewed on the local radio station and speaking on a DVD.

Here is what I came up with:

*Silhouetted Male*

*It doesn't matter who I am, where I am from or where I work...*

*The only thing that matters is that I am a male, aged between 24-44 and I live on the Central Coast...*

*Because of this I am at risk of suicide...*

*Each year as many as thirty males in this age group on the Central Coast die by suicide instead of reaching out for help...*

*I could be your brother, father, teammate or friend...husband, neighbour, son or colleague...*

*I could walk past you on the street, live in the same neighbourhood, play in the same sport team or work in the office next to yours...*

*We are nameless, faceless statistics who are afraid to ask for help...because that's not what we do...*

*As a male I am supposed to be thick skinned and tough...*

*I am expected to handle any stressful situation...*

*I am not supposed to show emotion or that I am not coping... otherwise I am considered weak or not 'blokey' enough...*

*Yet I breathe like everyone else...feel like everyone else...and bleed like everyone else...*

*I am too afraid to talk about my feelings because I am embarrassed about how I feel... worried of what you will think of me...afraid of how you will treat me...and scared that I will be less of a man...*

*I don't want to be judged or labelled...*

*I don't want to be a burden or inconvenience...*

*I just want to step out of the darkness and tell you how I feel...tell you that I am not coping...and for you just to listen...*

*I just want you to see me...and ask if I am okay...*

MALE SUICIDE – IT'S TIME TO
CHANGE THE WAY WE THINK...

Despite the stigma around the issue of suicide and the fact that I had opened up about how I was feeling, I was excited about being involved and was eternally grateful to Katie for that opportunity. During the forum I sat to the side listening to the many speakers and watched as my DVD was played to the audience. I felt so inspired by some of the stories that towards the end of the evening I went on stage and revealed myself as the 'silhouetted male.' I certainly didn't plan to make an appearance but believed that it was important, and not only for me, to be seen as well as heard. I felt that because of my experience as a police officer and as someone who had contemplated committing suicide that I had a unique point of view, which was gratefully received. It felt good using my negative experiences to positively assist other people in the same situation. Maybe there was something to look forward to in the future.

After the success of the forum and the failure of the spinal block, I placed my faith in a spinal cortisone injection to alleviate my pain, but again with minimal to no effect. Despite the physio, hydro, massage and medications, I wasn't improving and was beginning to realise that my chronic pain was something I would have to learn to live with. It certainly wasn't helping me mentally either. It had also been fifteen years since I started at the Police Academy. I didn't feel much like celebrating, just like I needed time out from the world, or at least a few days without the pain, flashbacks or feeling so vulnerable.

The fact that I was having so many issues with the insurance company coupled with a lack of 'duty of care' from the police really wasn't helping. After being off work for nearly twelve months and having been diagnosed with a recurrence of my PTSD not associated with my back injury I was informed that I had to submit a 'recurrence of injury form.' This meant I had to see an independent psychologist, which this time I understood was part of the process. The eleven-page statement he took from me led to the recurrence claim being accepted. But once the insurance companies for the NSW Police Force changed, that's when things got tough.

March was a particularly pivotal month for me. I had spent a lot of time contemplating my future both inside and outside of the police and realised it was time to make a final decision. I was worried that if I returned to work as a police officer, the likelihood of having another relapse was too high and that the consequences might not be something that I could live with. And the honest truth was that I was a 'shit magnet' and that trouble had a way of always finding me.

But conversely, it was hard to perceive that there was a life outside the police, and not being part of the police 'family' after nearly sixteen years was something that I couldn't comprehend. I was also concerned about what my wife, family, friends and colleagues would think of me if I didn't go back. What sort of role model would I be if I allowed myself to be consumed by this condition? For so long I had identified myself and been identified as a police officer.

Whenever anyone asked what I did for a living, I'd say, "I'm in the cops."

If I came across someone in need of help or doing the wrong thing, I could flash my badge and take control, as a cop. I'm known as the cop who lives down the street, the cop who raises money for charity and the cop whose friends come to him for legal advice. I met my wife in the cops. She's a cop. My kids know me as a cop. It's who I have been for nearly my entire working adult life. It's more than just a job. It was my life. It was who I was — my identity. It was not something I wanted to let go of.

I guess in a lot of ways my 'identity' was something I struggled with; being an identical twin, you are always compared to your sibling — who is smarter, who is better at sports, who is better looking… Looking back in hindsight now I can see that when the reality of having to make the decision to leave became real I started seeking vindication for all the sacrifices I had made in the police by seeking recognition and awards, because in that moment I felt like everything I had achieved, all the sacrifices I had made and the times I risked my life, had all been for nothing. I was angry, bitter and resentful.

But then I had a few life-changing realisations that made me realise that sometimes the hardest decisions in life are ultimately the easiest ones to make:

- *It's not what job you do that defines you, but who you are that makes a difference.*
- *A police officer is what I did as a job — it's not who I am as a person.*
- *I don't need recognition or awards to be grateful for the way I executed my duties.*
- *There is a difference between giving up and moving on.*
- *I would rather be remembered for how I lived than how I died.*
- *My kids don't care whether I am a cop or not, just that I am fair but kind, supportive and loving, that I am there when they need me and that I love them for who they are and what they will become.*

After weighing up my options and objectively balancing the reasons why I should stay or go, I made the decision, with the support of my family and specialists, that it was time to go (even though I thought about changing my mind a few more times). I had accepted that there was a difference between quitting and moving on. I had served my time. Nearly sixteen years in any job is long enough. Once I had made and accepted my 'final' decision, it was a matter of advising the police and letting the process of medical discharge begin.

Whilst the wheels turned slowly for my PTSD claim, I sought one last hope at improving my quality of life with my back through a pain management group that was held near Newcastle. It was three days a week, eight hours a day for three weeks, which I thought in itself was asking a bit much considering it was an hour's drive each way and I could only sit for fifteen minutes at a time. But I was desperate and trying to stay positive.

There were about ten of us in the class with chronic neck, shoulder and back injuries, all work-related, and we were all at that stage of hoping that this would work because nothing else had. There were a lot of sad stories told within the group of the effect that the chronic condition had had on them personally and professionally. But as a group we clicked, and what at first seemed pointless seemed to be having a positive influence on everyone, even the lecturers. We had a strong and supportive team of counsellors, physios and other professionals behind us who were focused on educating us about chronic pain and ways to manage the effects of the pain to help with everyday life, such as pacing, calming and stretches.

On the first day they recorded a video of us walking and doing certain activities so that at the end of the course we could compare our progress. It was good to look back and see just how much we had improved. Because we all got on so well, it was a lot of fun, and we encouraged each other and proved that laughter really is the best medicine. Personally, I was able to wean myself off of all medication and develop strategies to manage my pain and control any flare-ups. I certainly wasn't to the point of returning to work or running a marathon, but being able to sit and stand for more than fifteen minutes was a success for me. By the end of the course we all became good friends and promised to keep in contact. I learnt a lot from the course that I have been able to apply to my everyday life, although it is a lot harder when you're away from the group. I made some lifelong friends during those few challenging weeks, and deep down I know that what I have learnt I will be able to use to create a better and more functional lifestyle for myself in the future.

It wasn't long after the pain management course had finished and I had made the decision to seek medical discharge for my PTSD when I was informed by the new insurance company that my recurrence of PTSD claim had been "closed." Apparently because my recurrence of PTSD wasn't a "fresh" claim it was, for some reason, linked to my original claim in 2001, which was three insurance companies ago. To cut a long story short, they lost it. I was furious to say the least. The old insurance company assured me that it was open before it was transferred but wouldn't put anything in writing to help me, due to privacy reasons. As if I wasn't already going through enough with making the decision to leave, now I had to deal with the incompetence of alleged professionals who had my financial, and ultimately psychological, future in their hands. It took what seemed like an eternity of tearful phone calls, emails and faxes between my solicitor, insurance companies, work and me for the claim to be re-opened, but I was so relieved when it did.

## Chapter Twenty-One: The Decision

Months had passed, and there didn't appear to be any prospect of an outcome for my discharge in the foreseeable future. I really wanted it over before Christmas so I could make 2012 a new start. When I was referred to an independent psychologist in Sydney in August 2011, I was relieved that Rachael was allowed to attend with me for moral support. It was a long drive down, but we made sure we got there early. I was nervous, but having Rachael with me really helped. It was obvious that I was uncomfortable being in Sydney and having to relive all of my past incidents again, but I understood that it was part of the discharge process. Nonetheless, I was glad when it was over.

The specialist was very welcoming and didn't seem to have an agenda against me. He listened to what I had to say and took a genuine interest in how I was feeling. Rachael was allowed to have her say about how she thought I was going and the negative effect my condition was having on our family, our relationship and me. Towards the end of the sixty-minute interview it was apparent that I wasn't coping, and I was struggling to talk about the incidents and my thoughts of suicide, so he reassured me that he had already made his mind up in the first five minutes that he would be recommending medical discharge. Although it was quite a shock to see my career coming to an end, I felt relieved and confident that I had made the right choice. Now it was just a waiting game.

A few days later I wasn't feeling that positive anymore and ended up in hospital suffering from severe chest pains, most likely from stress. I vented on Facebook, writing that I was "So over feeling like this…friggin' sore back…screwed up in the head…chest pains… dizziness and feeling like crap…somebody just shoot me…"

My mood didn't improve much over the next few days either. It was August 16th, exactly fifteen years from when I attested as a Probationary Constable from the Police Academy so young, proud and full of enthusiasm; it was one of the happiest days of my life. But there I was sitting in my shrink's office when I received a call from work telling me I'd been recommended for medical discharge and that I couldn't be a policeman anymore—now one of the saddest days of my life. Although it was what I had been waiting for, to receive notification that my policing career was almost over on the same date that held such meaning to me as my attestation was like rubbing salt into the wounds. Luckily I had Rachael, some close friends and the PTSD group as a support network for me to turn to.

Following the success of the Suicide Forum earlier in the year, I was keen to do more to help break the stigma of male suicide. Thankfully, Katie invited me to assist her in organising a Suicide Prevention dinner in September. It was a distraction that allowed me to channel my thoughts into something positive. I made another DVD, but this time as Jeff Garland, where people could see me, hear my words and see the emotion on my face. I even had my 'mug' in the paper to promote the event, which was a big decision to make, having my face associated with male suicide. But I am glad that I did it. The night was a great success, with a celebrity guest speaker who had lost a friend to suicide. My wife and a group of close friends shared a table, and the evening really meant a lot, knowing that I had their support. I really felt like I was making a difference. I was on a buzz for a few days after that and was feeling more positive about the future, even though my discharge from the police may not have been too far away.

Thankfully, we had booked a ten-night South Pacific cruise twelve months earlier, which at that point was only about a month away. It was something the whole family was looking forward to and something I really needed, especially when I found out that my official last day of service would be whilst I was away on the cruise. It also helped knowing that my family would be there with me, and coincidentally my mate Mark was also on the cruise. Although I hadn't officially been told when my discharge date would be, I kept 'enquiring' and was told that it would be before the end of October.

"This shit just got real," as Martin Lawrence said in *Bad Boys II*.

It was time that I started getting my things and my thoughts together in preparation for that day. Despite thinking that I was doing better than I actually was psychologically, I was nervously terrified about this transition—what would I do? How would I cope? There was this heightened sense of vulnerability that I had never experienced before that threatened to undermine the strength I was attempting to muster. The flashbacks returned in waves as my whole career unravelled before me, but it wasn't just the critical incidents—it was everything, both good and bad: the memories, the friendship, the laughter and the whole experience. I really started to question whether I had made the right decision.

I also noticed that I had become hyper-vigilant about things that I could normally handle. I was overly alert and security-conscious at home and overreacted and became frustrated very easily. For me the biggest bugbear was P-plate drivers doing burn-outs in the streets near where I lived. It all started just before we went away on the cruise, and I couldn't control how angry and helpless I felt. Normally I would have just recorded the registration of the vehicles and rang them from work, charged them and made sure they were without a licence for a while. But that wasn't something I could do anymore. It wasn't an option for me and I couldn't take it. I didn't have control. I couldn't ring the police or even go to Court if I made a statement because of my PTSD, so I felt trapped. I would stay up late at night listening for them and looking out the windows. If I saw them driving around, I would record their registration on my phone so that I knew who they were. It was debilitating for me and caused many arguments at home.

"I guess you can take the man out of the cops but not the cop out of the man."

Despite that obsession, I was still attending my physio appointments and seeing my shrink every two weeks. I knew that Rachael was worried about me because she knew how hard this was going to be. But something inside me changed. I began to accept what was about to happen and felt comfortable with my decision, knowing that it was in the best interests of my family and me. So like I had done with my incidents throughout my career I decided to confront them and change what they meant to me before I was discharged. So in the month or so leading up to the cruise, I visited two of the locations where some of the more recent and more serious incidents had occurred.

The first stop was the footbridge where the young girl had drowned before Australia Day 2009. It was the first time that I had been back there since the incident, despite living not too far away. It was a lot less chaotic then I remembered, which was good because it gave me a chance to be alone with my thoughts. The only reminder of the tragedy was moulted flowers and snapshots of the young girl's life hanging next to the bridge. I took a moment to read the heartfelt messages that her friends and family had left and beheld the memories that had been captured in time through the eyes and hearts of those who knew her so well. Although it was confronting, I knew that it was something that I had to do, especially if I wanted to move on.

It was hard not to reflect upon what more I could have done that day. But regardless of how guilty I felt or how much we all wanted things to work out differently, the haunting reality was that they hadn't, and I needed to construct a new 'anchor' and change what this place meant to me. It didn't mean that I would ever forget — how could I? — but I needed to change my perception. And what better way than by celebrating Father's Day with my family in the park adjacent to the bridge?

The echoes of the children laughing and playing filled the afternoon skies as the water tranquilly flowed beneath the bridge, bereft of the innocence lost. My wife and I went for a walk along the shoreline and onto the bridge. We stood where 'she' would have jumped off, reading the tender messages etched into the timber railings. Initially I felt a sense of guilt for sharing such a special occasion so proximate to where she drowned, but gradually, as we settled down to a family lunch and played games in the park, I felt a familiar warmth and sense of security. The haunting memory of watching her life slip away and feeling so helpless began to fade. And now every time I drive through the area and see the bridge I am able to reflect favourably upon some happier memories, but still I will never forget how that girl, or that day, changed my life and those of so many others.

It was some weeks after I had made the decision to confront my demons from the Crackneck Lookout incident that I received the call confirming that I only had two weeks left as a serving police officer. Although I knew that it was going to happen and it was a decision that I had taken a lot of time to make, it was still very difficult to accept that it would soon be over after nearly sixteen years of dedicated and professional service. As I stood on the edge of the cliff and allowed the significance of that reality to sink in, the mosaic history of my career turned like pages in a book.

There were times when I was very proud, very brave and very scared. And times when I was very humbled and overwhelmed by what I had witnessed and experienced. The warmth, the strength and the unique bond of the policing family was one that you could only ever explain if you were courageous enough to be part of it. But every shift, every officer I worked with, every incident I attended to, every victim I helped, every crook I locked up, each and every one of those memories was what made me the officer I became, and they were all part of my journey from Student Police Officer to Senior Sergeant, from civilian to Retired Service Member and from a naïve youth to a more experienced, shrewder and tougher person.

Fortuitously, my last day of service happened to coincide with the final few days of the family cruise we had planned earlier in the year.

## Chapter Twenty-One: The Decision

Although I had been on one when I was a teenager, this was to be the first Garland family cruise for me as a husband and parent, sailing nine nights aboard the luxurious P&O Pacific Pearl, cruising the South Pacific and visiting the islands of Vila, Isle of Pines and Lifou. It was something we were all looking forward to, especially the kids, even though it would be somewhat bittersweet for me. It was strange to comprehend that I would leave Australia still a serving member of the thin blue line, be discharged in the middle of the Pacific Ocean and then return home as a civilian; but it was good timing nonetheless.

I remember a few days after the call pronouncing my last day of service as October 27th 2011 I received a letter from the NSW Police Force formalising the declaration that the Commissioner had reviewed my file and recommended me for medical discharge. Apart from a few administrative instructions, that was it.

There was no "Thank you for your service and sacrifice" or "Good luck in the future."

It wasn't even signed by the Commissioner or even a serving police officer, but by an acting Team Leader from the Death and Disability section. It was heart-wrenching to feel that after such a long career, which resulted in me suffering both a serious psychiatric condition and a chronic physical injury, I was still considered only a number (30763). It did reinforce that I had made the right decision and that it was time to start looking after myself.

It wasn't until about a month after my medical discharge that I received some form of acknowledgement from the Commissioner for my years of service when he wrote:

"I would like to thank you for the contribution you have made to the NSW Police Force and the community of NSW. It is regrettable that your condition precludes you from pursuing your chosen career as a police officer."

Now, if this had been in the first letter confirming my medical discharge, it would have made a world of difference.

The morning of our cruise we were all packed and very excited as we waited outside for our lift to Sydney to board the ship. Because it was our maiden voyage I wanted to make it a memorable experience, so when a luxurious stretch Chrysler limousine pulled up near the driveway the girls almost burst with excitement, especially when they saw all the flashing lights and free drinks inside. I must say that the 'big' kids were very impressed as well. It was a great start to our holiday.

We made our two-hour drive south along the F3 Freeway and along the Pacific Highway towards the CBD. As we drove over the Sydney Harbour Bridge we looked towards Darling Harbour, where the majestic P&O Pacific Pearl was docked, awaiting our arrival. Before long we had boarded, found our cabins and made our way to top deck. With drink in hand, spirits high and party music playing, we set sail along Sydney Harbour, gliding under the arched frame of the Harbour Bridge, passing the iconic Opera House, and out through Sydney Heads into the untamed and vast Pacific Ocean. Thankfully, the weather was fine, the skies were clear and the seas were calm. Maybe it was a sign of things to come for my future, too!

The Pearl had a lot to offer. It was thirteen stories of excitement, comfort, relaxation and entertainment. You could do a lot or do nothing. The girls had their own kids' club, with activities catered for each age group, which they really enjoyed going to. It also gave Rachael and me some quality time to indulge in other activities and spend some time together. The food was magnificent, with a wide range of buffet and restaurant dining. The staff were friendly and always willing to make you feel welcome. Despite my impending discharge, it was relatively easy to relax, and I even found myself at times not thinking about policing. But I knew that my last day of service wasn't very far away.

I remember the morning of October 27th. I didn't sleep too well the night before thinking about the enormity of the occasion, wondering if I would feel any different. I woke just before the dawn, moved towards the back of the boat and watched the sun rise over the horizon. The skies were so crisp and clear away from the smog-filled skies back home. I thought about what I had achieved, about what I had survived and about what I still had to offer to my family and my community. Although I had many months of pondering such emotions, it was important for me not to lose sight of why I had made the decision to leave. It was sad but at the same time cathartic knowing that I had served my time and been paroled to live amongst the general community, knowing that I had achieved nearly all I had sought to accomplish during my career. I sat watching the waves and feeling the morning warmth against my skin for about an hour before I went into our cabin and woke the family. It was a new day, a new life. A good day!

We spent most of the day hanging out together, enjoying each other's company and creating our own memories. With just the touch of her hand or the look in her eye I could see that Rachael was thinking about what I was going through, and even without words it spoke volumes for the woman she is and the bond that we shared. She was a massive reason why I was still around to savour my last day as part of the thin blue line. My girls were my life.

To mark the special occasion, Rachael had organised a romantic interlude for the two of us at Luke Mangan's acclaimed Salt Grill restaurant on-board the Pearl, where we had a chance to talk and reflect not only on my career, but also on our lives together. It was by chance that we were seated next to her uncle and aunty, who managed to imbue some words of wisdom and reassurance for the future. Unwittingly, or perhaps by some divine intervention, our friends Mark and Kate, who were also on the cruise, were able to change my neuro-association of what the day and occasion meant to me by announcing their engagement. So it will be remembered as not only my last day as a police officer, but also the day two close friends got engaged. It certainly was a time for celebration, and celebrate we did.

I woke up the next morning somewhat thinking what I had the day before, wondering if I felt any different. Rachael and the girls gave me the biggest cuddles, not just as a sign of support but because they loved me regardless of whether I was a cop or not. As of that morning I was not, and it was okay with me too!

I guess in a lot of ways it was like the threat of the Y2K bug on New Year's Eve 1999, which was supposed to cripple the world's computer network as we entered the twenty-first century. Amazingly, on January 1st, 2000 no major computer problems were reported and life went on as normal. Similarly, on October 28th, 2011 my world hadn't ended and "the only limits I had were the ones I placed on myself." It was time to go home and start contemplating life. After ten days at sea, it was good to be home. I mean, I knew that I was still going to have my good days and bad days, but at least I was a little more optimistic about what lay ahead. As for the foreseeable future, I was happy being 'Mr Mum' and helping our five-year-old daughter with her transition into kindergarten. Very exciting times!

Even though I had been off work for about seventeen months, it had taken only seven months from the date I decided to leave until my final medical discharge. I had heard of officers waiting over twelve months, and some whose application for discharge had been refused, so essentially I was one of the fortunate ones. Although getting to the stage where you are either physically or psychologically — or in my case both — unable to serve as a member of the NSW Police Force is devastating, having to make the decision, or being told, to leave may be overwhelming, yet the actual discharge process may even exacerbate your situation, especially if you decide to take civil legal action against the police or have to fight your claim in Court.

I found that there wasn't much information or support out there for police who were going through the workers compensation and medical discharge processes. Sure, you can search for things on the Internet, but from my experience, I found that speaking to other police who had gone or were going through it was the best source of advice and guidance. Whether you can find anyone and whether they are willing to help may be a different issue. It's the same with knowing how to deal with your PTSD symptoms. Sometimes your best information on who the best specialist is and what type of medication or treatment works best comes from sufferers or survivors of PTSD.

One thing I was really worried about was having a restricted life outside of the police and that it wouldn't be very fulfilling. I had been so proactive throughout my policing career as well as my charitable fundraising ventures. I didn't just want to exist. I wanted to live. And I certainly didn't want my physical or psychological conditions to prevent me from living a life with purpose and meaning. I already felt that I had lost my manhood because I wasn't able to be the 'man of the house.' I had to rely on my girls to mow the lawns, help around the house and do things that I should be doing as a dad and a man. I just knew that I had to be aware of my limitations, work harder and smarter and sometimes think laterally about how I could achieve the same goal a different way. I still have so many dreams and goals for the future, and I guess what will be is up to me.

I suppose that's why I have been trying to do my law degree since I have been off work. It was something I started, not because I was ever planning on getting out of the police and going into private practice, but just because it was something I had always wanted to do and I thought it might look good on my resume. It's been really tough, though. It was so hard to concentrate and find the focus and motivation to study because of the amount of pain and disruptive thoughts I had to deal with. Also, because I was completing the degree by correspondence, I had to attend two weekend schools for

## Chapter Twenty-One: The Decision

a semester to learn each subject, but due to the distance to Sydney and my inability to sit or travel for long periods, coupled with my reluctance to be around people, I had to learn primarily from the prescribed texts, which didn't make studying tax law or torts any more exciting or interesting. It also meant that I had to defer a semester or two because I couldn't study or travel or even sit long enough to complete the exam.

Thankfully, I successfully completed my law degree and passed all of my exams in July 2013, after almost eight years. Despite the setbacks caused by the incidents that ended my policing career and began my battles with PTSD, depression and suicidal thoughts, I made it! I couldn't have done it without the love, support and encouragement of my gorgeous family and friends.

Ultimately, I am not sure what value or assistance the law degree will have in my future. I spent a long time involved in the legal field as a police officer and working in the Courts as a Prosecutor; it might be time for a change. Of course, it provides options in the future and is certainly something I can come back to. I have even been offered work as a Defence solicitor from firms on the Central Coast and been asked to be instructing solicitor on a murder trial, which was a great honour. But after spending almost sixteen years locking the crooks up, there is no way I could ever stand up in Court and defend them, even though I understand that every person is presumed innocent until proven guilty.

## Chapter Twenty-Two:
# In My Opinion

I loved being a police officer. I thought it was the best job in the world. But it wasn't just a job. It was a career, an opportunity, a calling. I couldn't imagine doing anything else, even despite what had happened during my career. I mean, in what other job do you find people who are willing to risk their lives to keep you safe in the face of constant danger, media criticism and public scrutiny?

I had been a proud serving member of the NSW Police Force for nearly sixteen years. In my last eighteen months alone of frontline policing, I was almost killed twice in the line of duty whilst protecting our community and trying to keep our streets safe from 'lowlife' crooks who want to break into your home, steal your car, assault members of your family and deal drugs to your children.

The brave men and women who risk their lives on a daily basis to protect their local community are people too — they are mums and dads, brothers and sisters, football players, guide leaders, builders, photographers and athletes.

But they are more than that. They are true heroes — courageous, dedicated, role models. Without these brave officers, where would society be? Who would be there to uphold the law? In what other profession do people confront such brutal and high-risk situations, the worst of human behaviour and the very real possibility of being killed and never seeing their family again?

It is true that we have made the decision to become police officers in an effort to help make a difference and combat the tidal wave of crime and violence, in many instances without respect and without thanks. But it is because of that sacrifice that we are able to feel safe in our homes at night. They will risk their lives, will undergo counselling and physical rehabilitation to get back to work just to get back out on the streets and risk their lives again, if they can.

The police's job is not limited to law enforcement and keeping our community safe. They perform many functions during the course of their duties: being your 'mate' when you've had a few too many or need someone to talk to, offering you advice and educating you about the law, acting as a counsellor or mediator in attempting to sort out your domestic disputes, referring you to counselling, providing first aid to victims of assault or when attending serious motor vehicle accidents, fighting fires or running into burning buildings to search for and rescue people, acting as a lifeguard to save you from drowning or slowing you down on the roads to prevent you from becoming a statistic, acting as a bodyguard who will take a hit, punch, kick, knife or bullet for you to keep you safe.

I believe that police are unfairly criticised within our community because of the position that they hold. There is a perception that you only ever see them when you are in trouble or they have bad news to tell you. I can tell you that police hate giving bad news. It's one of the worst parts of the job. But just think about their daily duties: attending to serious motor vehicle accidents, murder crime scenes, natural disasters, dealing with distraught relatives and deceased persons at suicides, crowd control during protests and riots, violent assaults and chasing/wrestling with armed, violent, intoxicated/drug-affected or mentally ill people, no matter the weather or time of day. And let's not forget the never-ending mountains of paperwork and constant scrutiny from the media and community.

Police have to make *split second* decisions about what course of action to take to save themselves, their partner or members of the community, only for the media, management and external agencies to publicly grill them after having months and countless opportunities to review the evidence and dissect their every action.

Their reality is the worst that human life can cough up. Having to endure nightmares, anxiety, sleepless nights and depression is part of the 'policing experience.' But it also offers an opportunity for ordinary Australians to achieve extraordinary results, to make a stand for what they believe in and a difference in their local community. It offers excitement, diversity, camaraderie and pride. You become part of a family that you can rely on to watch your back.

# PTSD AND ME

When I started at the Police Academy in February 1996, there were about 13,100 police in NSW, and my registered number was 30763. The class that graduated from the Academy in December 2013 have registered numbers around 52,000, and the current actual strength of the NSW Police Force as of December 2013 is 16,311. This means that over the last eighteen years, nearly 22,000 students have graduated from the Police Academy, and yet the NSW Police Force has only increased in strength by around 3,200 Police. According to my calculations (22,000 extra registered numbers – 3,200 extra police (16,300 – 13,100) divided by eighteen years), that's an attrition rate of over 1,044 officers per year, or over eighty-seven per month. Whether by resignation, medical discharge, retirement, termination of employment or death, surely something more has to be done to prevent this exodus of knowledge, skill and experience.

Although the NSW Police Force and the NSW Police Association are silent on the number of police suicides, I have been able to obtain a report from the National Coronial Information System (NCIS) that reflects the seriousness of the situation. Statistics show that between July 1,st 2000 and December 31st , 2012, at least fifty-eight former or currently serving police officers nationwide have committed suicide. Almost half of these (twenty-five) are from NSW. This is nearly twice the number of NSW police officers 'killed' in the line of duty (fifteen, whether by murder, motor vehicle accident or illness/injury on duty) over the same period. This is also more than triple the number who were killed as a direct result of intentional physical assault/injury in the execution of their duty (seven).

Frighteningly, it seems from the research I have conducted that there are at least six further suicides by past or currently serving NSW police officers between December 2012 and June 2014. This is six times the number of NSW police officers killed or who have died on duty during the same period, and nearly six hundred times more than the suicide rate for the Australian population. Anecdotally, I have heard the figure could be at least thirteen in the last six months alone.

Let's not forget that for every successful suicide there are an estimated thirty people who attempt to take their own life but fail and an even greater amount who contemplate suicide on a daily basis.

Figures also suggest that there are hundreds of NSW police officers absent from work due to mental stress at any one time. This is reinforced by statistics obtained from the NSW Police Force website, the NSW Police Force Annual Reports (2009/10-2012/13), the Auditor General's Reports to Parliament (2010-2013) and the *Effectiveness of new Death and Disability Scheme 2014* report. These records indicate that:

Between 1 July 2006 and 30 June 2013 there were:
- approximately 3,299 officers medically discharged from the NSW Police Force (average of 471 per year);
- approximately 3,627 workers compensation claims made for mental stress (average of 518 per year).

Between July $1^{st}$, 2009 and June $30^{th}$, 2012 there were:
- approximately 1,223 partial and permanent incapacity claims made by NSW police officers;
- on average 79 percent (966) related to a psychological claim;
- on average 95 percent (1,162) contained a psychological component to the injury.

Further statistics that highlight the issues affecting police officers are:
- as of January $1^{st}$, 2012, there were approximately 1,357 sworn officers off work due to sickness or injury—reduced to 902 in August 2013, mainly due to medical discharge;
- as of May $2^{nd}$, 2014, there are currently 905 officers who are absent from work due to long-term sick leave (hurt on duty/workers compensation), extended/maternity leave/leave without pay or suspended or external secondments, and;
- as of May 2014, there were 402 officers on permanent restricted duties.

The fact that so many police are succumbing to the grasp of PTSD is evidence of the fact that policing is an inherently dangerous job and that there isn't enough being done to support police in general. Although I don't have any tertiary qualifications as a psychologist in this area or claim to know all the answers, from a personal point of view, from someone who has been both a victim and a survivor of the condition, I can convey to you my experiences, both negative and positive, in the hope that you may change your mind about this disorder, but more importantly, about your opinion of your friends, family or workmates who have succumbed to its torment.

There is nothing specific that can trigger it, which makes it so hard to prevent and detect. For some people it may be a single traumatic incident that they witnessed, whereas others may have been the victims of violence or experienced a life-threatening situation. For me it was the accumulation of a number of violent incidents that I was involved in during the execution of my duties where I was at risk of serious injury or death, in addition to some traumatic events that I witnessed or was involved in.

What aggravated my condition most was the fact that I felt I couldn't talk to anybody because it was 'un-police like behaviour' or a 'guy thing' to do, and so I bottled up my emotions until I had a breakdown and everything came to the surface all at once. I am sure things would have turned out differently for me if the policing culture wasn't so 'blokey,' where mates looked out for their mates and police weren't just treated like numbers.

It's also important to remember that the PTSD doesn't only affect those afflicted by the condition but also their families. I honestly don't understand why my wife decided to stay with me throughout this torment and my recovery. When I ask her, she humbly replies it's because she loves me. I'm a very lucky man! The rollercoaster ride of emotions I must have put her and the kids through is unthinkable — from being withdrawn and inconsolable, angry and edgy, to riding the highest of highs on my good days.

The families of those suffering and recovering from PTSD are secondary victims to this condition. They may not have been involved in the incident, been witness to the events or understand what their loved ones are thinking and feeling, but living with someone with PTSD can have enormous adverse impacts mentally and emotionally. It's important that families aren't forgotten and that they are educated about the warning signs, symptoms and coping strategies so that they know how to help not just themselves, but each other.

One of the biggest things you can do for anyone who is off work with PTSD is to keep in contact. Ask them how they are going and let them know that they are not alone. Some people may not want to speak to you about how they are feeling because it is too much for them or because they feel guilty about the way they feel and how it is affecting them. Some, maybe a lot of them, are embarrassed about what others think of them because they aren't coping. I know that each time I went off work sick with PTSD I felt isolated and alone and was so fearful and embarrassed of what others would think of me. When I didn't hear from anyone at work, whether it was due to a busy workload or the stigma that's attached to the condition, it made me withdraw more from the world around me because I felt that I had done something wrong.

Since I have been off work with this last episode of PTSD and had help starting up the PTSD Support Group, I am amazed by just how many other police, from all corners of NSW, different ranks, years of service and areas of expertise, have been diagnosed with PTSD and have been or are in the process of being medically discharged, some even unable to ever work again. I have seen tough grown men disabled by its overwhelming grip, crying hysterically and unable to leave the house, answer the phone or look after themselves. I have seen marriages break down, friendships dissolve and once energetic happy people become wretched and withdrawn.

Because of everything I had been through during my career, I honestly didn't know whether I had a future in the NSW Police Force. There were days when even the thought of going back to work was too overwhelming, and yet there were days when I was so proud to be a part of this family and couldn't wait to go back. It's something I really struggled with. I wasn't expecting to be incapacitated for so long or to be placed in a position where I may have to make such an important decision.

The truth is that I have had PTSD for the past thirteen years and had six relapses, each more severe than the last. The possibility of me going back to work and having another relapse is fairly high.

As my psychiatrist told me, "It's not a matter of if, but of when I leave."

I just didn't want to make the wrong decision, but I knew I had to do what was right for my family and me. I didn't want to return to work just for the rank, great salary or because I looked great in uniform (lol). I wanted to be an active participant in my own career and personal life. I have a loving and supportive family that wants to enjoy spending time and experiencing life with me. I want to prove that it's okay not only for police, but in particular for men of any age to admit that they are having a bad day or aren't coping and that it's okay to reach out for help.

I may have had PTSD since 2001, but through seeking help, positive actions in confronting my emotions and changing the way I think about those feelings I have been able to return to and get promoted at work, contribute to my community through large-scale fundraising events and be a loving husband to my wife and father to my children. Because I haven't given up, I have been able to resume some normality in my life, although there were times when suicide felt like the only option. But I am delighted to say that it hasn't been since around November 2012 that I have had such intrusive thoughts. I am very proud of what I have achieved, both in my career and in combatting the 'sadness' despite some very tough times.

It's time to 'change the way we think' about PTSD, depression and suicide. It shouldn't be a taboo subject but rather something that is openly discussed in order to reduce the stigma and perceptions that push ordinary people to the brink of giving up. We need to start re-educating everyone, from the students at the Police Academy to the Commissioner himself, so that the negative culture in policing is changed forever, and for the better. Policing is inherently dangerous, and therefore anyone within the 'thin blue line' is at risk and deserves to be protected, encouraged and supported. They are our greatest asset and sometimes the only line of defence against tyranny and chaos on our streets, in our society and in our homes.

## Chapter Twenty-Three:
# Reflection

The last six months have been both very exciting and very confronting for me. I have learnt a lot about myself, made some difficult decisions and achieved some milestones.

I turned forty a few days after Christmas. To many that is a scary prospect, but for me it was a chance to make up for lost time. Up until that point my life had been: child, student, twenties, PTSD, forties. I missed out on ten years of my life, my thirties, because I was suffering from PTSD. A whole decade of my life was spent lost in a void of depression, irrational suicidal thoughts and struggling with my own identity. I look back and can see the numbness that controlled my every thought and feeling. But now I feel like I have woken from that hibernation and am ready to reclaim those missing years. I don't feel old. I feel inspired and blessed.

I have taken control of who I am, how I think and the direction I want my life to go in. After finishing my law degree in July, I realised that it was time for a new beginning. I spent nearly sixteen years of my life engaged in law enforcement, almost half of that as a legal professional working in the Courts. I realised I didn't want to be working in that environment anymore, so I withdrew from my College of Law before getting my certificate to practise as a lawyer. It was a hard decision to make after spending so much time studying, graduating and then deciding to head in a new direction. Although my wife tried to convince me that completing the course was a good Plan B, I just saw it as an excuse to fail. I understood her concerns, but after making that decision I felt liberated and in control for the first time in a long time. Worse comes to worse, if I change my mind in the future I can always re-enrol. It's not a definite never-going-back, just not now.

At the same time of taking control and making some big decisions I had begun a journey of self-discovery by undertaking a number of personal development seminars and reading books by successful and inspirational people from around the world such as Eckhart Tolle, Brendon Burchard, Richard Branson, Ken Blanchard, M. Scott Peck and John Maxwell. Two people who have had a great influence upon me and given me strength, clarity and understanding are Tony Robbins and Scott Harris. Many people may have heard of Tony Robbins or attended his seminars, so they will understand what a profound effect he can have on your way of thinking, your perceptions and, ultimately, your life. I have listened to a lot of Tony Robbins' material throughout my career, which as I have indicated has had an enormous effect upon me personally and professionally. I know if it wasn't for Tony's insightful teachings I wouldn't have been able to return to work after the Ute incident or process my experiences as I have.

But as influential as this seven-foot giant guru was, the man who has made the most difference in my life is Scott Harris. When I first met Scott at a one-day property seminar I attended in Newcastle back in April 2013, he was bursting with life and energy and was outrageously passionate about what he was saying. He didn't just talk the talk, he was living it. He was very congruent with the way he was living his life and what he was teaching. It had an instant impact upon me.

Since mid-2013 I have had the privilege of attending a few of Scott's seminars on the Gold Coast and can honestly say that his wisdom, passion and honesty have saved my life and my marriage. I know that sounds melodramatic, but it's true. Although I had come to the realisation prior to my discharge that my identity wasn't defined by my chosen career, I still hadn't discovered what my new identity would be. I was really struggling with who I was and what my future would hold. I knew I wanted to help others suffering from PTSD and raise awareness about male suicide, but I just didn't know how or have the motivation to make it happen.

When I first started attending his seminars, I was feeling restricted and embarrassed about my past. They were defining who I was, the person I was becoming, and they were my excuse for everything. Scott not only taught me how to change the way I think and feel, but he also empowered me to believe that what had happened to me was meant to happen. It was my purpose in life—my ultimate destiny. I know it may sound 'foo-foo' (as Scott would say), and I promise I won't start chanting, but Scott made me realise that things happen in your life for a reason and that I could use those past experiences and the lessons I have learned to help others and make a difference to those who aren't coping. I also learned that you meet people for a reason: to grow and to help you become the person you were meant to be.

I never used to believe that we all had a destiny in life that had already been determined. I always thought that we created our own destinies based on the decisions we made and didn't make and the things we did or didn't do. That was until Scott taught me about the 'Feather, Brick, Truck Principle.' I had never heard of it before, and after I did it was like a light bulb had exploded in my head. It was also a revelation because I have never been a religious person, so to accept such a theory would require me believing in some divine intervention and power. Even though deep down I felt that there was something celestial that created us, I have never embraced my own spirituality until recently.

Without doing the theory too much injustice, it basically says that because we are all born with a purpose in life, the Lord (in whatever form your religious beliefs recognise that being to be) sends you some 'reality checks' or signs to see whether you are on the right track. These take the metaphorical form of a feather, a brick and a truck, which appear as a feeling, an action or an event. The 'feather' is a gentle nudge to remind you to focus on the journey that you are meant to be on. The 'brick' is less subtle and is designed to startle you into submission and getting back on-track. The 'truck' will just flatten you and force you to reconsider the direction you are following.

Once I heard Scott explain the theory, it made so much sense and appeared to explain why certain things had happened in my life and career. It made me realise that my purpose in life was to help others, raise awareness, and 'change the way we think' about PTSD and male suicide; it was something I already knew but did little about. Even though I had always been in touch with my philanthropic side through my past charitable events, this just made sense. Flashbacks started skimming through my mind, like connecting the pieces of a jigsaw puzzle. Upon reflection, I realise that my life and career has been full of these signs but that I just didn't have the awareness or courage to acknowledge them.

They seemed to come in waves during my career, first at Redfern and then later working in the Central Coast and Prosecuting. At Redfern, the 'feathers' were in the form of incidents that I was involved in. Not a specific incident, but rather the volume. I now understand that I was supposed to have those experiences in order for me to have a reference to understand and appreciate what it's like to feel overwhelmed, unable to cope, face death and survive and then use that for the greater good. As you have read, I was involved in a number of incidents at Redfern that made me confront my own feelings, which created a relevant broad reference base.

There were a few 'brick' reminders while I was at Redfern, which in hindsight I can see escalated over time. First there was the Black Market Murders. I still can't understand to this day why, after just murdering three members of an opposing OMGC, they didn't shoot and kill my partner and me when we were only a few metres away, sitting in our police vehicle and a serious threat to their liberty.

The next incident I can think of was 'Shots Fired,' where against my training and experience I drove down an alleyway after responding to a break-in at a local service station. That single decision prevented me from driving onto an adjacent street straight into the line of fire of another policeman shooting at the suspect escaping in his stolen vehicle. This was followed a short time later when a female suspect almost stole my firearm and shot me with it during a violent arrest in Eveleigh Lane.

Let's not forget the 'Signal One' incident where my partner and I chased an offender wanted for armed robbery through the rear of a house only to be assaulted and surrounded by members of the community who prevented our escape, or chasing and restraining the offender armed with the knife into Eveleigh Lane after committing an armed robbery only to be restrained and assaulted myself. There were even two 'brick' incidents that actually involved bricks—the riots on Australia Day 1998 and the Waterloo Riots of 2001.

I think after any or all of these incidents I should have gotten the message. But typically, as a bloke and a police officer I chose to ignore how I was feeling and that I wasn't coping. This of course led to the ultimate 'truck' reminder, which in this case took the shape of a Ute. That was God telling me it was time to go and get help. And I guess for a while it worked, until I made the decision to come back following the fatal accident I came upon on the way to a training day—yet another reminder that I was ready for some more learning. I had to go back as proof that not coping (being human) and reaching out for help isn't a sign of weakness but rather a strength of character.

Things went well for a while after returning to prosecuting and then transferring back to general duties at Tuggerah Lakes, until the signs returned. This time they were less subtle. The 'feather' reminder occurred one evening when I attended to a local beach carpark where a group of about a hundred intoxicated youths were causing trouble. When I got out of my police vehicle to speak to the youths I noticed that I had dropped my portable radio on the driver's seat. As I bent into the car to pick it up, a beer bottle bounced off the roof and smashed, right where my head and face would have been if I hadn't bent down. Yet again, I had someone watching out for me that night.

As usual, I just brushed that off until things started to spiral out of control again. That's when the 'bricks' started flying my way. First there was the incident at Crackneck Lookout, followed by the incident at The Entrance Channel. At least I was able to recognise that I wasn't coping and took some time off to get some help. It wasn't long after I returned to work that more 'bricks' headed in my direction—because I didn't learn. The incidents involving the drowning of the girl at the bridge and the guy who attempted to rip his own head off in front of us should have been enough. I knew I wasn't coping but didn't want to lose my identity by making the decision to leave the police. It was obvious that I wasn't listening and needed to be stopped once and for all. That's when the 'truck' ran right over me. It must have been a B-double truck it hit me with such ferocity.

The messages I was given through these incidents weren't sinking in, so the Almighty got physical with me—inflicting me with a chronic back injury, which led to a relapse of PTSD, forcing me to make a decision and ending my career.

Scott also taught me about the importance of being true to myself, that it was my responsibility (to respond with ability) to take control, to make a decision and to go after what I wanted in life—"Fuck it, no plan B." I have learned about the six human needs (certainty/security, uncertainty/adventure, love and connection, significance, growth and contribution), which explain why some people act out of character—to fulfil their primary needs. I learned about the importance of values and living every day in accordance with those values to become the "very best version of yourself," about relationships and the five love languages (Gary Chapman), about the psychology of wealth and how to create an abundant life, about how time management can expedite you to success and about how everything I need to be confident, happy, healthy, abundant, successful and extraordinary is already within me now!

I have learnt how to be grateful every day just for being alive and for the extraordinary people and gifts that I already have in my life that other people don't have and that we take for granted. Each morning I take the time to be grateful for the gift of life—for the experiences I have had, the mistakes I have made and the lessons I have learnt. I thank God that I have been granted the gift of sight, hearing, taste, touch and smell, for a brain that can think, a heart that loves and forgives, for my good looks and, obviously, good sense of humour.

I am hoping that through Scott's support and guidance that I will be able to start doing my own public speaking and fulfilling my purpose in life.

One of the things I regret most about having PTSD is the way it has affected my relationship with my wife. When we first met, there was a lot of romance, quality time and intimacy. But over time, things have changed. I admit that most of it was my fault because I succumbed to my demons battling with depression and my PTSD symptoms. I was no longer the happy, carefree and positive person I used to be that she fell in love with. I became sullen, moody and very withdrawn. I don't know how or why she stayed with me.

One of the most confronting and valuable lessons I learned from Scott and Tony was about our relationship and how the status quo had changed. I was no longer a masculine male because I was struggling and feeling overwhelmed and alone. Over the past few years, I also lost my masculinity because of my back injury, which prevented me from helping around the house. Even the most mundane task seemed like a challenge. This meant that Rachael had to adopt the more assertive and supportive role in our relationship, stripping her of her feminine character. Don't get me wrong, she is still the most gorgeous girl I know, but her identity as a woman was lost because of what I was going through. She had to be strong because I was weak; she had to be happy because I was sad; she had to be in control because I was out of control. She had to become the masculine person in our relationship, not because that's who she was but because I had become the feminine person. It took me so long to realise that, but once Scott and Tony explained it to me it was like a revelation. It was time for me

## Chapter Twenty-Three: Reflection

to step up and be the man again, to treat my wife like a queen, spend quality time with her, show her how much she meant to me and be the man I once used to be.

It hasn't all been easy, and understandably there has been some resistance to change because we have been that way for the majority of our sixteen years together. There have also been a few times when we almost ended our marriage. Sometimes it was because we were butting heads as we both tried to be the masculine partner in the relationship (through her habit and my efforts), and sometimes I thought that it would be easier to move on (and that she deserved better). But because of what I have learned, I have been able to wrestle my masculinity back and encourage Rachael to embrace her feminine side. Now our relationship has never been stronger or more positive.

One of the other great people I have met during my journey over the last six to eight months is Mark Rolton. He is the leading expert when it comes to property options in Australia. His company, Massland, has helped me find direction and the confidence to begin building (or developing) an in-depth knowledge of property investment, acquisition and development. Both Scott and Mark have been a source of inspiration as mentors for me in their own way, and I look forward to forging an ongoing relationship and friendship with them in the years to come.

When I read the experiences of former police officers, PTSD survivors and published authors, such as Esther McKay's *Crime Scene and Forensic Investigator*, Al Sparkes' *The Cost Of Bravery*, and Paul Horner's *Jack Knife - The Crashing Of A Policeman* and saw what great efforts they were making in providing support and education to sufferers and survivors, it encouraged and inspired me to get my book published and to start telling my story when and where I can.

As you know, I have known Esther for a few years. She has been a great source of support for me in completing this book and is responsible for the creation of PTSD Support Groups. Unfortunately, the support group that I started on the Central Coast only lasted only twelve to eighteen months. However, I have recently been able to establish a Central Coast/Hunter PTSD Support Group for past and present members of the NSW Police, Fire, Ambulance and Rural Fire Services from the Central Coast, Lake Macquarie and Newcastle/Hunter areas, which meets the fourth Thursday of each month, thanks to Esther and her volunteers from the Police Post Trauma Support Group. Although it has been a struggle and the interest is not reflected in the lack of attendance, rather than giving up, it has made me resolute and passionate to do more.

I haven't had the honour of meeting Al Sparkes, but I really enjoyed his book and commend him for his involvement with Beyond Blue and the public speaking he does relating to PTSD and suicide prevention. I have, however, been privileged to attend a public speaking event of Paul Horner after reading about his experiences. I flew to Queensland in early February 2014 just for the day to hear him speak about his experiences and provide me with some motivation. I'm very glad I made the effort.

I guess whatever happens from this moment is up to me. Despite everything that has transpired throughout my career, the depths of depression and despair that I reached, my near-death experiences, the overwhelming thoughts of suicide and pain it has caused me personally and within my relationships, I wouldn't change a thing. I have no regrets about making the decision to become a police officer or about executing my duties the way I did. And, if I am honest with myself for a *split second*, I do miss being a part of the thin blue line, but more, I believe, for the idea of it than the reality of it. It is part of me and the reason I am the person who I am today.

I have found strength in my past and am now able to use my darkest moments as a source of courage to help others. My relationship with my wife and girls has never been stronger, and I am surrounded by friends who love and support me as I endeavour to take a new path in life. I have also been lucky to meet and befriend a number of amazing people and mentors from all over the world who have added purpose and direction that I have been missing.

Although my direct experiences relate to incidents surrounding my duties within the field of emergency services, the lessons and skills I have been able to learn, develop and apply can relate to any person suffering from stress, anxiety or depression, and/or the loss of identity, whether it be a result of losing your job, a breakdown of a relationship or the death of a loved one.

My continuing journey of self-discovery and personal development has revealed a universal opportunity for me to use my experiences to make a difference in the lives of so many people. This is the moment. This is the time...

I am so grateful that I have gone through what I have. I don't look upon it as a negative anymore. I didn't suffer—I grew. I wasn't weak—I was strong, brave and courageous. I am a survivor.

## Lessons I Have Learned

- Being a police officer is a dangerous and difficult job. Be proud of what you have achieved and of making the conscious decision to make such a serious commitment.
- You are not defined by the job you do (or the relationship you are in).
- Being a police officer is what I did as a job - it's not who I am as a person. I am courageous and kind, loving and understanding, good-looking, funny, awesome, amazing, and inspiring.
- There is life after the police. At the end of the day it is just a job.
- Recognise when you are not coping—it is not a sign of weakness but a reflection of your strength and courage to know you deserve better.
- Acceptance is the first step on the road to recovery.
- Talk to someone or ask for support—family, friends, workmates, counsellors, EAP, doctors, psychologists, and psychiatrists.
- Write down what you are feeling—it gets it out of your head and gives you a new perspective.
- Don't use alcohol or drugs to numb your pain. They're only a temporary solution and can aggravate your situation or condition.
- Accept that it's a normal reaction to a stressful situation (you are only human). It wouldn't be normal if you weren't affected.
- Attend a Support Group meeting. Even if you only take the first step and make contact—even the longest journey starts with a single step.
- Exercise—look after your body. It's amazing how much better you feel when you take time out for you. Healthy Body = Healthy Mind.
- Change your state—get up and move—do something physical, make a dramatic movement (jump, dance, sing).
- Change your focus—think about something positive that you enjoy doing. Think of happy memories and times when you felt alive.

- Change your language — don't use negative words or phrases. I am worth it. I am awesome. I am courageous. I am a survivor. This doesn't happen to me all the time. I can make a difference.
- Don't lock yourself away from the world — spending too much time alone dwelling on how you are feeling will only make you feel worse. Do something spontaneous, catch up with friends, do something active.
- Remember that you are not alone — there are so many people grateful for your courage who are willing to help. Use your experiences as a blessing to help others who aren't coping. Remember other people have suffered and survived.
- Change your story — do something that will change your view about what happened — use it to make you a stronger, more caring, confident person.
- Read a book on personal development.
- Suicide is not the answer — it is not an option. You don't want to die, just to escape from the pain. Think about the people you are leaving behind and the effect it will have on them. Be remembered for how you lived, not for how you died.
- Be grateful for all of the extraordinary people and gifts you have in your life.
- There is such a thing as a police family — but it comes with the negative connotations (like being forgotten, ignored, ridiculed, bullied and judged), as well as the positive (camaraderie, mateship, purpose, love, security and a sense of belonging).
- You can only get better if you want to get better — you are in control.
- Meditation - find time to focus on the now, slow your mind and breathing down - relax and listen to the sounds around you.
- Have something to look forward to - plan a holiday, an event or a get together with family/friends. It creates excitement and motivates you to start living again.
- It's all part of the experience — life is like a game where we live, learn and grow. We make mistakes, wrong decisions and take chances. Sometimes when we try we succeed, we simply learn. We are the only ones responsible for the meaning we give to each and every experience.

# Epilogue

It was a great journey for me to undertake this book. Partly it was a form of therapy that allowed me to confront all the fear and denial I have contained within me over the years. But it was also a chance to express my feelings about the job I loved. It was an opportunity to promote the bravery and camaraderie of my brothers and sisters within the NSW Police Force, past, present and future, and to allow others an insight into life as a frontline cop behind the thin blue line.

I am not attempting to glorify my career, as I am sure that there are millions of other officers around the world who execute their duties as professionally and bravely as anyone else. I admit that I have made mistakes, and I have learnt a lot from my experiences and from listening to other police, both senior and junior.

I am glad to see that the police culture is changing and becoming more receptive to officers admitting that they are not coping, accepting that they are human and not expecting to perform their duties like a robot. But the frontline police themselves need to accept that it is okay, too.

As I have discussed, throughout my career I have gone through a roller coaster ride of emotions, from the depths of depression and fear to pride and fulfilment. I have accepted that I cannot change what has happened in the past but can use my experiences to help others. I must remember the important things in my life, especially my family and that at the end of the day this is just a job.

Whilst I have been writing this book I have cried and felt angry. My chest has ached and my hands have shaken. But through this pain I have found resilience of character and been able to confront my demons and move through the barriers, lowering my walls and letting you all in to see and hopefully changing some negative attitudes and opinions about police.

At times this has been a very tough battle, and I am still here because I have never given up. I have been called names from "fucking white copper cunt" to "super-cop" and heard rumours and innuendo, criticism and condemnation from my 'customers' and colleagues, but from those who count, nothing but support, love and understanding.

Within a blink of an eye your world can be turned upside down. Life's pretty fickle like that. But it's all about opportunity, and I've always been one to strive to be the best I can be and never to quit.

There have been times throughout my career when I've thought about giving the job away and others when it has almost cost me my life. For whatever reason I've made the decisions I have, it was because I believed in what I was doing and the office I swore to uphold. Basically, "I was doing my job," and you can't take that away from me.

To those officers with whom I have had the privilege and honour of working throughout my career I would like to extended my warmest and sincerest gratitude for the experiences we have shared and the lessons that you have taught me. Particularly the officers involved in the incidents that I have referenced throughout these pages, you have had an enormous impact on me, both personally and professionally, and I will be eternally grateful for your guidance, support and mateship. You have made this journey one to remember!

So, having experienced life behind the thin blue line and now looking from the outside in, I still believe that anyone considering applying for the NSW Police Force should take the chance and just do it. You never know unless you try it for yourself. Regardless of what I have been through in my career, I would never discourage anyone who wanted to join the rank and file of the NSW Police Force, as long as they are armed with an awareness of PTSD, how to recognise and cope with symptoms and encouraged to reach out and seek help without fear of retribution or being isolated. These are my experiences, and every location is different. Every officer has his or her own story to tell.

Although there are experiences I haven't included that I could have, such as being at the Thredbo disaster (my first time in the snow), chasing offenders across rooftops and being embarrassed at the Sydney Mardi Gras by a 'performer' on rollerblades with a feather, there is nothing I have included that I feel I shouldn't have. It's raw; it's honest; it was my reality. This isn't a job where you can walk away and delete what you've seen. It becomes part of who you are. I will always remember the names, the faces, the locations and the way they made me feel. Sometimes forgetting is harder than remembering.

Finally, I just want to say a massive thanks to my family and friends, especially to my Benamba Street family (see picture page 297), who have been so supportive of me along this journey and had to put up with more than what they deserve. Without their guidance and understanding, who knows how this story would have ended up? I will always be eternally grateful and will never forget what you have done for me.

What direction my life takes from this point is up to me. The most important thing is that I have control. After living with and surviving the grip of PTSD for the majority of the twenty-first century thus far and struggling with chronic back pain for the last thirty months, I believe I have reached an impasse where I am confident about my future. Although there is an underlying sadness about the experiences I will miss out on, I am looking forward to making a difference and 'changing the way we think' about mental health, PTSD and suicide within the policing culture and society in general. I am proud to say that I no longer suffer from flashbacks or nightmares and am able to manage my pain sufficiently to allow myself to maintain a relatively normal lifestyle. I have recently started exercising again to strengthen my core and improve my fitness and have already lost fifteen kilograms, which makes me the lightest I have been in ten years.

They always say that the first step is the hardest, and writing this book has been just that for me. I hope you have gotten as much out of reading this book as I have in writing it over the last thirteen years.

Thanks for listening.

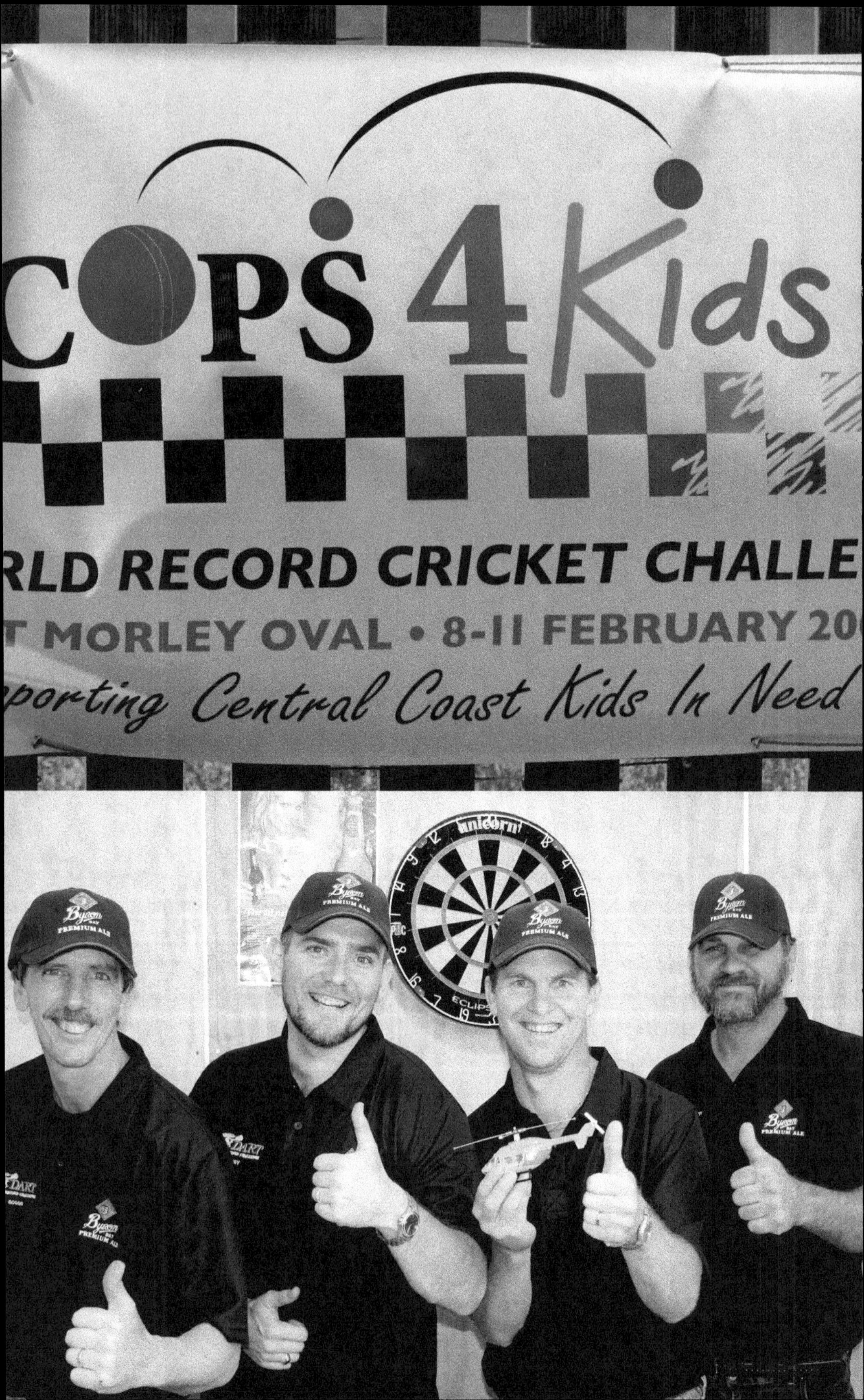

COPS 4 Kids
RLD RECORD CRICKET CHALLE
T MORLEY OVAL • 8-11 FEBRUARY 20
porting Central Coast Kids In Need

Jeff Garland, 17, left, and ███ ██████, 18, both of Belmont, will ride to Queensland to raise money for a centre for Newcastle's homeless youths.

## Belmont students plan 1000km ride to raise money for homeless youths

FAILURE is not a word in 17-year-old Jeff Garland's vocabulary.

The Belmont youth is juggling the demands of studying for the Higher School Certificate and organising a 1000km bicycle ride to Southport, in Queensland, to help raise $100,000 for a centre for Newcastle's homeless youth and is confident of superb results.

Jeff will be joined in the gruelling venture by Belmont friends ███████ ██████, ███████ Dunn, 17, and ███ █████, 18.

The fundraising quest, named Ride For Nobody's Children, will start on December 5 from the Belmont City Centre.

The riders have allocated eight days and will have a support team of 11, including a masseur and a St John Ambulance officer.

They will raise money along the way by selling T-shirts specially printed for the event and ask for individual donations and sponsorship for every 15-20km ridden.

A long-standing desire to help those who need it has prompted Jeff to try to raise $100,000 so the Salvation Army can establish a centre for homeless youths.

Jeff said the money would be raised over six-months.

He has organised a ball to be held at Belmont 16ft Sailing Club on November 2 and will organise a large concert for mid-June.

People who want to help Jeff and his team can contact him on ██ ████.

Preparing to do time: The Entrance officers Sen Constable Mark Waddell, Chief Insp Tony Long, Sgt Paul Battley, Constable Nicole Coombs and Sen Constable Jeff Garland Officers get in some practice. Picture: Gary Graham

# Charity cricket game a hard slog

IT'S a far cry from the defining moments seen at the SCG, MCG or even the WACA ground, but on a sleepy morning next month Bateau Bay's Pat Morley Oval is set to become part of cricket history.

Twenty-four police officers from the Tuggerah Lakes local area command are in training to break the Guinness world record for the world's longest cricket match, to raise money for Central Coast Kids In Need.

Tuggerah Lakes Senior Constable Jeff Garland, who is also co-ordinator of the cricket marathon record attempt, said officers were aiming to play for 68 hours from February 8 to February 11.

The group is aiming to break the current Guinness record set by New Zealand's Cornwall Cricket Club, which played for 55 hours last year.

"For me it's not about the world record — I just think a world record is a great way of raising money for charity," said Sen Constable Garland. "It gives people something to work towards."

The group is aiming to raise $5000, although Sen Constable Garland, who has also been involved in world record darts and golf endeavours, said any extra would be more than welcome.

The cricket marathon will kick off about midday on February 8. For more details or to make a donation, contact cricketmarathon@bigpond.com.

Sen-Constable Jeff Garland and keeper Sen-Constable Mark Waddell play on to make the world record for the longest game of cricket.

# Record 67 hours, not out

ORGANISERS of a charity 67-hour long cricket match say they have been "blown out of the water" by the community's support.

Tuggerah Lakes Area Command Sen-Constable Jeff Garland organised a Guinness world record attempt for the longest cricket match to raise money for Central Coast Kids In Need.

The game started at Pat Morley Oval, at Bateau Bay on Sunday and finished at 8am on Wednesday.

The two teams of 12 people were hoping to play for 68 hours but missed 51 minutes of play because of a thunderstorm.

"On Sunday we played through one of the hottest days of the year, then through a thunderstorm and then through temperatures of 15C," Sen-Constable Garland said.

He said everyone was in high spirits after the game but most people had sore and swollen feet.

"Everyone's a bit tired but we're all in high spirits," he said.

He said they had people cheering them on and donating money.

"I wanted to say a huge thanks to everyone involved, the guys who played, the public, family members and everyone who helped out," he said.

Sen-Constable Garland said the game raised more than $5000 and would go to Central Coast Kids In Need. It will help families with sick children and travelling to Newcastle or Sydney for treatment.

monday, september 1, 2008 | dailytelegraph.com.au

Champions: Jeff Garland (right) and his team    Picture: Gary Graham

## Quartet set darts record

THERE are no international-standard sporting facilities in Wyee Point, no Olympic pool, no velodrome but four knockabout blokes from the town finally realised their dreams of international sporting glory yesterday — snatching a new Guinness world record for the longest darts marathon.

The group beat the previous record of 25 hours and 34 minutes set in the UK last year by an hour and a half, and in doing so, helped raise more than $3000 for the Westpac Rescue Helicopter.

Jeff Garland, Tony Gafa, John Goggin and Ian Van Veen began their 27-hour odyssey at 10am on Saturday at The Hive, Erina Fair. It ended at 1pm yesterday after playing more than 70 straight games under a makeshift marquee through the wind and driving rain.

"It was a little cramped in here but we got through the worst of it," Mr Garland said. "We raised a little more than $3000 before we started and we've been passing the tin around all day so we hope to finish with about $5000."

No stranger to world records, Mr Garland previously held the 2002 Guinness title for playing 1728 holes of golf in seven days.

The four hatched the plan for a tilt at the record while playing a regular game of doubles at Mr Gafa's house.

### Contact us

**PHONE**
News/Sport:
4323 5014/8058
Photo sales: 1300 301705
www.newsphotos.com.au

**ADDRESS**
Lot 18, Bowen Crescent,
West Gosford, NSW 2250
FAX 4323 5016

**HAVE YOUR SAY**
extra@dailytelegraph.com.au

**WEATHER**
TODAY: Sunny and mild. Winds light, NNE. Max: 19
TOMORROW: Mostly sunny but mild. Winds SE. Max: 19

## Knife used in hold-up

A WOMAN accused of holding up a service station with a knife will face court today.

The woman, 42, of Umina Beach, allegedly wore a balaclava as she entered the service station on Ocean Beach Rd, Umina, about 8pm brandishing a weapon.

She allegedly demanded money before fleeing with cash and chocolates in a nearby car.

She was arrested at Ettalong Beach a short time later and taken to Gosford police station where she was charged with armed robbery.

She was refused bail and was remanded is to appear at Gosford Local Court today.

# Golf record raises $8000 for kids

Last December Snr Cst Jeffrey Garland, now attached to Legal Services, set out to break the Guinness World Record for playing the most holes of golf in seven days, and raise money for a local television telethon.

Snr Cst Garland had to play more than 1706 holes at the picturesque Morisset Country Club to achieve his goal.

Despite 22 hour days battling extreme heat and bushfire haze, darkness and a leg injury sustained in the first 24 hours, Snr Cst Garland managed to complete 1728 holes (96 full rounds) within the allotted time and raise more than $8000 for sick and underprivileged children.

"Looking back at what I did, I am very glad it's all over. It was a while before I picked up a golf club again, but it was all worthwhile," he said.

"One of the things that amazed me was the level of community support I received. Cars would pull up on the side of the road to watch me play and other golfers applauded as I played through. It was great encouragement.

"I was surprised at how well I was able to control my fatigue. I only had 10 hours' sleep all week.

"I was able to average a round of golf in just over an hour which didn't leave much time to aim my shots. My scores weren't spectacular but I still managed a few pars and birdies, and even fluked an eagle. I think over the whole week I hit about 10 500 golf balls, which is more than most would do in a lifetime."

Snr Cst Garland said he collapsed just five rounds short of the record.

"I allowed myself to relax once I realised the end was in sight, which was a big mistake. I was extremely dehydrated and remember seeing little green men running across the fairways," he said.

*Last December Snr Cst Jeffrey Garland broke the Guinness World Record for playing the most holes of golf in seven days*

"But thanks to the support of my friends and family I regained my bearings and finished.

"The biggest buzz was when I played my last hole and there were 150 people standing around the green cheering me on. It made the pain and sacrifices all the more worthwhile.

"I want to thank my family and the volunteers who selflessly gave of their own time to help and for keeping me in line. But mostly I want to thank my wife Rachael, Insp Jason Sharp and his wife Natalie, Steve Vanspronssen and the Police Media Unit for their support. I am hoping to be mentioned in the 2004 Guinness World Record Book."

This year, Snr Cst Garland will concentrate on his new career as a police prosecutor, and is hoping to publish his book 'Blue Armour' about his police experiences.

# HONOUR ROLL

During my career there have been twenty-one brave NSW police officers killed in the line of duty:
- Constable David Carty (1997)
- Constable Peter Forsythe (1998)
- Senior Constable Ronald McGowan (1998)
- Senior Sergeant Raymond Smith (1998)
- Constable Matthew Potter (1998)
- Senior Constable James Affleck (2001)
- Student Police Officer Robert Brotherson (2002)
- Senior Constable Glenn McEnally (2002)
- Senior Constable Chris Thornton (2002)
- Constable Kylie Smith (2003)
- Detective Sergeant Mark Speechley (2003)
- Detective Inspector Mark Day (2003)
- Constable Shelley Davis (2004)
- Student Police Officer Steven Rosser (2006)
- Sergeant Colin McKenzie (2006)
- Senior Constable Gordon Wilson (2006)
- Senior Sergeant Loreto Finucci (2006)
- Constable William Crews (2010)
- Senior Constable David Rixon (2012)
- Detective Inspector Bryson Anderson (2012)

Each of these officers died in the execution of their duties and is listed on an Honour Roll. They died doing something they loved. Two of the officers killed, S/C McEnally and S/C Thornton, were people I knew of and admired. I had the opportunity and the privilege of being touched by their experience, their kindness and their selflessness. They will always be remembered and never be forgotten.

Many, many more officers who haven't been killed in the line of duty are left with the psychological and sometimes physical scars of what they witness and experience on a daily basis. Let's not forget them either.

Sadly, too often another brave officer's name is added to the Wall of Remembrance. On Police Remembrance Day, September 27th each year, I choke back tears of relief as I reflect upon the list of courageous comrades who have made the ultimate sacrifice and realise just how lucky I am and how close I have come to becoming one of them.

Here is a poem, written by an unknown author, that captures the essence of what it's like to be a police officer.

### *The Final Inspection*

*The policeman stood and faced his God,*
*Which must always come to pass.*
*He hoped his shoes were shining.*
*Just as brightly as his brass.*

*"Step forward now, policeman.*
*How shall I deal with you?*
*Have you always turned the other cheek?*
*To My church have you been true?"*

*The policeman squared his shoulders and said,*
*"No, Lord, I guess I ain't,*
*Because those of us who carry badges*
*Can't always be a saint.*

*I've had to work most Sundays,*
*and at times my talk was rough,*
*and sometimes I've been violent,*
*Because the streets are awfully tough.*

*But I never took a penny,*
*That wasn't mine to keep....*
*Though I worked a lot of overtime*
*When the bills got just too steep.*

*And I never passed a cry for help,*
*Though at times I shook with fear.*
*And sometimes, God forgive me,*
*I've wept unmanly tears.*

*I know I don't deserve a place*
*Among the people here.*
*They never wanted me around*
*Except to calm their fear.*

*If you've a place for me here, Lord,*
*It needn't be so grand.*
*I never expected or had too much,*
*But if you don't.....I'll understand.*

*There was silence all around the throne*
*Where the saints had often trod.*
*As the policeman waited quietly,*
*For the judgment of his God.*

*"Step forward now, policeman.*
*You've borne your burdens well.*
*Come walk a beat on Heaven's streets,*
*You've done your time in hell."*

# Service History

18 February 1996: Police Academy Goulburn

16 August 1996: Attested as Probationary Constable of Police

19 August 1996: Commenced Duties at Gosford Patrol

16 February 1997: Transferred to Redfern Patrol / LAC

19 January 2003: Transferred to Legal Services

17 June 2007: Transferred to Tuggerah Lakes LAC

19 April 2009: Transferred to Legal Services

27 October 2011: Medical Discharge

## Promotion History

18 February 1996: Student Police Officer

16 August 1996: Probationary Constable

16 August 2002: Senior Constable

Relieved as Sergeant:

July 2000 – October 2000: Redfern Intelligence

September - October 04 / April - October 05 / January – May 07: Legal Services

October 07 – November 08: Tuggerah Lakes LAC

19 April 2009: Senior Sergeant

## Awards/Notations

**October 1997:** Notation: In recognition of officer's actions, initiative and resourcefulness following an armed robbery

**July 1998:** Notation: For professionalism displayed in detaining and searching male armed with a samurai sword

**September 1998:** Notation: For good work in the detection and arrest of two suspects for armed robbery

**December 1998:** Notation: For good work in arrest of suspect wanted for robbery offences

**December 1998:** Notation: For excellent police work in arrest of suspect wanted for numerous indictable offences, including armed robbery

**May 1999:** Notation: For good police work in arrest of suspect wanted for numerous indictable offences, including armed robbery

**August 1999:** Notation: For good police work in arrest of suspect wanted for a number of serious offences

**February 2000:** Notation: For excellent collation and analysis of intelligence resulting in arrest of suspect for large number of steal from person and robbery offences

**August 2000:** Awarded 'Commander's Certificate of Appreciation' for excellent police work in the identification, arrest and charging of offender wanted for numerous armed robbery offences on taxi drivers

**February 2001:** Awarded 'Commander's Certificate of Merit' for arrest of male for numerous armed robbery offences

**March 2001:** Notation: For the excellent police work in the arrest of an escapee

**March 2001:** Awarded 'Commander's Commendation' in recognition of excellent teamwork and dedication while engaged in apprehension and charging of suspect for armed robbery offences

**November 2003:** Awarded 'Commander's Certificate of Appreciation' for professional performance during prosecution and subsequent conviction of suspect accused of two armed robberies

**February 2007:** Awarded NSW Police Medal

**June 2007:** Awarded Hunter/Central Coast Storm Emergency 2007 Medal

**October 2008:** Awarded Rotary 'Pride of Workmanship' Award

**October 2011:** Awarded 'Commander's Certificate of Merit' for the arrest of an offender armed with a knife in Eveleigh Lane, who was wanted for numerous armed robbery offences

**October 2011:** Awarded 'Commander's Certificate of Merit' for the arrest of an offender for theft offences: Ute incident

**October 2012:** Awarded 'Bronze Medal' from Royal Humane Society for incident at The Entrance Channel

**November 2012:** Awarded 'Commissioner's Certificate of Merit' for the incident at Crackneck Lookout

**November 2012:** Awarded 'Commissioner's Commendation/Medal for Courage' for the incident at The Entrance Channel

# About The Author

Jeff Garland is a dedicated and decorated retired Senior Sergeant. And, more importantly, he is a father, a husband and a survivor whose passion to make a difference has led him on an incredible road to self-discovery. His story, determination and courage about how he overcame the depths of depression, thoughts of suicide and PTSD will inspire and move you.

Jeff had always dreamed about making a difference. To him there was no greater purpose in life. Whether it was organising large-scale fundraising events to raise money for charity, attempting Guinness World Records, serving on the NSW Police Force's frontline, or being a public advocate for change Jeff knew from an early age what he wanted his legacy to be – hope!

"For as long as I can remember, I have always had the passion to help other people and make a difference in their lives. It makes me feel so alive and grateful…. One of the greatest lessons that I have learnt is to never give up hope. Tomorrow is another day! Things happen in our lives, but it's not the event but the meaning that we give it that has the greatest affect – change the meaning; change your life."

Jeff's inspirational journey began as a child; whereas a twin he struggled with a sense of identity. His search for self and purpose guided him on a philanthropic path of discovery, understanding or consciousness, and contribution. His endeavours to raise funds and awareness for those 'less fortunate' or 'forgotten' are testament to his character and commitment.

The resilience and fortitude that Jeff has displayed in serving as a Police officer, overcoming PTSD, depression and thoughts of suicide and writing about his experiences over the last thirteen years reflects the congruency of his words with his actions. His message is simple and sincere: We need to change the way we think in order to make a difference. Help A Mate Before It's Too Late!!!

www.ingramcontent.com/pod-product-compliance
Lightning Source LLC
Chambersburg PA
CBHW071857290426
44110CB00013B/1176